MAKING HISTORY

MAKING

HISTORY

ALUTIIQ/SUGPIAQ LIFE
ON THE ALASKA PENINSULA

Patricia H. Partnow

University of Alaska Press
Fairbanks, Alaska

CATALOGING-IN-PUBLICATION

Partnow, Patricia H., 1949-
    Making history : Alutiiq/Sugpiaq life on the Alaska Peninsula / Patricia H.
    Partnow.
        p. cm.
    Includes bibliographical references and index.
    ISBN 1-889963-38-0 (cloth : alk. paper) — ISBN 1-889963-39-9 (pbk : alk. paper)
    1. Pacific Gulf Yupik Eskimos—History. 2. Pacific Gulf Yupik Eskimos—social
life and customs. 3. Alaska Peninsula (Alaska)—History.
E99 .E7 P24 2001
979.8/004971 21

                                                                    2001054044

International Standard Book Number
Cloth   1-889963-38-0
Paper   1-889963-39-9

Library of Congress Catalog Number: 2001054044

Printed in the United States of America by Thomson-Shore, Inc.

This publication was printed on acid-free paper that meets the minimum requirements for the American National Standard for Information Science—Permanence of
Paper for Printed Library Materials ANSI Z39.48-1984.

Publication co-ordination and production
    Deirdre Helfferich, University of Alaska Press

Design
    Deirdre Helfferich and Dixon Jones

Index
    Paul Kish, Kish Indexing Services

Cover illustration
    Deirdre Helfferich and Dixon Jones

Front cover
    Chignik River Fish Weir. Photo by Pat Partnow.
    Alutiiqs on Chignik Dock, Early 1900s. Courtesy Anchorage Museum of History
    and Art.

Illustrations
    The ornament used on chapter headings is a petroglyph found on Afognak Island,
    Kodiak Group, Alaska. Taken from Looking Both Ways by Crowell, Aron L.,
    Steffian, Amy F., and Pullar, Gordon L. (Eds), Fairbanks, University of Alaska Press,
    2001.
    Maps on pages 18, 20, 23, and 28 were created by Vanessa Summers and belong to
    Patricia Partnow.

I dedicate this book to my parents, Ruth and Dean Hartley, whose fascination with the interplay between place and event shaped my own personal history, and to my children, Seth and Alix, who give me joy in the present and hope for the future.

CONTENTS

PREFACE

Consider these two stories from Alutiiq history:

> After years of abuse and exploitation at the hands of fur traders, the Alutiiqs finally hire a shamanic hit man to execute the Russian king. The assassin shoots his target through an open window, then disappears, never to be seen again.

> A ne'er-do-well drifter shoots and kills the competent and generous fur company manager who is enjoying a friendly meal with associates. The murderer escapes, probably with the help of local Natives.

Here is a description of a single event from two points of view, one Alutiiq and the other nineteenth-century American. Underlying the differences are contradictory assumptions about guilt, responsibility, and justice. Alutiiq history is made up of many such instances, when incompatible premises result in contrary accounts. History also contains examples of reasoned compromises, brilliant adaptations, unwilling capitulations, resolute dissent, and unconscious adherence to custom. Each vignette represents the way people experienced, understood, and recounted the stories of their lives. The results are a history that is made, not merely reported.

All humans make history: most, simply by being alive; a few by affecting the course of events over vast regions or changing the lives of thousands. But in a more direct way, we fashion and retell our personal stories within the context of our time, society, and culture. The Alutiiq people of the Alaska Peninsula, who also call themselves

Sugpiaq, have made history in all three ways. This book is an account of both their collective and individual histories, filtered through personal narrative, archaeological evidence, and written record. Its sources range from artful oratory to dry prose, each element deriving from a created view of reality.

Making History is a story of the Alutiiq people of the Alaska Peninsula over the course of some 9000 years. The story begins with the earliest archaeological evidence of human habitation—not demonstrably ancestral to today's Alutiiq population, but occupying the same territory—and extends to World War II, concentrating on the 200 years between first contact with Russians and the beginning of the war. Although history continued beyond the war, I followed the lead of the tradition bearers who tutored me in stopping at the dawn of the current era. I note only as postscripts the most recent events such as the baby boom, Alaska statehood, the Alaska Native Claims Settlement Act, the institution of a limited entry fishery, the *Exxon Valdez* oil spill, and the importation of television and computer.

The Alutiiq story is complex, wrought from the many voices that tell it. Each voice offers a different interpretation of the story's meaning and import. Its contents are the disorderly, often conflicting criss-crossing paths of people, ideas, and technology. If Alutiiq history could be represented by a single utterance, it would be more like the jumbled sum of all transmissions sent simultaneously over a fiber-optic cable than a harmonious musical composition. Distinct voices, some beautiful, others shrill, at times rise above the overall babble, but there is always background noise to confuse and obscure the piece.

Usually the history of a people who are socially, demographically, and ethnically in the minority is written in a single key: tragic, uplifting, promising, or instructive. The story I present in this book contains elements of all four. Reducing it to a single theme would disguise the richness of the Alutiiq experience.

The first key, tragedy: As often told, the Alutiiq story is the tragic one of a formerly self-sufficient people who were conquered and enslaved by foreign governments and capitalists. From their subjugators they learned to replace their traditional concern for the community with self-serving individualism. Some forgot their ancestral oneness with the land and become as rapacious toward it as the worst Europeans and Americans. As generally told, this narrative begins its descent with the arrival of the first Europeans, and, following the conventions of the narrative form, can have no happy ending. Even though individual Natives may prosper in the current system, to succeed they must give up their Nativeness.

A second, alternative key, triumph: Outstanding Alaska Native individuals, consummate communicators or artists, break through cultural barriers and teach lessons from their ancestral cultures to the non-Native newcomers around them. Intelligent, creative, perceptive, they achieve status in both cultures. This second story emphasizes continuities with the past rather than death and disruption. It is a hopeful and triumphant narrative.

But out of cataclysm comes new life, not just for a gifted few but for whole villages, the vestiges of a still living culture. The good of the community as a whole is still an overriding concern to many rural inhabitants, and this outlook underlies a third key, hope. Villagers still continue to respect the plants and animals that provide for them, and still teach their children the ancient stories that impart age-old values. Children still grow up honoring their elders, and still become skilled in solving the problems their natural surroundings present to them.

A fourth key, reflective, sees in the history of Alaska Native cultures the inevitable changes that all peoples have experienced throughout the history of humankind. By our nature humans like to design new ways to do things. We are excited by the novel, especially if it makes our lives easier. We are active participants in our destiny, at once reacting and causing additional changes. This story teaches that cultural change does not necessarily mean cultural death. Alutiiq culture in the twenty-first century will be different from nineteenth-century Alutiiq culture, but there will be threads of continuity between the two.

Not only is the history presented here multivocal—though not, I believe, as chaotic as the noise that travels over a fiber-optic cable—

it is also unfinished. This is partly because we have only limited information about the past. Each written record and oral narrative derives from a single perspective, mirroring a particular authorial goal. The writers of history were usually the bosses, victors, or teachers who had traveled to the Alaska Peninsula to accomplish a specific task. Rarely can we learn how the subjects of their policies experienced events. But even when an Alutiiq perspective is available through oral testimony, it is similarly one-sided. For instance, the stories I heard about folk heroes depict them as single-minded, focused humans. In life, each was a confused mixture of good and bad, thoughtful and selfish, hopeful and self-destructive. But because of the nature of oral tradition, much of this complexity is lost in the retelling. What is remembered is a clear lesson that can instruct future generations, and whatever does not is left out. This clarity makes for good moral instruction, but it oversimplifies history.

The story told here is unfinished, also, because history continues into the future. I infer from my study of the past that in the future Alutiiqs will choose from among a number of strategies for dealing with change. Some will embrace twenty-first century American values and charge into city life. Some will give up trying to adapt—or even survive—after a lifetime of change and victimization, and they may retreat into substance abuse. Some will choose to live in villages where they can be close to their cultural past and use the skills that allow them to thrive in that setting. Some will migrate between city and village, seeking a balance between the material wealth of the one and the natural and spiritual riches of the other. Each choice will add to the history of the future.

Finally, this tale is unfinished because of the information that is available, there are an immense number of stories about Alutiiq history, but only a few could be included here. Yet I hope that in its very multiplicity and inconclusiveness this account will communicate an appropriately rich and complex sense of the history of a unique people, and the recognition that they have been, are, and will continue, making history.

INTRODUCTION

HOW THIS BOOK CAME ABOUT

Alutiiqs educated in American schools treasure the world they hear described in the old stories. They also recognize that their knowledge of Alutiiq history is incomplete because they can neither understand the language of their grandparents, listen to the elders long gone, nor read the old stories, for they have never been printed. I wrote this book in large part for these younger generations as a way to communicate in a lasting and accessible way Alutiiq oral traditions and outsiders' observations about life in the past.

It was Alutiiq elders who suggested that a book be written. At first they merely agreed to let me, a non-Alutiiq anthropology student, record their oral traditions for posterity and the university archives. As I continued recording and learning and coming back for more, people began to see the value of a publication based on the oral traditions. As the person with the tape recorder and an interest in their past, I was given the task of researching, writing, and editing what I had heard. What began as personal research toward a doctorate in anthropology led to a collaborative exploration of the history of Alaska Peninsula Alutiiqs.

I first visited the peninsula villages in the Chignik and Perryville regions from my home city of Anchorage in 1990. I was a graduate student in anthropology at the University of Alaska Fairbanks. A dozen times over the next eight years, I flew the 500 miles from Anchorage to the villages of Chignik Bay, Chignik Lagoon, Chignik

Lake, Perryville, Ivanof Bay, and South Naknek. I spent from one to four weeks in the villages during each visit, staying in homes or sleeping on schoolroom floors. I observed, questioned, interviewed, recorded, worked, played, worshipped, ate, and lived with my hosts.

As generally happens when one enters a new cultural landscape, only after the visitor listens to people for a while does she realize what they are saying. Through the stories they told me, the elders were not merely recounting events of the past. They were also expressing a unique attitude about history in general and about Alutiiq history in particular, showing how the past gives meaning to the present and future and validates their identity as a people. It became clear to me that I needed to include this attitude, as well as the stories themselves, in the book.

Although elders recorded many of their oral traditions in the Alutiiq language, they asked that the book be written in English for the benefit of their children who speak only the language of schools. The volume was to be detailed enough for adult enlightenment and enjoyment, yet at a reading level suitable for high school students. This publication results from a two-way translation, first from Alutiiq to English, and second from oral performance to written transcript. At best the translation can only be an approximate portrayal of the narratives. It would be far better for the elders to tell their stories themselves, in the language they find most comfortable, at moments when the audience is most receptive. This book is a substitute, an adaptation to the fact that schoolbooks, television, and the internet are rapidly replacing the storytelling venues of the past.

HISTORY AND ETHNOHISTORY

Besides the oral traditions of the Alutiiq people of the Alaska Peninsula, this book contains information from a number of printed sources, including records of archaeological digs, letters and papers of Russian and American fur traders, explorers, and visitors to Alaska, and official government documents. This combination of sources yields a unique kind of history called *ethnohistory*.

Ethnohistories are different from traditional histories in two ways. First, they include information from the people themselves which is not usually part of the official written record. Besides offering a different perspective, this can add life to otherwise dull data. For instance, United States Census Bureau reports for the Alaska Peninsula tell the number of people who lived in particular villages and how they were related to members of their households. But the records do not indicate other personal information—such as which children were cousins, which men were hunting partners, which women were village midwives. Nor does official data describe how the people felt about each other, who was respected, who feared. This kind of information can only come from the oral traditions people tell about their ancestors.

The second distinguishing characteristic of ethnohistories is the way they look at the topic of history itself. All humans think and talk about the past, but people from different cultural backgrounds explain it differently. In Europe and mainstream America, history is usually understood as a line of events dating from the first written records and extending to the present. Everything that happened is seen to fit somewhere along the line. People from other cultures have other ways of reckoning time and talking about the past, and their histories reflect these practices. Many traditional societies concentrate not on the march of time and the changes that time brings—often seen as "progress" in Western histories—but on the continuity of seasonal or life cycles.

For instance, in the past as the summer salmon fishing season arrived, Alutiiq elders would explain to the children how to harvest the fish. They would also tell them how to show respect for the life force, the *sua*, of the salmon so that the fish would return the following year. Adults would recount stories about past individuals who disobeyed the rules or acted foolishly during fishing season. In this way Alutiiq children learned lessons about the past *when and as often as they were meaningful*. Chronology—for instance, when the rules were first codified—is irrelevant to the story.

This approach to teaching about the past is different from a history-book method in which a student might learn about George

Washington's wintertime camp at Valley Forge during September or May in a tenth-grade history course, and at no other time. Since according to this perspective events happen only once, teachers need to talk about each event only once during a child's education.

Alutiiqs have two ways of grouping narratives about the past, and neither is strictly chronological. Either they tell stories in groups according to topic—for instance, one *awuláq* [a bigfoot-like creature or "hairy man"] story usually leads to another, one war story to a second—or they talk about different genres of stories.[1]

The oldest stories, which were once commonly called *unigkuat* [singular *unigkuaq*], took place in a time long ago when the world was different from today. It was different not just because there were no four-wheelers or airplanes, but because the very nature of the relationship between humans and animals was different. In those long-gone days, animals and people could communicate with each other directly, using the Alutiiq language. Animals could transform themselves into human-looking beings by taking off their animal skins. Humans could put on animal skins and become animals. In this distant time, humans learned how to treat animals respectfully, avoid wasting game, be careful with animal bones or skins, and many other rules that still apply today. *Unigkuat* may seem magical or supernatural to some listeners today, but elders do not consider them fictional fairy tales. Alutiiqs explain that the stories are not invented, but have been learned from parents and grandparents, generation after generation. The elders say that the human-animal interactions that are described in *unigkuat* are extremely rare nowadays but that in the past they happened to everyone. The animals have not lost their ability to understand humans, but few humans can now understand messages from the animals.

Although *unigkuat* seem to refer to the days before Europeans came to the Alaska Peninsula, they cannot be placed at a particular date along the historical time line. Elders don't know, nor do they guess, when the events described in *unigkuat* took place. They only say that it was "long, long ago."

There are more recent stories, usually called *quliyanguat* [singular *quliyanguaq*], which happened in the past, but are about people whom living Alutiiqs remember personally or remember hearing about when they were children. Some of these narratives are similar to *unigkuat*. For instance, many *quliyanguat* that tell about events in the days before the 1912 Katmai eruption describe supernatural or paranormal occurrences. But *quliyanguat* are also different from *unigkuat* in that some of them *can* be assigned dates on a timeline. When an old woman tells a *quliyanguaq* about her girlhood experiences trapping ground squirrels, she can remember how old she was when she trapped, and so remember the season and the approximate year. Similarly, if a man remembers when his father's hunting partner was fatally mauled by a brown bear, he knows how old he was when it happened and can date the event accordingly. I have tried to reflect this Alutiiq way of understanding *unigkuat* and *quliyanguat* in this ethnohistory.

HISTORY AS INTERPRETATION

Like all histories, this one is not just a statement of dates and events, nor merely transcripts of oral performances. It is an interpretation of data fashioned into a collection of stories. All humans must interpret their own pasts and those of the people around them because so much happens in a single lifetime that only a small part of it can be remembered. The human mind remembers by relating new experiences to older understandings and assigning a meaning or interpretation to those new experiences. One result of this process is that humans may forget things that do not make sense to them at the time or that do not fit into their preconceived ideas about how the world works. Another result is that subconsciously people may invent interpretations to match information they had previously learned. Memory is especially malleable during times of disaster or extreme emotion. Author Norman Maclean's explanation of the memory of a particular catastrophic fire in Idaho is pertinent:

> it would be hard to make a map from [the participants'
> experiences] and then expect to find ground to fit the
> map. It has the consistency more of a gigantic emotional
> cloud that closes things together with mist, either

> obliterating the rest of the objective reality or moving the remaining details of reality around until, like furniture, they fit into the room of our nightmare in which only a few pieces appear where they are in reality.[2]

The memories of participants, whether crystal clear or within clouds of emotion, along with what newspaper reporters or government officials record, become the data that eventually are transformed into history. Histories are therefore interpretive and subjective because they are based on the experiences, attitudes, and understandings of the historians themselves and what somebody in the past thought was important enough to record.

This ethnohistory of the Alaska Peninsula Alutiiqs is triply subjective. In the first place, it depends on the memories that the Alutiiq people felt should be passed on to others. People such as Ignatius Kosbruk of Perryville, Vera Angasan of King Salmon, and Doris Lind of Chignik Lake chose to tell certain stories and not others. Aware that they were recording for the future, they purposely excluded information that might embarrass or hurt others. As a result, in writing this book I could not include all parts of remembered history.

A second part of the history of the Alaska Peninsula, that based on recorded impressions of outsiders, was limited by the skills and interests of those outsiders. For instance, Russian American Company (RAC) officials recorded population figures and shipping dates, but no one wrote in detail about a typical day in the life of an Alutiiq sea otter hunter or his wife. Therefore on some topics this history cannot go beyond what non-Alutiiq people of the past thought was important.

Third, in pursuing my own interests I shaped this book according to what I understand best and find most interesting. For instance, I have included rather more on questions of economic pursuits than government regulations. I also have omitted events or opinions told me in confidence.

I see this book as an opportunity to contrast perspectives from various participants or observers. Sometimes I have achieved a balance, other times merely a multisided picture. Nevertheless, for this underreported region and these little-known people, the necessarily partial picture presented here is far better than a blank canvas.

HOW THIS BOOK IS ARRANGED

Most Alutiiq stories are not concerned with dates, but instead with topics, lessons, or entertainment. Still, the oral traditions make more sense to a modern audience if they are heard or read in context. Listeners need to be able to picture the houses, people, weapons, tools, and animals that are part of the stories and understand what the characters in the stories think about certain things. For instance, do they consider gambling fun or evil? Do they think killer whales are good luck or bad omens? Are they afraid of shamans or grateful for their healing abilities? These types of information are not usually contained in the stories themselves, so I introduce each narrative in this book with a discussion of some of its cultural and historical context.

The book is arranged roughly in chronological order, following what has become the standard division of Alaska's history into the pre-contact era (before 1741), the Russian period (1741–1867), and the American period (after 1867). However, I made a few exceptions to this scheme in keeping with Alutiiq ways of considering the past. As a first step, I placed each narrative into one of the three historical eras. Then within each era, I placed the stories according to the topic they cover, but not necessarily according to a particular date. For instance, the story Ignatius Kosbruk told about the shaman Puglálria's conversion to Christianity appears in this book immediately following the discussion of the 1830s introduction of Russian Orthodoxy to Alaska Peninsula Alutiiqs. Puglálria probably lived not in the 1830s but in the 1880s or early 1900s, but rather than guess when the events in the story happened, I placed the narrative alongside its clarifying context.

In general, *unigkuat* are concerned with the old way of life as it existed before the coming of Europeans, dealing, for instance, with warfare against other Native peoples, the spiritual and natural properties of animals, and the challenges facing humans who live off the land and sea. These narratives seemed to fit best within the discussion of the pre-contact era. However, I did not place all *unigkuat* in the pre-contact section. As mentioned, several deal with Christianity or with parts of the Russian fur trade, and so appear in Chapter Three, The Russian Period.

Most *quliyanguat* fit into either the Russian or American period, but some are not easy to date. Alutiiqs were involved in sea otter hunting during both the American and Russian periods, and it is not always clear whether a given otter hunting story took place in one era or the other. I was able to assign other *quliyanguat* to a general period after a bit of research and thought. For instance, one narrative recounts a long walk down the coast of Bristol Bay. I concluded that the trip was made after the sale of Alaska to the United States but before the Katmai eruption. The travelers' destination, a fish cannery, was the first clue. No canneries were built on the Alaska Peninsula until the 1880s, so the story had to take place during the American era. The second clue was the route the men took. They portaged from the Pacific side of the peninsula down the Naknek River to the shores of Bristol Bay, a route no longer navigable after the Katmai eruption.

Still other *quliyanguat* can be dated precisely. Ignatius Kosbruk's tale of the death of Macintine refers to events and dates that are described in written records. This story is about a murder that occurred in Kodiak on November 1, 1886.

In general, then, I placed the narratives within appropriate chronological eras following the Euroamerican practice of using timelines, but surrounded by cultural and historical context, in accord with the Alutiiq way of remembering stories.

THE STORYTELLERS

Some narratives included here were recorded long before I began work on the Alaska Peninsula. I thank local residents and linguists for supplying me with copies of these tapes. I recorded the rest on audiocassettes, usually as the storytellers and I sat over cups of tea at kitchen tables. Sometimes the narrator's spouse or children were present and added comments or details. The people who recorded or recounted the oral traditions for this book include the following.

Perryville

The most prolific storyteller was Ignatius Kosbruk, the recognized storyteller of the village of Perryville (see map of Alaska Peninsula Alutiiq settlements, p. 20). He was instructed in his youth by three knowledgeable and important men. His father, George Kosbruk, was known as a dramatic storyteller with a keen sense of his audience. Ignatius's foster father, Harry Kaiakokonok, was an Alutiiq Russian Orthodox priest who was known as an effective teacher and excellent storyteller. Ignatius's mentor, Wasco Sanook, used to hold nightly storytelling sessions in his

Ignatius Kosbruk of Perryville
Lisa Scarbrough, Alaska Department of Fish and Game

own house that were attended by the young boys in the village. From him Ignatius Kosbruk learned most of the Alutiiq narratives he told me, both *unigkuat* and *quliyanguat*. Ignatius died in the summer of 1998 at age eighty.

Polly Shangin, in her eighties and the oldest resident of Perryville when I interviewed her, was universally respected and loved in the village. She spoke only Alutiiq, although she understood a great deal of English. She recorded parts of her life history in Alutiiq and through translators answered many questions I posed about life on the Alaska Peninsula at the beginning of the twentieth century. She died in the summer of 1997 at age eighty-seven.

Ralph Phillips of Perryville was in his midsixties when I worked with him, and claimed that he was less knowledgeable about traditional lore than Ignatius Kosbruk had been. He was formerly the bilingual teacher in the school and his interest in the Alutiiq language continues. He skillfully translated and helped me transcribe Kosbruk's Alutiiq stories. He also recorded a number of village traditions and personal memorates (narratives based on personal memories) of his own.

Elia and Mary Phillips were also from Perryville, though Elia's father was originally from the village of Mitrofania. Elia himself was church reader and very knowledgeable about both church lore and village history. He died in the spring of 1994. Mary, the sister of Father Harry Kaiakokonok, recalled much about her childhood in Perryville.

Ivanof Bay

In Ivanof Bay, Olga Kalmakoff and her eldest son Joe recorded several tapes with me. They, along with Olga's daughter Arlene Shugak, shared family photographs and recorded personal and family memorates.

Chignik Lake

In Chignik Lake, I was helped by Christine Martin, who recalled much about her upbringing in Perryville. She also remembered several Alutiiq songs that she had sung as a girl. Christine knew the histories and genealogies of many local families, and helped me keep characters straight in stories told by others. She passed away in early 2000.

Doris Lind, now nearly eighty, was the bilingual teacher at Chignik Lake in the late 1970s and early 1980s. She is still fascinated with both the language and the lore and told me many old stories, but agreed to record only local and family oral histories and traditions. She protested that she couldn't remember traditional Alutiiq stories completely enough to record them. She often referred to individuals, now deceased, who *really* knew the stories and should have been recorded. Like Ralph Phillips in Perryville, she skillfully translated and helped me transcribe Alutiiq language tapes recorded by others.

Doris's husband Bill was known for his knowledge of hunting stories and skill at telling them. The son of Chignik Lake's founder, Dora Andre, Bill was the village chief for many years. He excelled as both a hunter and as a village representative to state and federal agencies. At the request of a nephew, Bill recorded several memorates and traditional stories. He expressed great interest in preserving oral traditions and carefully read transcripts of recordings other Alutiiqs had made. Bill died of cancer in the summer of 1993.

Virginia Aleck, niece of Bill Lind, spent her younger days in her mother's home town, Perryville. Nancy Shangin Lind died when Virginia was a young girl, so Nancy's mother, Barbara Shangin Sanook, took care of the children and moved with them and their father, Andrew Lind, to Chignik Lake. Virginia was the health aide in Chignik Lake for many years and was known as an excellent hunter. Because she was raised by her grandmother, Virginia knows much traditional information that others of her generation had not had a chance to learn.

Barbara Shangin Sanook was Virginia Aleck's grandmother. Known as "Old Gramma" in Chignik Lake, she had survived the Katmai eruption. She was known as a healer, midwife, and excellent cook. She spoke little English, but passed on much information to her grandchildren before her death in the 1970s. She left a recorded tape of reminiscences about the Katmai eruption.

Dora Lind Andre, Chignik Lake's "Young Gramma," is one of the village's founders. Although I never met her, it was apparent that she was a remarkable woman. Widowed with young children, she hunted and fished to support them until she married her second husband, John Andre. She is remembered as hospitable, kind, generous, knowledgeable, and intelligent. She recorded reminiscences about her life on several occasions. Dora passed away in 1990 before I began work in the region.

Emil Artemie was the younger brother of Christine Martin. Born in Perryville and raised in Chignik Lake, he lived in the Lower 48 as well as various parts of Alaska. Emil was village president for several years and had worked with federal and state bureaucracies to benefit the village. He had a quirky sense of humor and recorded a number of personal memorates about growing up on the Alaska Peninsula at a time of much technological change. Emil passed away in 1995.

Chignik Bay

Spiridon Stepanoff was known by many in the Chignik region as "Grampa Down the Bay." Originally from the small village of Eagle Harbor on Kodiak Island, as a boy he had moved to Mitrofania with his family, then to Chignik Bay. His memory and skill at storytelling were remarkable. He is also re-membered as a gracious host and generous man. He recorded per-sonal memorates and oral history in 1969 for the Chignik Lake teachers shortly before he died.

Walter Stepanoff of Chignik Bay
Patricia Partnow

Walter Stepanoff, Sr., is Spiridon's nephew. Walter lives in Chignik Bay, where before his retirement he was a successful commercial fisherman and skilled photographer. His parents were originally from Kodiak Island and later Mitrofania, but Walter and his brothers and sister grew up in the Chignik area. Walter is an excellent storyteller who recorded personal memorates for this project.

Port Heiden

Aleck Constantine lived in Port Heiden, but was raised at the now-abandoned villages of Ilnik on the Bristol Bay side and the Old Village at Chignik Lagoon. He was related to several Chignik Lake residents, and it was in Chignik Lake at Christmastime in 1993 that I met him. He recalled life in Ilnik as well as tales told him by Spiridon Stepanoff. He died in 2000.

Chignik Lagoon

Mike Sam lived in Chignik Lagoon when I first met him; he later moved to Anchorage. Mike was the bilingual teacher at Chignik Lagoon school for many years. A generous and hospitable man, Mike recorded oral traditions as well as personal memorates for this project. He remembered much that his grandfather, Innokenty Kalmakoff, had told him. Mike died in 1998.

August "Skinnix" Pedersen was the grandson of a Danish fisherman and an Alutiiq woman. Both his parents were "Scandinavian Aleuts," descendents of fishermen who came from Northern Europe at the turn of the century and stayed on to live and marry Native women. Born and raised in the Chignik area, Skinnix lived in Chignik Lagoon until his death in 1991. He had an excellent memory for places and events related to both commercial fishing and subsistence practices. He recorded some of his memories when I visited him in the summer of 1990.

Bureau of Indian Affairs anthropologists also interviewed knowledgeable elders from Chignik Lagoon. Julius Anderson and Clements Grunert shared much information about area land use and trapping practices with them.

South Naknek

Vera Kie Angasan is the matriarch of a large, well-known family from South Naknek. Born in Ugashik of an Alutiiq mother and Japanese father, Vera spent her formative years in New Savonoski and Kittiwik, a seasonal fishing and hunting camp at the mouth of Brooks River in what is now Katmai National Park. After the death of her father and remarriage of her mother, she lived with Pelegia Melgenak and her husband, One-Arm Nick Melgenak. From them,

Vera Kie Angasan of King Salmon and South Naknek
Patricia Partnow

Vera learned about both life in Old Savonoski before the 1912 Katmai eruption and contemporary subsistence practices. I interviewed Vera at her home in King Salmon.

Pelagia Melgenak
National Park Service

Teddy Melgenak, now of King Salmon, was also raised by Pelegia and Nick Melgenak. The youngest of many foster children, he felt privileged to hear stories of life in pre-eruption days and learn hunting and fishing techniques from the recognized experts of the area. Teddy is now in his early sixties and continues to visit the old site of Kittiwik through his job with the National Park Service at Katmai.

I also interviewed Vera Angasan's two oldest children, Fred Theodore Angasan, Sr., and Mary Jane Angasan Nielsen, both of South Naknek. They grew up first in New Savonoski and then in South Naknek, learning from Pelegia and Nick Melgenak (whom they call "Gramma and Táta") as had the generation before them. Both are also students of the history of the region and were extremely helpful in pointing me to important sources of information about the Naknek River drainage.

Finally, I interviewed Carvel Zimin, Sr., the son of a Russian immigrant who arrived in Alaska via Hawaii, and a Scandinavian-Aleut mother. Like Vera, Teddy, Ted, and Mary Jane, Carvel spent most summers and many autumns in Katmai National Park, learning about its human and natural history and harvesting its resources. An observant and involved man, Carvel provided much insight into the current political situation as it relates to subsistence harvests.

Other Storytellers

The people listed above, along with three others mentioned below, were considered among the most knowledgeable tradition-bearers in the region by their fellow villagers. There are other people whom

I did not interview formally, either because we never happened to be in the same place at the same time, or they were too busy with family, job, or subsistence activities to sit down in front of a tape recorder. But there is a woman and two men in particular whom I wish I had been able to record. Each possesses a wealth of information about the peninsula's history.

The first is Ivanof Bay's patriarch and founder and Olga's husband, Artemie Kalmakoff. As a young man he was a formidable brown bear hunter. His children remembered hearing many exciting tales about his younger days, but he was not interested in recording them. He died in 1999.

In Chignik Lake, Mary Boskofsky, sister of Bill Lind, knows many traditional rituals and taboos and remembers much history told her by her mother, Dora Andre. People go to Mary for advice on everything from recipes to child raising to moral advice to the proper way to follow traditional customs. She shared some of this information with me, but did not wish to be recorded.

Finally, Harry Aleck of Chignik Lake, nephew of Dora Andre, was raised in the Bristol Bay village of Ilnik and moved to Chignik Lake with his wife and children in about 1950. He is now nearly deaf so rarely tells stories any more. People are concerned that his vast knowledge will be forgotten. It is with regrets that the stories of these people and many others are not included in this book.

NOTES

1.   Throughout this volume I have used the Alutiiq orthography proposed in 1999 for the Chugachnuit Curriculum Project by Jeff Leer, after consultation with Sally Ash, Sperry Ash, Fiona Sawden, Seraphim Ukatisch, and Rhoda Moonin.

2.   Maclean 1992: 212.

1

ALUTIIQS AND THE LAND

The Alaska Peninsula is little known and less visited. The images broadcast by fishing and hunting lodges show huge brown bears, Bristol Bay red salmon and herring catches, and the moonlike Valley of Ten Thousand Smokes in Katmai National Park. Most Alaskans know nothing of the terrain, natural resources, or human history of

Valley of Ten Thousand Smokes.
Patricia Partnow

the Alaska Peninsula, for it is remote even by Alaska standards. No roads tie peninsula communities to the rest of the state or each other, so casual tourists never stumble in. The peninsula is sparsely populated except during the frenzied fishing seasons of late spring and summer. And its history is largely unpublished, residing either in the memories of elders or archival records of defunct trading companies and abandoned churches.

Yet the human history of the Alaska Peninsula is long and varied. People have lived off its resources for some 9000 years, waging uncounted battles, traveling unimagined distances, and adapting themselves to changing circumstances. Recorded history began a scant 200 years ago when a handful of Russians, the first visitors from an alien continent, built fur-trading posts on the shores of the peninsula. Today's residents can claim ancestry from these immigrants, but also from Yupiit (the autonym of the people of Southwest Alaska, commonly called "Eskimos"), Unangan (Aleuts of the Aleutian Islands), Athabaskan Indians, and later arrivers born in Scandinavia, Italy, Greece, Japan, and points beyond. Each group has contributed to the region's story.

In short, the Alaska Peninsula is a place whose story needs to be told. This book contributes to that story with the history of one particular set of peninsula residents, those who today call themselves *Sugpiaq, Alutiit,* or Alutiiqs.

THE LAND

The narrow Alaska Peninsula, 475 miles long and averaging 50 miles wide, extends from Iliamna Lake in southwestern Alaska to Unimak Island in the Aleutians. The entire length of the peninsula's southeastern Pacific shore is dominated by the rugged volcanic Aleutian Range. The northwestern Bering Sea/Bristol Bay shore of the peninsula, in contrast, is a flat, lake-studded tundra. The peninsula enjoys a maritime climate with an average annual temperature of forty degrees Fahrenheit and a yearly precipitation of from twenty to seventy-five inches, depending on location. The wind is almost

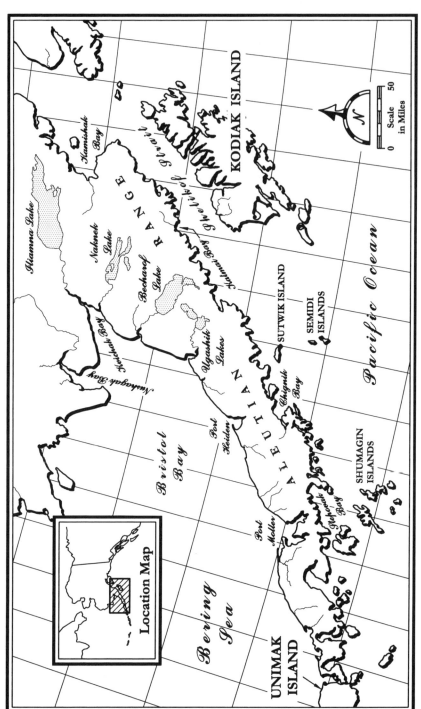

The Alaska Peninsula

continuous, often gusting above forty miles per hour. The region is rich in salmon, halibut, and herring. Local sea mammals include seals, sea lions, sea otters, orcas, beluga whales, and occasionally baleen whales. Common land mammals are caribou and Kodiak brown bears, as well as smaller animals such as beavers, marmots, and ground squirrels. Many species of waterfowl nest in the peninsula's lakes and shores.

In the past, people traveled often and far as they journeyed from location to location on the Alaska Peninsula, but they traveled slowly. Before contact with European explorers—a time that historians call the "pre-contact era"—people either walked or used skin boats for transport. During the early twentieth century, dogsleds, sailboats and fishing dories came into use. Even today a journey to the Alaska Peninsula is no small undertaking. With no roads between communities, the traveler must fly in a small twin-engine twenty-seater aircraft to the town of King Salmon. The route from Anchorage, Alaska's largest city, follows the coast of the Kenai Peninsula, crosses Cook Inlet, passes over Kamishak Bay with the active volcano that forms Augustine Island, climbs over a portion of the Alaska Range, traverses huge Iliamna Lake, and eventually follows the Naknek River valley to the runway. In good weather the territory that was once known only to the Alutiiq hunters of Katmai and Savonoski is visible beneath the plane on the approach to King Salmon. As the plane glides or bumps above mountain passes and river rapids, its passengers can imagine people hauling sleds or portaging skin-covered kayaks along the route below.

King Salmon itself is just barely on the Alaska Peninsula, on the edge of Alutiiq territory. To get to most of the villages inhabited by Peninsula Alutiiqs today, one must hop aboard a small single-engine plane and scoot down the Naknek river to South Naknek or take what locals call the "milk run" down the coast of Bristol Bay toward one of five villages in the Chignik and Perryville areas. The route crosses vast stretches of tundra, often providing glimpses of swans, caribou, or brown bear. The first stop is Egegik, which during the summer boasts a large concentration of commercial fishers from Seattle as well as Bristol Bay and the Alaska Peninsula. Residents consider theirs an ethnically mixed community devoted not to

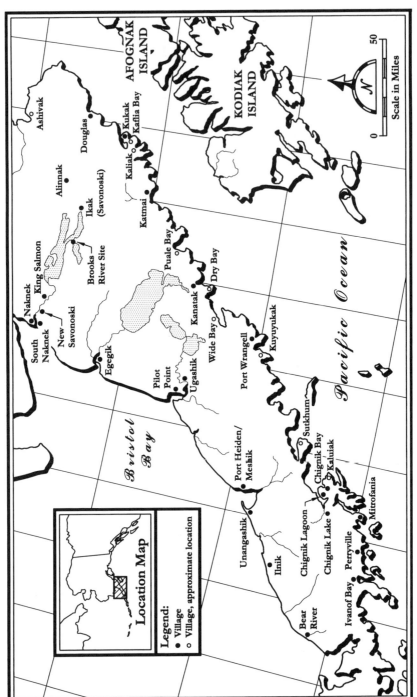

Alaska Peninsula Alutiiq Settlements

traditional lifeways but to commerce. People with ancestry from various European and Asian countries live alongside Yup'ik-speaking people and a few Alutiiqs.

The plane bumps along the gravel runway, then takes off to the southwest for the next village, another ethnically diverse place called Pilot Point. This too is a busy fishing village in the summer, and during the winter is the home for several dozen Yupiit, Inupiat (northern Eskimos) brought to the region to herd reindeer in 1910, and, again, Alutiiqs.

From Pilot Point it is a straight shot down the coast to Port Heiden. During World War II, this town was a bustling hive of army barracks and Quonset huts. It is now a transportation hub for the more southern villages of the Alaska Peninsula as well as for Sand Point in the Shumagin Islands and Aleutian Island destinations. Two generations ago Port Heiden was known as "Mashiq" ("Meshik" in modern spelling), and was a small Alutiiq village. The population of about a hundred now consists of a number of Caucasians as well as the descendents of earlier Alutiiq and Unangan residents.

From Port Heiden the plane finally crosses back over to the Pacific side of the peninsula, climbing to clear a mountain pass. The route to Chignik Lake is always turbulent—so much so that at a certain point the plane is said to pass through the "Chignik bump." Passengers sometimes report bruised heads from the sudden bounces and pitches of the small plane, but the pilots seem to enjoy the diversion. If travelers fly to Chignik Lake in the summer or fall, they often see brown bears below, and the pilot obligingly banks steeply to allow a closer view. The plane follows the ancient portage route between the Pacific and Bristol Bay sides of the peninsula. Beneath the aircraft stretches first Black Lake, then winding Chignik River, which in turn empties into Chignik Lake. The village of Chignik Lake lies at the far end of the lake, at the narrow point where it enters the second part of Chignik River.

Chignik Lake was the site of an ancient village or hunting camp. Local beachcombers have found dozens of stone projectile points, knife blades, skin scrapers, incised pebbles, and arrowheads. When

Village of Chignik Lake.
  Patricia Partnow

the new school was built in the 1980s, workers uncovered what local residents describe as a sizable site with many artifacts, including a large bowl-like stone oil-burning lamp. During the twentieth century the area where the village is now located was a heavily used trapping, hunting, and fishing ground, inhabited seasonally. Today's Alutiiq residents established a permanent year-round village only about forty years ago when a few parents decided that their children needed a local school. It is not clear whether the earlier stone-tool-makers were the ancestors of today's Alaska Peninsula Alutiiqs or were a different group of people altogether. What is clear is that the Black Lake/Chignik River portage is an ancient and well-traveled route across the peninsula.

Beyond Chignik Lake, the plane follows the twists of the short eastern segment of the Chignik River to the large saltwater lake called Chignik Lagoon. On its southeastern shore is the village by the same name. During the summer, the lagoon is packed with fishing boats from all over southwestern Alaska waiting to take advantage of the huge red salmon runs that head through the lagoon and up the river.

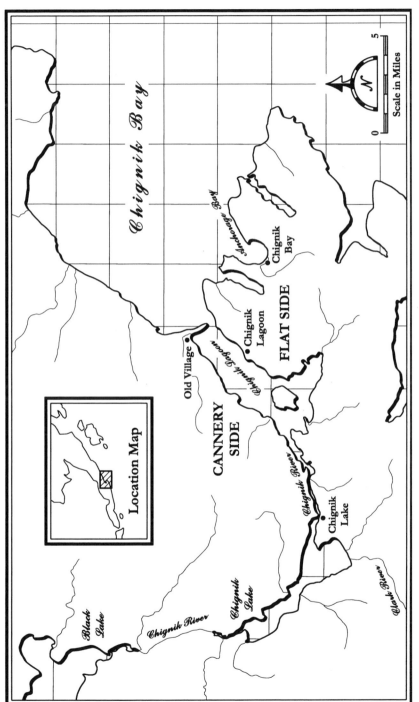

Chignik Area

Chignik River fish weir near the village of Chignik Lake.
Patricia Partnow

Until 1959 when fish traps were banned, massive permanent log and wire structures, each capable of holding thousands of fish, jutted out of the water at four or five locations within the lagoon and outside its protecting sandspit. Nowadays, fishing is regulated by the Alaska Department of Fish and Game, which allows for escapement of enough fish up the river to ensure future populations of salmon. In the winter, the village of Chignik Lagoon is sparsely populated, consisting of Alutiiq and non-Native fishermen and women who have decided to winter over, or whose families have lived there for several generations.

The town of Chignik (also called Chignik Bay), just around a point from the village of Chignik Lagoon, is the financial center of the region. It is located in small, protected Anchorage Bay, which is part of the larger body of water called Chignik Bay. The town's canneries employ a number of seasonal workers, many of whom are college students flown in from other parts of Alaska or the Lower 48 states. One cannery operates year-round, taking advantage not only of summer salmon fisheries, but also cod, crab, and pollock.

The town of Chignik, 1900.
  Patricia Partnow

Chignik, also called Chignik Bay.
  Patricia Partnow

Perryville, from Perryville School.
  Patricia Partnow

The community has a mixed population of Caucasians, Alutiiqs, and a large contingent of Scandinavian-Aleuts.

There are two additional Alutiiq villages on the Alaska Peninsula: Perryville (which airplanes approach either through harrowing mountain passes from Chignik Lake or Chignik Bay or along the longer and less exciting coastal route) and Ivanof Bay, southwest of Perryville. Both villages are young settlements, but the ancestors of their inhabitants have lived on the peninsula for thousands of years. Perryville was established in 1912 by the refugees from the destroyed Alutiiq villages of Katmai and Douglas, and the saltery site at Kaflia Bay far to the northeast. The eruption of Katmai Volcano had killed wildlife and covered the entire northeastern portion of the peninsula in several feet of ash. Aided by the U.S. Revenue Cutter Service (the predecessor of today's U.S. Coast Guard), the people chose a new location for their village, built homes, and began to live off the land and sea in this new and unknown territory.

Like the four other villages on the Pacific side of the peninsula, Perryville is located in a spectacular setting. In contrast to the flat tundra on the Bristol Bay side, the terrain on the eastern coast is broken by countless fjords, inlets, and bays. Mountains jut out of the water in straight vertical lines. Only a few flat areas provide sites for villages, and one such area is the setting for Perryville. A long volcanic black-sand beach curves from the salmon-bearing Kametolook River in the northeast to the rocks of shellfish-rich Three Star Point to the southwest. The wide bay in front of the village is protected by Chiachi Island, whose name is a derivative of *chaika*, the Russian word for seagull. Behind the village a wide coastal plain rises for twenty miles toward the foothills of volcanic mountains dominated by active Mount Veniaminov.

From the earliest days of Perryville, its residents used Ivanof Bay to the southwest as a hunting, fishing and trapping area. In the mid-1960s six families decided to leave Perryville for Ivanof Bay permanently, not only to be closer to the natural resources they depended on but also to establish a religious colony of converts to the Slavic Gospel Mission. Most of those who stayed behind in Perryville have remained Russian Orthodox.

ALASKA PENINSULA INHABITANTS

The picture was very different when Russians first set foot on the Alaska Peninsula in the eighteenth century. Rather than stable villages of 100 residents, they found a number of smaller settlements, many that were used only seasonally. The people of the Alaska Peninsula spoke several different languages, each centered in a different area. West of Port Moller, including the offshore Shumagin and Sanak Islands in the Pacific, were Unangan speakers who shared the language and culture of their Aleutian Islands neighbors, but not of the Alaska Peninsula Alutiiq speakers (see map, Precontact Ethnic Relationships, next page). In the northeast lived Dena'ina Athabaskan Indians, inland Kiatagmiut (Yup'ik speakers), and recent Yup'ik immigrants from the Kuskokwim area who called themselves Aglurmiut. Also in the northeastern part of the peninsula, primarily along the Pacific coast, were the villages of speakers of a fourth language, who then called themselves *Sugpiat* (meaning "authentic, real people"),

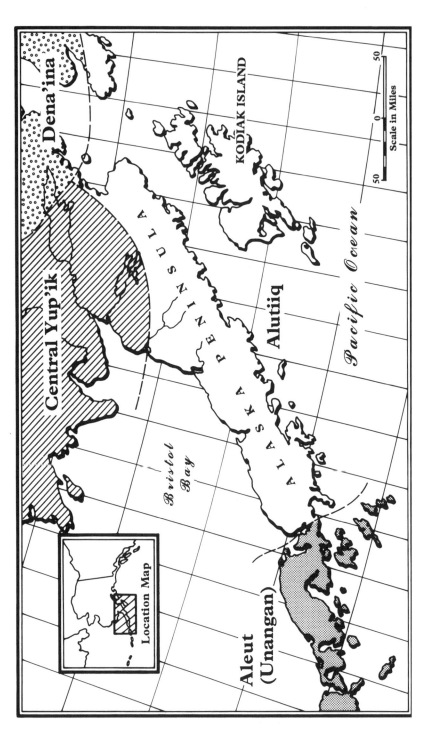

Dena'ina

Central Yup'ik

KODIAK ISLAND

ALASKA PENINSULA

Alutiiq

Pacific Ocean

Bristol Bay

Location Map

Aleut
(Unangan)

Scale in Miles

50   0   50

Precontact Ethnic Relationships

but whose descendents today often use the term *Alutiiq*. Linguists classify Sugpiaq/Alutiiq (also called Sugtestun) as an Eskimo language. Indeed it is so closely related to Central Yup'ik that some Alutiiq speakers can understand Yup'ik speakers who live as far north as Bethel. Sugpiaq/Alutiiq is in the same language family as Unangan, though very distantly related, but it is not at all related to Dena'ina, which is in the Na-Dene family. When the Russians arrived they found that the Alutiiq language was also spoken by people on Kodiak Island, the southern part of the Kenai Peninsula, and the shores of Prince William Sound.

Oral tradition indicates that during precontact days, there were only two recognized ethnic boundaries on the Alaska Peninsula. The first was between the Eskimo-speaking peoples (the ancestors of today's Yupiit and Sugpiaq/Alutiiqs) and the Unangan speakers to the west and southwest (see map, facing page). The Alutiiqs called the Unangan people *tayawut*, after the Unangan word *tayaĝux̂*, meaning "man." The Unangan, in turn, called the Alutiiqs of the Alaska Peninsula and Kodiak Island *Kanaagin*. Russian pronunciation turned *Kanaagin* into *Kan'iag*, and the island's name into *Kad'iak*. In modern spelling, these terms have become "Koniag" and "Kodiak" respectively.

The Unangan and Alutiiqs were bitter enemies. Stories of bloody battles are still told today. Both peoples now call themselves "Aleut" when speaking English, but neither used this name in the days before contact with Europeans. Eighteenth-century Russians labeled them "Aleuts," ignoring the people's names for themselves: Unangan, Alaska Peninsula Sugpiaq, and Kodiak Sugpiaq.

The second firm boundary on the Alaska Peninsula in precontact days was between the Eskimo speakers (Yupiit and Sugpiaq/Alutiiqs) and the Dena'ina Athabaskans to the northeast (see map, opposite page). Like the Unangan, the Dena'ina were enemies to the Yupiit and Alutiiqs. Nonetheless, Yupiit, Alutiiqs, and Dena'ina Athabaskans occasionally traded with each other.

Nowadays Alutiiqs and Yupiit acknowledge differences between their languages and cultures, but their ancestors did not think of themselves as separate peoples. First, their languages were so close that they merged into a single dialect somewhere in the northern part of the peninsula, probably at about the point where Egegik is located today. Second, before Russian days the Native people of Alaska did not conceptualize "tribes" or "nations" or even "groups." Instead, each village was a separate political unit. Villages might temporarily band together for wars against a common enemy, but there were no paramount chiefs of all the Alutiiqs, nor of the Yupiit, nor of any group of Natives. The only leaders were heads of their families or villages or temporary war leaders.

The Russian newcomers began to change life on the peninsula, first by introducing European goods and money, and later by converting the people to their religion. They built two trading posts on the Alaska Peninsula within Alutiiq territory, the larger one at Katmai and a small post at Sutkhum (see map, Alaska Peninsula Alutiiq settlements, p. 20). Through a combination of force, persuasion, and novelty, the eighteenth- and nineteenth-century Russians convinced the Alutiiqs to hunt and trap fur-bearing animals for the European fur trade, and in exchange gave the hunters goods such as cloth, metal, sugar, and tea. By the mid-1800s, Russian priests were making regular visits to the Alaska Peninsula settlements, all of whose residents had been baptized into the Russian Orthodox church.

The Russians also introduced a more subtle change to Alaska Peninsula simply by renaming the people they met. They called the Alaska Peninsula "Aliaksa" or "Aliaska," and often called the Alutiiq speakers who lived there "Aliaksintsy" [Alaskans]. They sometimes called the Alaska Peninsula Alutiiq speakers "Kan'iagi" [Koniags], borrowing the Unangan name *Kanaagin*. In some ways, this was appropriate, for Kodiak Islanders and Alaska Peninsula peoples spoke the same dialect of Sugpiaq, their cultures were very similar, and they believed themselves to be related to each other. The Russians often modified their catch-all term "Aleut" with geographic adjectives. For instance, they called one group of Unangan the "Fox Aleuts" (after the Fox Islands in the Aleutian Chain) and the Koniag and Alaska Peninsula peoples "Koniag Aleuts." The name "Aleut" eventually caught on among the people themselves, so that today the

Alaska Peninsula and Kodiak Island autonym, *Alutiiq*, is simply the word *Aleut* spoken in the Native language.

The Russians had other effects on old ethnic boundaries. Beginning at the turn of the nineteenth century, the Russian-American Company, which owned the trading posts on the peninsula, moved Koniags and Prince William Sound Alutiiqs to the peninsula posts, and peninsula Alutiiqs to Kodiak or southeast Alaska posts. Whole villages moved from their old winter sites to former summer camp sites to be closer to the Russian settlements. Native people began to live peacefully with old enemies. They met new people and learned new ideas from them.

The formation of a new class of people, the creoles, complicated the question of who was an Alutiiq and who was not. Creoles were the children or descendents of Russian fathers and Native mothers. During precontact days they would have been accepted as village members without questioning their genetic heredity. However, under an agreement between the Russian-American Company and the government of Russia, these children were considered of a class separate from their Alutiiq cousins, and awarded more privileges than either Alutiiqs or local Russian inhabitants. For instance, creoles could not be forced to work for the company, unlike Natives, nor did they need to pay taxes, unlike Russians. In addition, they were given the chance to obtain a free education at company expense, as long as they promised to work for the company after graduation.

Today's Alaska Peninsula Alutiiqs are the descendents of these eighteenth-century Sugpiaq speakers, creoles, and other immigrants who traveled to Alaska and decided to stay. Their written history begins with the reports of early Russian explorers, but their past stretches back much farther than the eighteenth century. It is that earlier period, before written records, that the next chapter considers.

2
THE PRE-CONTACT PERIOD ON THE ALASKA PENINSULA

ORIGINS

Elders no longer recall stories about the distant era when the world was made. However, long ago the people of the Alaska Peninsula probably told a myth similar to the following, recounted on Kodiak Island to the Russian Orthodox official Hieromonk Gideon at the beginning of the nineteenth century:

> There was once upon a time a Kashshiakhiliuk *[kaḻagalek]*, a sage, a trickster. At that time there was neither day nor night. He began to blow through a straw, causing land to begin to emerge gradually from the water and imperceptibly to spread. Then, while he still continued to blow, the sky opened, the sun appeared, and in the evening the stars came out and the moon rose. Finally they saw animals and people.[1]

Nor have records of traditions about the origins of the people of the Alaska Peninsula survived. Again, Gideon reported a legend that was probably shared by peninsula Alutiiqs:

> The Kad'iak folk, according to the legends recounted by the old people, moved to Kad'iak from Aliaksa [Alaska Peninsula]. Their ancestors formerly lived on the north side of Aliaksa near a great river, the Kvignak. They had

an anayugak [leader, *angayuqaq*] named Atlivatu. He had
an only, well beloved daughter who disappeared without
a trace. He set out with his command to search for the
girl, and also persuaded another angayuqaq, Iakunak by
name, to join him. They wandered over many places for
a long time. Nearing the southern side of Aliaksa, they
sighted land and called it Kigikhtak *[Qikertaq]*, which
means in their language "an island." This name was ap-
plied to Kad'iak until the arrival of the Russians.

Later on, Atlivatu and Iakunak became curious, in-
vestigated, and all sorts of advantages [on the island]
persuaded the rest with their families to resettle on
Qikertaq.

The affinity of the languages of Kad'iak and Aliaksa
inhabitants lends support to such [a sequence of] events.[2]

For a century, geologists and archaeologists have asked the questions considered in these oral traditions: how was the land formed
and where did the people come from? With each new batch of evidence, the answers become more detailed, the past clearer. The first
indication of a human presence was the discovery of tools found in
the Ugashik narrows region on the Bering Sea coast. The tools date
to about 9000 BP (Before Present). Because no human skeletons were
found with the tools, it is impossible to determine whether those
who made them were ancestral to today's peninsula Alutiiqs.[3]

The distant past of the peninsula's other coast was, at first, even
more puzzling. Early archaeological findings were misleading; researchers found few prehistoric sites, especially when compared with
the numbers being unearthed in the Kodiak Island group. Archaeologists reasoned that the coast's rich marine environment with
numerous bays, inlets, and salmon streams, coupled with its inter-
mittent portages into the peninsula interior, should have been as
inviting to people as was heavily populated Kodiak.[4] It was not until
restoration measures following the 1989 *Exxon Valdez* oil spill allowed
researchers to survey the coast for environmental damage that archaeologists discovered dozens of new sites. These show that, indeed,
the Pacific coast of the Alaska Peninsula was far more heavily populated just before contact with Europeans than it has been since. In
fact, the region experienced a steady population growth for some

6000 years until 1500 BP. From that time to the eighteenth century, the population grew at a more rapid rate still, so that much of the coast was inhabited by the years immediately preceeding European contact.[5] Locations especially favored for settlements were those with a variety of resources available throughout the year and sufficient shelter to allow easy sea travel in skin kayaks.

The earliest Pacific Coast Alaska Peninsula sites, dating to about 6000 BP and located near Katmai, are similar to sites from the same period on Kodiak Island.[6] The people on the two shores of Shelikof Strait lived on sea mammals, shellfish, and fish. Their tools were made of chipped and flaked chert and basalt.

The earliest sites found along the Naknek drainage north of Ugashik date from 4500 BP. They show marked differences from the Kodiak and Pacific coast peninsula sites. Tools were made not just from flaked stone but also from polished slate. Oil lamps rather than firepits supplied heat and light, and caribou remains are more common than bones of sea mammals. People on Kodiak Island and the Pacific Coast of the peninsula added ground slate tools to their tool kits shortly after 4500 BP, probably a result of contact with these Bering Sea people.[7]

It was at this time, roughly 4500 BP, that sites in Bristol Bay, Ugashik River, and Naknek River shared with more northern peoples the Arctic Small Tool Tradition, an assemblage of artifacts that extended north along the Bering Sea and was ancestral to Eskimo culture. During this period, the sites on the two coasts of the peninsula show many similarities, suggesting that people traveled from shore to shore. Nonetheless, there are still enough differences between Pacific and Bering Sea coast sites to suggest that each was home to separate peoples.[8]

Meanwhile, people were also living at the southwestern end of the Alaska Peninsula and along the Chignik coast. Their sites are similar to those that later developed on the Aleutian chain, though they also show contact with peninsula residents to the northeast and across the peninsula at Port Moller.[9]

By 2200 BP the Chignik region had begun to be used heavily, but the unique tool assemblage found there differs from those found at

Brooks River barabara reconstruction near Naknek Lake.
National Park Service

Ugashik and Naknek River regions as well as those from the Katmai
coast. In fact, it was not until about 1000 BP that the Chignik area
people used substantially the same tool kits—with the exception of
pottery, which has not been found in this region—as the people who
came to speak Sugpiaq and inhabit the upper peninsula.[10]

In short, over the years, periods of isolation between the Pacific
and Bering Sea coasts of the Alaska Peninsula alternated with periods of contact, with a long-term trend toward more contact. By 1000
BP (about AD 1000) the people of the Bering Sea and Pacific coasts
of the peninsula at least as far south as Chignik Bay, as well as people
of the Kodiak Island group, were in frequent and continuous contact. In fact, thousand-year-old sites on the Pacific side of the
peninsula look almost identical to those on the Bristol Bay side. The
tool kits and settlement patterns on the two coasts began to look
alike quite suddenly, indicating that communication and transportation between Bristol Bay and Kodiak Island had opened up in a very
short time. People must have begun to travel across portages from

the Naknek and Ugashik rivers to the Pacific coast regularly, either moving into villages inhabited by others or for trade. They seem to have overcome some unknown barrier that had kept them from exploiting the Chignik coast as well. In doing so they introduced many Eskimo tools and ideas. Scholars believe that it was at this time that the Yup'ik-like language that later came to be called Alutiiq or Sugpiaq became dominant on Kodiak and the peninsula.[11]

From AD 1000 until the eighteenth century the people of Kodiak Island and the Pacific coast of the Alaska Peninsula continued to develop and revise their tools and way of life, in the process developing a unique culture anthropologists call "Pacific Eskimo." When Russians first visited the peninsula they found Alutiiq-speaking people using skin boats, oil lamps, complex stone, bone, and ivory tools, and skillfully crafted skin clothing. The inhabitants built square semisubterranean houses and located their villages on beaches. They spent summers at fish camps, some within a day's travel of the winter settlements, others farther away, and traveled far to hunt, trade, and engage in battle.

Unfortunately, archaeological investigation cannot uncover the languages in use by the earliest toolmakers, nor how the people themselves were related to each other. Scholars have no way of knowing what the people of the Alaska Peninsula spoke before they adopted Sugpiaq in about AD 1000. Linguists do know that three of the peninsula languages the Russians encountered—Unangan, Sugpiaq/Alutiiq, and Yup'ik—developed from the same parent language, which they call "Esk-Aleut," and share some aspects of grammar, vocabulary, and a phonemic system. However, Alutiiq and Yup'ik are so different from Unangan that it is as if the people who spoke them separated 4000 years ago.

PRECONTACT CULTURE AS REPORTED BY THE RUSSIANS

Almost from first contact, the Russians realized that the Alaska Peninsula Alutiiqs considered their neighboring Unangan speakers enemies. The cultural border on the Pacific side was likely at about Kuiukta Bay, northeast of the present village of Perryville and just south of Chignik Bay.[12] On the Bering Sea side, Port Moller (see map, p. 20) is the most probable easternmost boundary of Unangan territory. Much of the land between that bay and the Ugashik River was either uninhabited or dotted only with seasonal sites.[13]

The first Russian visitors to the Pacific side of the Alaska Peninsula found that most of coastline between Stepovak Bay to the south and Katmai to the north was used only as seasonal hunting and fishing grounds by Unangan and Alutiiqs. One Russian document reports that Katmai Alutiiqs regularly traveled to Sutwik and Semidi Islands, sometimes journeying even further west toward Unimak Island to hunt sea otters, seals, and sea lions.[14]

On the Bering Sea, the village of Ugashik, slightly inland along the Ugashik River, is the southernmost mentioned in early Russian sources. During the first part of the nineteenth century, Ugashentsy (the people of Ugashik) traveled regularly across the peninsula to the Pacific side to hunt the abundant sea mammals.[15]

Although accounts by Russian and American travelers sometimes conflict, it appears that at the time of contact the people living along the Bering Sea coast of the Alaska Peninsula north of Ugashik spoke Yup'ik, while those between Port Moller and Ugashik possibly spoke a language intermediate between Yup'ik and Alutiiq. It is clear that the Ugashentsy were a group distinct from their Yup'ik-speaking neighbors, particularly the recently invading Aglurmiut—but whether they spoke the same language is not clear. In the 1830s Russian-American Company Chief Manager Wrangell explained how the Ugashentsy had been displaced south from the Nushagak River by the Aglurmiut, who in turn had been pushed out of their homeland. Wrangell wrote,

> the Agolegmiuts [Aglurmiut] and the Kuskokvim [Kuskokwim] are enemies, since the former were driven from their homes on the banks of the Kuskokvim.... They finally moved away to Nunivok [Nunivak] Island and another island at the mouth of the Nushagak, where they settled under the protection of the commander of the [Novo] Aleksandrovskii Redoubt and were safeguarded from the attacks of the Kuskokvim.... For their part, the Agolegmiuts expelled the natives living at the mouth of

the Nushagak, and these wandered as far as the eastern
half of the Aliaska Peninsula and are now known as the
Severnovtsy (Northerners) and Ugashentsy.[16]

Many Yup'ik legends tell about the time in the 1600s and 1700s
when peninsula people were pushed southward and inland by invading Yupiit from the north. This so-called period of the Bow and
Arrow Wars involved the Yup'ik people from the mouth of the Yukon
River to the Bristol Bay area.[17] Nick Abalama of Egegik told part of
the story to Bureau of Indian Affairs researcher Marie Meade, who
translated the account:

> He [Nefoti] used to tell me stories of the warring time. When
> the enemy comes they would flee to the area. And those that fled
> would stay and probably establish settlements. And at that time
> in the spring and summer when a cuicuicuaq [a kind of bird] sings
> out they would move on even in the middle of the night. They
> were afraid of the warriors....
>
> They probably populated that area [right along Becharof Lake]
> there....
>
> It is those darts. They say there were two fathers—the two boys,
> the children of theirs, were playing a dart game. One of the boys
> accidentally struck the other boy. The father of the other boy—
> perhaps they were *kumeglutek* [angry?]. Then the father of the
> other boy quickly poked the child's eyes. It was from that inci
> dent the fighting and killing began.
>
> It was out there—from someplace there, perhaps it was above
> the Kuskokwim area or in the Kuskokwim area itself. I don't know.
> They say it began out there and the fighting moved towards here.
> They were killing people. When they reached a settlement they
> would kill the people or take all their food supplies and perhaps
> they do something to their fish. They reached down the coast
> somewhere—I don't know where. Perhaps they stopped when
> there were no more people.[18]

According to archaeological evidence, oral tradition, and the reports of Russian explorers, after the wars ended and shortly before

the Russians arrived, Yup'ik-speaking people joined the Alutiiq-speaking residents of several Naknek Lake settlements to form a group that the Russians called the "Severnovtsy" (northern) people. Alutiiq apparently remained the dominant language in these settlements, and in fact the language's stronghold on the Alaska Peninsula extended along the Pacific coast of the Alaska Peninsula from Kamishak Bay southwest beyond Katmai to the Chignik area, inland to the Severnoskie villages, and probably west to the Bering Sea coast village of Ugashik.[19]

At least from the earliest Russian days, and probably long before, the same dialect of Alutiiq (now called Koniag Alutiiq) was spoken on the Alaska Peninsula and Kodiak Island. People who lived on the southwestern tip of the Kenai Peninsula and the shores of Prince William Sound spoke a different dialect of the language, today termed the Chugach dialect.[20]

The first Russian visitors found that the peninsula Alutiiqs were similar to Kodiak Alutiiqs in more than language.[21] Like Koniags, Alaska Peninsula Alutiiqs fished, collected intertidal shellfish, and hunted sea mammals from skin-covered kayaks. In addition, the mainlanders hunted a variety of land mammals, including caribou and brown bear.

The two groups believed they shared a common origin: one Kodiak myth held that a female dog on Kodiak and a large spotted male dog on the Alaska Peninsula had mated. Their offspring were the original Koniags. Iurii Lisianskii, a naval officer who wintered in Kodiak midway through a voyage round the world, heard a similar story during the winter of 1804–05. The Russian Orthodox Hieromonk Gideon, a fellow traveler with Lisianskii, heard still a third story, which led him to conclude, "The affinity of the languages of Kad'iak and Aliaksa inhabitants lends support to [the migration of the original Kodiak Islanders from the Alaska Peninsula]."[22]

German physician and naturalist Georg Langsdorff, who was in Alaska in 1805–06, also noted similarities between Kukak Bay inhabitants on the Alaska Peninsula north of Katmai and those of Kodiak. He said,

> The customs, the manners, and in a great degree the
> clothing and language of the Alaksans [*sic*] are the same
> as those of the people of Kodiak. The object in which
> they diverge the most from each other is in their food.
> The Alaksans joining on to the continent catch a great
> many reindeer and wild sheep; these constitute a princi-
> pal part of their food and clothing.[23]

There were other minor differences between the cultures of the
Kodiak archipelago and the mainland: Alaska Peninsula *baidarkas*
[kayaks] were shorter and narrower than those of the Koniags or
Unangan, and peninsula bows were sinew-backed, carved, and skillfully decorated, like those of the neighboring Dena'ina Athabaskans.
The boots and masks made on the two sides of Shelikof Strait were
slightly different.[24]

A sinew-backed bow, probably from the Alaska Peninsula, 1867.
National Museum of Natural History, Smithsonian Institution (NMNH 2528)
Photograph by Carl C. Hansen

Like Koniags, the Alutiiqs of the Alaska Peninsula located their
villages behind headlands and in bays. The perfect village site was
on the coast but protected from storms, near a freshwater salmon
stream, and fronted by a smooth, wide beach. A rocky promontory
nearby provided an endless supply of sea urchins, mussels, octopus,
and chitons, a plain behind the village was populated by caribou,
fox, or bear, and a sea mammal rookery was within paddling distance. A portage behind the village led inland and eventually to the
Bering Sea coast. Large driftwood logs were regularly found beached
in front of the village. Finally, the ideal village was located near a
lookout hill and was defensible from marauders coming by sea while
providing an escape route should defensive measures fail.

Naturally, not every site contained all these attributes. Often a
group inhabited two sites, one in the winter and one in the summer;
many villages were positioned near refuge islands with steep cliffs

Anchorage Bay, Alaska Peninsula, a good settlement site.
Patricia Partnow

leading to a grassy flat top, to which villagers could retreat in case of an attack.

Each village consisted of several semisubterranean sod-covered houses, which the Russians called *barabaras*. The size and shape of the family homes varied, depending on the number of inhabitants. Some barabaras were large enough to house twenty people and consisted of a large central kitchen and work area surrounded by attached private family rooms. Other side rooms were used for sweat baths with the addition of hot rocks. The dirt floor was covered with cut grass or grass mats.

In addition to individual barabaras, many villages had a larger, centrally located barabara called the *qasgiq*, similar in function to today's community hall. Religious and social dances, ceremonies, and celebrations were held here, particularly during the winter. Because most Alutiiqs converted to Russian Orthodoxy within a generation of sustained contact, the exact nature of the precontact ceremonies is not known. However, early Russian observers on Kodiak Island did note masking festivals, thanksgiving rituals, whaling ceremonies,

Mask from Douglas on the Alaska Peninsula, 1884.
National Museum of Natural History, Smithsonian Institution (NMNH 74694) Photograph by Carl C. Hansen

memorial feasts for the dead, invitational feasts at trading time, rituals preceding battles, and the presentation of a new village leader. The *qasgiq* was considered the property of the village leader, since he and his relatives built and maintained it.[25]

The Russians reported few eighteenth-century Alaska Peninsula Alutiiq villages, although more may have existed before Russian cartographers recorded their locations.[26] Villages noted by Russians include Kaliak (south of Cape Douglas), Katmai, and Kukak on the Pacific side and the Severnovskie settlements of Alinnak and Ikak along the Naknek River system.[27] People living in the peninsula Alutiiq villages were probably closely related to each other, forming alliances during times of battle.

In precontact days people traveled extensively for trade, warfare, and hunting. Even in Russian days small settlements with populations of about twenty often arose, some temporarily, as people moved around the area. The inhabitants of these new settlements maintained affiliations with their former villages. Through their travels the people established kinship and trading relationships. From Kodiak Island the mainlanders obtained amber and dentalium shells, while Koniags received sinew and caribou skin in exchange.[28]

Warfare between the Alaska Peninsula and Kodiak was as common as trade, usually carried out for the sake of booty, prisoners, or revenge. The peninsula's most common Koniag enemies hailed from the northern and western parts of the island, areas which also supplied their primary trading partners during peacetime. Holmberg described the warfare the Alutiiqs engaged in as follows:

> The wars of the Koniags were by surprise attack where...the prisoners were either tortured to death or enslaved. War was not only fought with neighboring or alien tribes but also amongst one another.[29]

The Orthodox official Hieromonk Gideon noted that the idea of a raid might originate from a single individual, who then attempted to convince others to join in the enterprise. An unsubstantiated report of a 1782 meeting of Russians, Unangan, and Alutiiqs near the Alaska Peninsula describes one method of summoning wartime allies. The author, A. Polonoskii, quotes a Katmai Alutiiq as follows:

> How can we be in agreement with such people [Russians and Unangan] or even submit to them while we are feared by all our neighbors who are subordinate to us? When needed, we call on them for help by lighting fire signals, and we, too, aid others.[30]

Besides the Koniags, peninsula Alutiiqs fought wars against others. The most bitter enemies of both peninsula and Kodiak Alutiiqs were the Unangan from the tip of the Alaska Peninsula, the Shumagin Islands, and the Aleutian Islands. Elders tell many stories of raids between the Alutiiqs and the Unangan. Orthodox priest Father Ivan Veniaminov (later Saint Innocent) reported the situation from the Unangan point of view:

> But with the Kad'iak people they [the Unangan] had constant wars since time immemorial. The Aleuts considered the Kad'iak people to be their irreconcilable enemies. The very word enemy, *Angadutix*, was used instead of the *Qanagix*, an inhabitant of Kad'iak and vice-versa [spellings as in original].[31]

War stories are still popular in peninsula villages, and usually depict the Alutiiqs as victorious. Ignatius Kosbruk of Perryville told one story about a war between Katmai Alutiiqs and Aleutian or Shumagin Island *tayawut*. The following piece is an English translation of a narrative told in Alutiiq. Italicized portions were originally spoken in English.

Here's another story I heard. Long ago, people used to have wars; they fought *like today*. Today that's how people live. Aleuts are different people; they used to fight with our relatives, the Alutiiqs.

Well, they were fighting like that. They say they were killing each other; *like the Civil War, I think*.

Now one time one from that village was named Melquq. He was a liar. Those people didn't believe him, he was always lying. People of that village didn't believe him, because they used to know the kind of person he was. He lied. That one lied. That one lied to them. Melquq—Melquq means liar. Never tell the truth, Melquq.

So then there in the village he had a wife. He had children; he must have been married. There in the village, he was living among them. One time he was walking along the beach looking for bow stem parts for his kayak, walking along the beach looking for wood. Maybe the Katmai beach. It's a long beach. He was walking along the beach. Just before he got to the end, he looked to one side, seeing something. Suddenly he saw them there—people. Lying on their stomachs. They were across the creek under— *under the bank he was looking, and he pretend*—then he pretended not to see them, continuing his walk on the beach. *Thousands of people were gathered along the bank, but he managed all the way to the end. And he didn't get excited.* He didn't rush, but passed by there. He passed them by as if he didn't see them. When he got to the end, then he came back, *did the same thing. He didn't get excited. But he seen all those people lying along the grass and he didn't see no kayaks or nothing. They hide their kayaks too in that river, inside that river.*

Then he pretended not to see them, walking the beach, on his way back. Then when he didn't see them any more, he walked fast, returning to the village to his people. He went to the head council, the bosses, the war lieutenants. *Officer in charge, I guess. He told him about them tayawuqs.* He told that village to pack up. There were lots of Aleuts on the end of the beach lying on their stomachs.

And the people didn't believe him. They didn't believe him.

"Melquq, that's how he lies. He's lying. *He's telling a lie." The people didn't believe him. So he took his family, all his kids and his wife and went up to the hill, and hide—hide away from them enemies.* Then he listened to them; suddenly in the night, suddenly they screamed. They cried—*making all kinds of noise, and here the tayawuqs were, march right in, they caught them while they were sleeping. And clubbed every one of 'em, killed 'em all.*

And towards morning the village was so quiet. And when the day break they went down. Every one of 'em were killed. The whole village.

They killed them. Then he took his family and went down. *And when he get to the road he seen a dead body, without head. He kicked the head and say, he tell them guys,* "That's how Melquq lies!" *But the whole village was conquered by the tayawuqs. Not one soul left.*

And then from there they notified the other village. There used to be another island someplace and them guys know where it is. Our army then, they capture them. During the night they cleaned every one of 'em, the tayawuqs. Some run into their kayaks. You know them tayawuqs used to have a kayak open on the [stern] end and drain the water out, and leave them like an angle so the water will drain out on the end?

Then they opened the end and drained it, on the end of the kayak. They tied—*they keep 'em tied up and when they land they drain the water out.* And when the army arrived that's how they captured 'em. *Without* their knowing, in the night, they got them, *the same bunch.*

That when that army left, they got there, clubbed them, and used bows and arrows. *Taya'uqs never used to have war bow and arrow. They didn't know nothing about it. They just clobbered 'em. And some that tried to survive, they ran into their kayaks and go out. As soon as they get halfway down in the sea they sank backwards because they didn't have a chance to tie their drainage in the end of their kayaks. They drowned themselves.*

Boy, that used to be a big story, about them....

That's all.[32]

Aleut kayak.
Drawing by John Webber, 1778, courtesy of the Alaska State Museum

This story contains an interesting detail that is corroborated by the ethnographic record: the presence of a drawstring at the stern of Unangan kayaks. In fact, museum specimens collected during the nineteenth century in the Aleutian Islands exhibit this distinctive marker.[33] But more important than this detail are the interethnic relationships described in the story. Alutiiqs expected trouble from the Unangan. They were dismayed, but apparently not shocked, to find their enemies hundreds of miles from home. And they were familiar enough with them that they could disable their kayaks in quick order.

The story also contains an overt lesson, as did most of those in Ignatius Kosbruk's repertoire: It can be dangerous to judge a person by his past actions or attributes. Like "the boy who cried wolf" in European folklore, Melquq was considered untrustworthy by his neighbors. But they dismissed warnings from that unlikely source at their peril. Ignatius seems to be cautioning his listeners that Alutiiqs must remain alert to all dangers, from all quarters, if they are to survive.

Two other stories illustrate the type of battle waged when residents of a village were forced to seek safety on an isolated "refuge" island. The first, recorded by Mike Sam of Chignik Lagoon and Anchorage, is said to have taken place at Spitz Island near Mitrofania, south of Chignik:

> Mitrofan Island, a little bit west of it, is a small little island. There's only one place you can go up it, that's on the west

side of it where there's kind of a little valley with grass growing all the way up. I don't know if they planted the grass or not. All the rest of the island is rocky, and there's grass up on top.

People were hunting around [Spitz] Island and they saw those Aleuts [Unangan] from the islands coming. You could see a long way; there's a lot of water between the islands. So they hid their kayaks and they landed there, went to the top, and hollered down to the Aleuts, "We're up here! Come get us!"

There was a big log up there with big spikes, like nails. They rolled it down the grassy slope. There was no way the Aleuts could jump aside because it was rocky on both sides of the grassy valley. The log was about twelve feet long and they'd roll it down and get every one of them.[34]

In October 1975, Father Harry Kaiakokonok was interviewed in Perryville by Katmai National Monument rangers. He told a story much like Mike Sam's, except that he said it took place on a small island off the coast of Katmai, not at Spitz Island. Father Harry did not identify the enemy as *tayawut*.

According to all these people, our fathers used to tell, the island had only one place where a person could get on top. And so wide, not too wide a place. Nice place. And this village was located on top. And used to be war from northward and westward and southeast and the people used to have several logs and them pieces of hard wood attached like pegs.

And when the warrior get inside [the village], their commander hollers them, "We are caught, we are caught! You fellows got us, we are helpless! How are we gonna do that? We have no weapons. We don't have enough men to fight you. You can come up slaughter us the way you like. We're free to you!"

Well, there's several people waiting with big logs. And the commanding officer telling [the enemy], "You come up and do what you like with us. We ready to die. Because we don't have enough men. We got no weapons."

Their people laughing. They just pull up their kayaks and all put up their weapons, spears, arrows. They go up laughing and making fun of them, "How easy we gonna slaughter you people when you are helpless though you said go up."

Just about a little ways from the top, the commander holler, "Release!" and that log, big log, roll down and get everybody. There lot of men on top. They don't show them. Let only one commanding officer talking from the top, and that's how it works, show how few people there were and let them come up to slaughter us. Just before they come up on top "Release!" and the log roll down and kill everyone.

They claim this island to be rough. That their people fix it so it will be smooth all the way down. Smooth, so when the log roll down, nobody can go through underneath. You can find out that there's one island, one spot that's no other place you can climb.[35]

Like the stories told by Ignatius Kosbruk and Mike Sam, this narrative recounts an occurrence said to have happened before the Russians arrived, indicating a long history of enmity between neighboring peoples on the Alaska Peninsula. As might be expected, war tales told by Unangan and Dena'ina narrators often describe themselves, rather than the Alutiiqs, as victors.

Little information about precontact subsistence practices on the Alaska Peninsula survives, but similarities in tools and implements indicate that the same techniques were in use as on Kodiak Island. Like Aleutian Islanders, Alutiiqs were known for their skill in building, maneuvering, and hunting from their skin kayaks. They built both one-hatch and two-hatch boats, adding a third hatch after contact to accommodate Russian travelers. From these boats they hunted sea lions, seals, sea otters, and, though direct evidence does not exist, perhaps whales as well.[36] A wide array of weapons and tools had been developed for hunting, harvesting, and processing food, each ideally suited to a particular species, technique, and purpose. Men wore beautifully carved and painted wooden helmets, cone-shaped hats, and bentwood visors while on the hunt as a way of

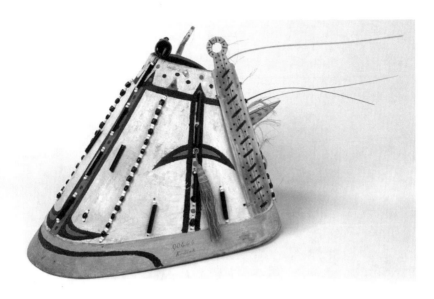

A bentwood hunting hat from Katmai, 1883.
National Museum of Natural History, Smithsonian Institution (NMNH 90444)
Photograph by Carl C. Hansen

communicating respectful intentions to their prey.[37] Salmon, halibut, and cod fishing were essential economic activities, and caribou and bear hunting were also important. Bear intestines were sewn into beautiful waterproof coats needed for sea mammal hunting on the open ocean. Ground squirrels were trapped for their skins, which were made into both fancy and serviceable parkas. Ducks, geese, and other birds were hunted for their skins and meat, and their eggs were gathered. Women and children were expert shellfish gatherers, bringing in huge amounts of edible mollusks and urchins. Berries and roots were harvested and preserved in seal oil during the winter months.

The Alutiiq people saw in all these resources not just sustenance for themselves, but representatives of entire worlds that existed below the surface of the sea and land or outside the limits of human sight. In each plant, animal, stream, and natural feature resided a

Portage Bay barabara, 1909. Woman and child are wearing ground squirrel parkas.
Alaska State Library, Flamen Ball Collection, PCA 24–109

part of the whole universe. Each had a spirit, called a *sua*, which was its life force. It was necessary for humans to maintain good relationships with the *suas* of the animals they needed for survival, for otherwise the animals would make themselves scarce and the people would starve. The only way humans could convince the *suas* they were worthy was through respectful treatment such as maintaining personal cleanliness while hunting, disposing of the unused parts of the animal in the appropriate manner, and performing ceremonies of thanksgiving each winter. A *sua* sometimes became visible to people when its animal, stream, or feature took on human form; in fact, elders explain that this continues to the present day in unusual circumstances.

In addition to individual *suas*, Kodiak and Peninsula Alutiiqs believed in a deity they called *l̩am sua*, translated as "spirit or personification of the universe," but there is no record of ceremonies directed toward this supreme being. At the least, each person was responsible for abiding by proper rules of conduct and could communicate directly with some *suas*.

Fienup-Riordan's remarks about Central Yupiit are doubtless appropriate to Alutiiq cosmology:

> Yup'ik Eskimos traditionally viewed the relationship between humans and animals as collaborative reciprocity; the animals gave themselves to the hunter in response to the hunter's respectful treatment of them as "persons" in their own right…. All living things participated in a cycle of birth and rebirth in which the souls of both animals and humans were a part, contingent on right thought and action by others as well as self.[38]

Many traditional and modern Alutiiq stories show this respectful relationship between humans and the resources they used for survival. The following story, told by Ignatius Kosbruk, tells about one such human/*sua* interaction:

> But I heard lot of stories about the bear. And the bear one time, I think it's one time there was a young man, went out hunting, and he was hunting porcupine. And the bear took him in. The whole winter. Took him in his cave.

And he told him, "Don't wake me up like this when you're hungry." [taps him on the shoulder] He had all the *mingciqs* [dried fish] and *ququs* [oil or fat] all over.

And one day he [the man] was hungry, and he was scared. He was scared to wake him [the bear] up. He shook him up on his shoulder, he wake him. Boy, then he [the bear] woke up and he was mad! "Didn't I tell you not to touch my body to wake me up? Club me on my backside!" [laughs]

Finally then again he get hungry. And he took a club and clubbed him on the back. Boy, he [the bear] got up smiling [laughs] He was glad. He wasn't mad then. And then in February and March, he turn around towards the sun. And about March month, in March and April, he start to get up, wake up. In April month he took the palm of his hands and put 'em out of the hole. And smelled them.

He tell his stranger, "The spring must be coming now, the birds are coming." Just by smelling his hands. And then he let him [the man] go home again after that. But he told him, before he left, not to tell nobody where he was for the whole winter.

But the people knew that they took him. The people knew right away. So like we all [do], mens always get excited right away. So they stayed in the village and when the spring come, when the man get home, they knew right away that the bear took him. And they all get excited. They wanted to hear the story and where he was.

But he was advised from the bear not to tell nobody where he was during the winter. But how anxious to hear the story, finally he break up and told them that he stayed with a bear whole winter.

And then he went up. He lead them to the burrow where he was. Just before they sit down and watch them. They didn't even have a chance to shoot him [the bear]. He didn't touch those other persons. He just grabbed that [man] and tore him all to pieces.

They didn't have no chance to spear him or shoot him. He was that quick. And tore him all to pieces.

Awayi nangnguq [it's finished].[39]

This is the story of a man who betrays the *sua* of a bear. Little was asked of him in exchange for a winter's shelter—only to observe bear rules (e.g., "clobber" rather than tap the bear to wake him) and keep the bear's confidence. The penalty for breaking faith was death. One obvious lesson is that humans need to maintain good and respectful relationships with animals, and that the relationship is reciprocal. The action in this *unigkuaq* is played out in what is straightforwardly portrayed as an unremarkable setting, the place between the corporeal and spiritual worlds.

Another bear story recorded by Kosbruk expands on the spiritual dimension in human/animal interactions. It is remarkably similar to one reported by the Russian visitor Gavriil Davydov in 1803, having an identical situation and plot. Its surprise ending, an innovation that was added sometime in the past two centuries, indicates both the persistence of oral tradition and its contemporary vitality. Kosbruk recorded the story in English. The italicized introduction is a synopsis of the story that he provided before I turned on the tape recorder:

One time a group of Katmai women went out berry picking. One of them disappeared. The others returned to the village to tell what had happened. Everyone agreed that a bear must have gotten her.

It was—it wasn't a bear that attacked her, it was a shaman that done it.

But after that, [the victim's two brothers] went into the river and exercised themselves so they could be strong enough to fight the bear. They pull the trees down. The alders. That's how they were. They started to exercise in water and on the land. So they could attack the bear if they charged them. They were practicing for a whole year. A whole year. Exercising themselves so they could be strong enough.

Finally when they thought they were strong enough, the older brother told [the younger], "I think we're strong enough." And examined themselves when they start to pull the trees from the ground, roots and all. And he said, "That's enough. I think we're good. We could start now." They pulled the trees up right off from the ground. Roots and all. How strong they were.

So when the spring came, when the bears were out from hiberna-tion, they started to look for the bear. And they attack every bear that they see and let the bear charge on them. So they kill every bear they see.

And finally they found one. It wasn't so big, he said. It wasn't so big a bear. And he hollered to his brother to use tongs to keep the bear down on his head. And he did. And he couldn't, he couldn't press him down to the ground. So he hollered to him "Use a spear! If you can't find his heart, his heart must be on his left hand side, on his top of his hand."

They struggled for a long, long time. And his brother said that he's getting tired. And his older brother was spearing [the bear] for a long, long time. He couldn't find the heart. He kept on spear-ing him and spearing him and finally his brother hollered to him that his heart must be on the top of his hand. On the left hand side. To put the spear on his left hand side. Soon as he put the spear on, fall dead.

So, it was made [to hap-pen] by the shaman. And they tore that bear up all to pieces. And they finally found his stomach. They opened the stomach, and found their sister's beads. And they tore him all to pieces. I don't know how small they were. Every bit of it. And they brought the necklace back to their home. And keeped it for their souvenir. It was the end.

It wasn't the end. And when they first got this American food, I think they were poisoned by them food, corned beef.[40]

Woman's necklace made from glass trade beads, Ugashik, 1879–82. This is the type of necklace that provided proof of the bear's identity in Kosbruk's bear story.
National Museum of Natural History, Smithsonian Institution (NMNH 72467) Photograph by Carl C. Hansen

In this telling, Kosbruk vividly illustrates the point that animals are more than they appear on the surface. Not only are they powerful in themselves, but their forms may also be enlisted as shaman spirit helpers. Nonhuman creatures must be treated as intelligent and sometimes evil or crafty beings.

The surprise ending in which the men are killed by tainted corned beef may be ironic (i.e., even strong men can be felled by an innocent-seeming agent), or cautionary (the shaman's power was finally unleashed against the bear's killers through the agency of bad corned beef). Either way, the story indicates continuity between ancient tradition and the modern world.

Davydov's 1803 version is the same in all but two respects: the ending and his inference of the story's meaning and import. The Russian traveler frames the narrative as evidence of whether Alutiiqs love their families:

> It is difficult to say for sure whether the islanders love their family or not; the latter would seem nearer the truth. There have been cases of vengeance being sought for them, but this can be found amongst other peoples. One case was very extraordinary; a bear killed and ate a little girl and her two brothers proposed to take vengeance on the bears for this; they would kill them all until in the stomach of one they found the earrings which had been in the girl's ears, or some other sign. Both of them were famous hunters, and they killed many bears on Kad'iak, and then crossed to the Aliaskan Peninsula where in one bear it is said they found the things the girl had been wearing. It is difficult to know how the bear, which ate the girl on Kad'iak, came to be in Aliaska, because the straits separating these two places are forty versts wide; but it could be that some unfortunate girl there, wearing the same things, was overcome by the same fate. I do not deny the veracity of this tale, but it is almost the only one which illustrates the love of the islanders for their relatives.[41]

Davydov, a child of the Age of Enlightenment, sought scientific, rational explanations for his observations. In this case, he was conducting ethnohistoric research of his own, hoping to learn the nature of Alutiiq kinship and emotional ties from the evidence provided in oral tradition. He makes no mention of the supernatural realm. The most interesting fact about the story to a twenty-first century audience is its persistence across time and space, which suggests that the peoples of Kodiak and the Alaska Peninsula were in close contact, probably continuously for the last 200 years. A modern reader might also see in Kosbruk's recording substantiation that today's Alutiiq elders believe that their ancient *unigkuat* are as relevant today as in the past. The story shows that the basic nature of the world has not changed, nor have the dangers facing the young.

The spiritual practices of the precontact Alutiiqs extended beyond belief in the *suas* of animals and the ability of humans to interact with them directly. In fact, three types of spiritual specialists mediated between the complex human and spiritual realms: the shaman, the healer, and the wise man.[42] The *kalagelek*, usually translated as "shaman" or "medicine man," could forecast and control the weather, help ensure a successful hunt, cure ailments, and observe over space and time. Both men and women could be *kalagelget* (plural of *kalagelek*). They were feared as well as respected, for on occasion they manipulated the universe toward selfish ends (see, for example the *Puglálria* narrative in the next chapter). The *kalagelek* often performed behind a mask or in face painting and costume, though sometimes he was naked.

Healers, often women, were knowledgeable in the use of herbs and roots, massage, midwifery, and blood-letting or acupuncture. Since physical illness was considered an expression of a spiritual sickness, these healers were considered to be spiritual, as well as medical, specialists. They often treated their patients in the steambath. A few elderly women on the peninsula are still sought for their knowledge of massage and herbal remedies.

The third religious practitioner, the "wise man," or *kasaq* [plural *kasat*], was in charge of the continuation of ceremonies and religious knowledge. He composed poetry and advised villagers on spiritual matters.

Aside from brief statements by European observers, we have only hints of precontact Alutiiq power structures, decision-making techniques, and group dynamics. At the beginning of the nineteenth century when Russians first observed the area, there was no region-wide territorial government on Kodiak or the Alaska Peninsula. The village was the basic political unit. There is evidence on both island and mainland of widespread though temporary alliances among villages at the time of contact. Unfortunately, these alliances were unequal to the superior military power of the Russians when the latter secured a settlement at Three Saints' Bay in 1784. Even in precontact days, each village's leader had power only over his extended family. Gideon reported that the Alutiiqs called this leader an *anayugak*, each of whom had his own *qasgiq*. The office of *anayugak* was hereditary, often passed down to a son or a son of one of the chief's sisters.

In spite of his limited power, this man was shown deference by all villagers. He was invariably a persuasive speaker who served as the primary counselor in both war and peace.[43] German physician Carl Merck, visiting Kodiak in the 1790s, wrote,

> The strongest and most intelligent man of a village is acknowledged as the leader *(ngayokak)* among the people. But he has no real power, because no one can command anyone but his relative.[44]

Archimandrite Iosaf Bolotov agreed that the indigenous leaders the Russians called *toions* had

> gained fame in war, and have numerous prisoners whom they treat with arbitrary power.... But they have no power over their neighbors and have no power to punish crimes. No force could bring their peers into submission, but they lead by maintaining good order, a show of concern and care for their fellows' wellbeing, by favors, and various political means.[45]

Leaders also formed temporary political alliances with families living in nearby villages as well as within their own settlements. By the nineteenth century these alliances were limited to marriage agreements; however, as Polonskii's account cited on p. 43 indicates, in precontact times they also included wartime pacts.

The Russians realized the importance of the village *anayugak-ngayokaks*. They soon deputized these men, seeking to use the existing power structure to maximize company profits by influencing the rest of the population to cooperate in the fur trade. According to Davydov, their plan was only partly successful. He noted,

> Nowadays the company's administrators have taken the place of the native toen and they nominate others for the post at will—but they do not command the same respect as those that have been ousted.[46]

The Russian merchants also capitalized on the fact that in the nineteenth century the Alutiiqs had no government beyond the village, since this lack of organization made them ineffective enemies. Davydov claimed, "Lack of unanimity amongst the islanders has been the main factor in [their inability to overthrow the Russians], rather than caution on the part of the Russians."[47]

Traditional Alutiiq marriage practices allowed men and women a large degree of freedom in their personal lives. Both could have more than one spouse, though this was rare because of practical difficulties. If a man had two wives, he had to hunt for food and clothing for both of them, as well as the children of both. If a woman had two husbands, she had to make clothes, prepare the catches, and cook for both. Marriage was generally a matter of choice for the man, though arranged marriages also occurred. Women sometimes were forced to marry the man chosen for them by the father or family leader. Brides might come from a groom's own village or another. Lisianskii explained one method of choosing a spouse:

> A young man, on hearing that in such a place is a girl
> that he thinks will suit him, goes thither, carrying with
> him the most valuable things he is possessed of, and pro-
> poses himself for a husband.... The husband always lives
> with the parents of the wife, and is obliged to serve them,
> though occasionally he may visit his own relations.[48]

To this Davydov added, "After some time has elapsed the newly-weds go off to their own house—but if the girl does not want to she remains living with her father."[49] Wives were also sometimes obtained as booty in raids. Wrangell wrote, "I will only remark that the Chugach and Kadiaks have intermingled with the American tribes, whose women they steal."[50]

When the Russians arrived in Alaska in 1741, they were met by a people who had a highly developed society and complex understanding of how they fit in the universe. It took only a generation for massive changes to occur in that culture. And yet in the midst of the ensuing cultural, social, and economic upheaval, much of the old way persisted.

NOTES

1.   Gideon 1989: 59.

2.   Gideon 1989: 59.

3.   Henn 1978; Dumond 1981.

4.   Cf. Dumond 1987: 153, 159; Erlandson et al. 1992: 54, 57.

5.   Erlandson et al. 1992; Crowell and Mann 1996.

6.   Henn 1978; Dumond 1981.

7.   Dumond 1981.

8.   Dumond 1971.

9.   Dumond 1995.

10.   Dumond 1995.

11.   Dumond 1987, 1988. It remains unclear whether the Yup'ik language spoken on Kodiak Island and the Pacific coast of the Alaska Peninsula, which is now called Sugtestun, Sugpiaq, or Alutiiq rather than Yup'ik, was introduced because of a large-scale movement of people

into the area, or was the result of a small-scale physical movement accompanied by a shift in culture and language. Aside from conquest by a major military power (for which no evidence exists) it is difficult to conceive of a process of whole language replacement that does not involve massive human immigration as well.

12. Nineteenth-century French explorer Alphonse Pinart was told by Native informants that the border between Koniag and Unangan had historically been at Kuiukta Bay (1873a: 12).

13. Yesner 1985.

14. Polonskii n.d.

15. Davydov 1977: 196–7.

16. Wrangell 1980: 64.

17. Fienup-Riordan 1990: 153 ff.

18. Abalama 1990.

19. I have used Russian endings throughout this book when referring to the Russian-era settlements, collectively called "Severnovskie." For instance, the plural ending is "ie," the neuter singular, "oe," and the masculine singular, "ii." During the American era, the spellings were changed to an Anglicized "Savonoski." The people of the Severnovskie settlements were called "Severnovtsy."

20. Krauss 1980: 44; Leer 1985: 77.

21. See Davydov 1977; Lisianskii 1968; Gideon 1989; Langsdorff 1968; Holmberg 1985.

22. Gideon 1989: 59.

23. Langsdorff 1968: 236.

24. Davydov 1977: 202; Desson 1995.

25. Cf. Davydov 1977: 107–111, 183–184; Gideon 1989: 40.

26. Cf. Clark 1987.

27. Vasiliev 1832–3 in Litke 1835.

28. Davydov 1977: 151; Gideon 1989: 57; Holmberg 1985:38, 57; Ellanna and Balluta 1992: 18, 21, 58.

29. Holmberg 1985: 56.

30. Polonskii n.d..

31. Veniaminov 1984: 205.

32. Ignatius Kosbruk 1992a.

33. Zimmerly 1986: 16.

34. Sam 1992.

35. Kaiakokonok 1975b.

36. Some whale bone has been found at archaeological sites along the Katmai coast, but the bones may represent drift whales. Early sites yielded long slate bayonets similar to those used much later on Kodiak Island for whale hunting but, again, these may not have been used for whale hunting (Crowell personal communication; July 10, 1998; G. Clark 1977).

37. Black 1991.

38. Fienup-Rordan 1990: 167.

39. Ignatius Kosbruk 1992d.

40. Ignatius Kosbruk 1992e. See a forthcoming article co-authored by Jeff Leer and myself about this story in Fienup-Riordan and Kaplan (eds.) *Words of the Real People*, Seattle: University of Washington Press (in prep.).

41. Davydov 1977: 167.

42. Pinart 1873: 677 discusses the shaman and the wise man.

43. Gideon 1989: 40–1.

44. Merck 1980: 109.

45. Black 1977: 84.

46. Davydov 1977: 190.

47. Davydov 1977: 188.

48. Lisianskii 1968: 198.

49. Davydov 1977: 182.

50. Wrangell 1980: 59.

3

THE RUSSIAN PERIOD
ON THE ALASKA PENINSULA:
1741 TO 1867

EUROPEANS LEARN ABOUT THE ALASKA PENINSULA

Europeans first saw the Shumagin Islands off the southern shore of the Alaska Peninsula in 1741. That September, Vitus Bering sailed his ship Saint Peter among the islands and was greeted by Native people, probably Unangan, who paddled out in kayaks to inspect the ship.[1] The Saint Peter was sailing under orders from the Russian government to explore and describe the land that lay across the sea from Siberia. As the government's representative, Captain Bering claimed the territory for Russia. For the next 126 years Alaska was to be called Russian America.

Four years after the meeting in the Shumagin Islands, Russians began trading for furs in the Aleutian Islands. It was another seventeen years before the first Russian ship visited the Alaska Peninsula. In 1762, the *Saint Gabriel*, owned by the merchant Ivan Bechevin and skippered by Gavriil Pushkarev, sailed through False Pass, which separates the first of the Aleutians, Unimak Island, from the Alaska Peninsula. The ship's crew spent the winter on the peninsula in what came to be called Bechevin Bay, near an Unangan settlement.[2]

In 1768 a Russian expedition under M. D. Levashev and P. K. Krenitsyn set out to explore the new Russian discoveries, including the Alaska Peninsula. They probably used a rough 1767 Russian admiralty chart as their guide. It was not a particularly good guide, however, for it showed the Alaska Peninsula as a stunted, featureless land mass jutting for a short distance into the Pacific (then called "Northeast") Ocean.³ Ten years later the contours of the peninsula were well known to Russian navigators, in part due to charts made on Levashev and Krenitsyn's expedition.⁴ When England's Captain James Cook sailed along the Pacific coast of the Alaska Peninsula mapping its shoreline, he may have had access to these new Russian charts.

Russian exploration of the Alaska Peninsula continued for the next half century in fits and starts. In 1791, the Russian navigator Dmitrii Bocharov traveled by *angyak* or, in Russian, *baidara* [large open skin boat] along the northwestern Bering Sea/Bristol Bay shore of the peninsula, paddled up the Kvichak River, returned to Bristol Bay, ascended the Egegik River to what is now known as Becharof Lake, and finally portaged to the Pacific coast. From Portage Bay (later the site of the village of Kanatak) he journeyed across Shelikof Strait to Karluk on Kodiak Island.⁵ On Bocharov's chart of that voyage four dots show that a settlement was located at the mouth of Katmai River, although the settlement's name is not given.⁶ Almost a century later, U.S. census taker Ivan Petroff reported that the settlement's precontact name had been "Yukutmak."⁷ The last generation of Alutiiq inhabitants—those forced out by the 1912 volcanic eruption—called it "Qayihwik."

The shores of the Alaska Peninsula had been fully charted by the 1830s. In 1828, the naval officer Mikhail Staniukovich had surveyed the peninsula's northwestern Bering Sea coast.⁸ In 1831, Ensign Ivan Vasiliev was instructed to map the Pacific coast of the peninsula from Cape Douglas southwest. He did not complete the task, and the next year the Russian-American Company Chief Manager Ferdinand Wrangell ordered him to continue his survey of the "Aliaska shore." Later that year, Wrangell criticized Vasiliev for not covering enough ground during the previous year. The explorer was told to leave his wife and in-laws at home in the future, and not to oppress the inhabitants and *baidarshchiki* (literally, "boatsmen" or "boat skippers"), who at the time served as local crew chiefs for the Russian hunting crews and later became managers of trading posts.[9] Also in 1831, the cartographer Obriadin was ordered to map the Shumagin Islands and the southwestern coast of the peninsula.[10] In 1836, Vasilii Voronkovskii mapped the Pacific shore of the peninsula south of Chignik. This completed the mapping of the coastline of the Alaska Peninsula.[11]

RUSSIAN ECONOMIC INTERESTS
IN THE ALASKA PENINSULA

1780s to 1818

Russian fur trading companies began sending ships to the Alaska Peninsula for a single goal: to obtain the rich pelts of fur-bearing animals for trade in European and Asian markets. Although in the first few years of Alaska's fur trade the Russians themselves hunted sea mammals, they were never able to master the skin-covered kayaks that made the hunt possible. Nor were they as skillful at hunting as the Unangan and Alutiiq men. So from the middle of the eighteenth century until 1818, when the practice of forced labor was forbidden by the Russian government, Russians compelled Unangan and Alutiiq men to hunt for them.

Until 1799 several rival fur-trading companies worked the waters of Russian America, but in that year the tsar awarded the Russian-American Company a monopoly for the North American trade. The Russian government issued a twenty-year charter that allowed the company not only to obtain furs in Russian America but also to act as the government's representative in the colony. During the years the first charter was in force, from 1799 until 1820, the RAC was allowed to run its business and the colony largely as its directors saw fit without interference from the government. However, the second charter placed restrictions and requirements on the company as of 1821. For instance, the RAC was required to hire workers rather than force Natives to hunt for fur-bearing animals. The change may not have been noticeable to the Unangan and Alutiiq hunters themselves, for virtually all those within the areas surrounding RAC settlements continued to work for the company. This meant they also had to schedule their nonworking time according to the requirements of the company's hunt, a situation that continued as long as the fur trade was the economic base of the region, until the end of the nineteenth century.

The luxurious pelt of the sea otter was valued above all others, but sea otter populations quickly declined as a result of overhunting. Nonetheless, the fur was so valuable that men continued to hunt the animals until required to stop by a 1911 worldwide ban on sea otter hunting. In addition to buying sea otter pelts, company agents paid Alaska Peninsula hunters for the skins of river otter, bear, fox, wolf, beaver, lynx, wolverine, marmot, fur seal, sea lion, and waterfowl. Meanwhile, the 500 or so Russians living in the colony helped build and fortify settlements, sailed ships to and in Alaska, oversaw company stores, and defended trading posts and forts.

As soon as they realized the wealth to be obtained from the furbearing animals in the region, Russian merchants sought to establish permanent Alaska Peninsula *artels,* or resident work crews. One nineteenth-century report by Russian researcher A. Polonskii asserts that as early as 1782 Russian businessmen tried to form an *artel* with peninsula Alutiiqs. Polonskii wrote that Dmitrii Polutov and Dmitrii Pan'kov traveled along the Alaska Peninsula coast and among its offshore islands in May of that year. They had recently finished trading in the Aleutian Islands and were traveling with a large group of Unangan hunters. At "Sanikliuk Island" [modern name unknown] off the shore of the Alaska Peninsula, the Russians, accompanied by 200 Unangan *baidarki* [kayaks], met a group of unfriendly "Koniags" from the Native village of Katmai. According to the account, after trading beads for a few sea otters, the Russians demanded that the Katmai people become Russian subjects. A battle and long siege followed, resulting in many deaths. Finally Polutov and Pan'kov gave up, leaving the area without establishing a long-term trading relationship with the Katmai Alutiiqs.[12]

The Golikov-Shelikhov Company, precursor of the RAC, established *artels* at Katmai and at Sutkhum on Kujulik Bay only a few years later. In 1784 the Russian merchant Grigorii Shelikhov had secured a Russian post and village at Three Saints Bay (site of the

village of Old Harbor) on Kodiak Island, and by the next year the
company used the Alaska Peninsula as a hunting ground for
Kodiak and Aleutian Islanders. In 1786, Shelikhov ordered that an
artel be formed at Katmai on the Alaska Peninsula opposite Kodiak
Island.[13] Greek shipper and trader Evstrat Delarov, who became chief
manager of the American settlements of the Golikov-Shelikhov
company the following year, was probably the founder of the Katmai
artel.[14]

RAC records indicate that the *artel's* early years were difficult.
For instance, in September 1787 skipper Gerasim Izmailov of the
Three Saints noted in his vessel's log that he had received word that
"*baidarshchik* Maksimov and the men of the Golikov-Shelikhov *artel*"
stationed on the Alaska Peninsula near the Native settlement of
Katmai had been killed by Natives of that village.[15]

By 1792, at least part of the Alaska Peninsula was under Russian
control, for in that year a census of peninsula residents yielded a
count of 814 people. Unfortunately, surviving records do not tell
which settlements were counted nor whether the people counted
were local Natives or immigrants from Kodiak or the Aleutian Islands.[16] The next year the Golikov-Shelikhov Company Chief
Manager Aleksandr Baranov wrote that he considered the peninsula
Natives "dependent"—that is, the men hunted for the company
whenever and wherever the company wanted.[17] Within less than a
decade, the peninsula had become a source of both furs and hunters
for the Russians. By 1798 at the latest, a second Russian settlement,
Sutkhum (see map, p. 20), was in operation in Alaska Peninsula
Alutiiq territory.[18]

During his term with the Russian-American Company, Aleksandr
Baranov required that each village supply men and women to work
for the company, either to hunt furbearing animals, fish for food,
gather berries and roots, or sew clothing and kayak covers. In the
beginning the RAC obtained these workers by force. A common
method of securing the adults' cooperation was to take their children as hostages, agreeing to return them to their parents only if the
village would deliver hunters in exchange.[19] By the early 1800s, hostages were not necessary, for the Alutiiqs no longer rebelled against

forced labor and in fact had come to depend on and enjoy the goods they received in exchange for animal pelts.

RAC records for the years before 1817 have been lost, so there is little direct information about the early days of the Katmai post. If Katmai was like other *artels*, its income derived from four categories of Alutiiq workers. First, most Alutiiq men who lived in Katmai and in nearby villages were forced to hunt and trap for the RAC. Their furs went directly into company coffers. Second, the company required men from outlying villages within the Katmai region to join hunting parties.[20] RAC traders recruited these hunters through appointed village representatives called *toions* (singular *tuyuq* in Alutiiq). RAC agents were told to choose the *toions* from among the respected leaders (the *anayugak* that Gideon had described) in their communities and give them gifts and silver medals. The Russians hoped the new *toions* would have enough influence to force or convince their fellow villagers to work for the company. Although their aim was to model the *toions* on traditional Alutiiq leaders, the Russians gave them a different type of authority and power than their predecessors had enjoyed. Previously there had been no village chiefs; instead, each family had had its own family leader. Under the Russian system, the *toion* represented the entire village in most dealings with the company. He negotiated the fate of hostages. He chose and sent the required number of hunters on each trip. He received the village's trade goods at the end of the season and gave them to the various village families.[21] In the Katmai region, as elsewhere in southwestern Alaska, *toions* operated as the RAC agents intended, providing the company with a steady labor force from the various villages.

The third group of Natives who dealt with the company in the early days were called "free Aleuts." These were people who lived in outlying areas yet willingly traveled to the *artels* to trade furs or sell fish. They could not be forced to work for the company because they lived too far from Russian settlements to be controlled.[22]

A final category of Native company employees included the workers who supported the hunting parties. Some were *kaiurs*, or Native workers. These people had formerly been slaves or hostages from Native settlements taken to ensure that their relatives would hunt for the Russians. They gathered food, sewed, hunted, helped run the posts, and transported Russians.[23] Other support workers were the local wives, children, and aged parents of the hunters. Women sewed gut parkas and kayak covers for the hunters and processed bird skins for clothing. Men repaired kayaks and gear, made spear points and paddles, and chopped wood. Workers of both sexes caught and dried fish to feed the hunters. They gathered berries, eggs, and edible roots to be stored for winter use. These workers were paid in skin and manufactured clothing rather than money.[24] According to company records, in the early 1800s each female *kaiurka* on Kodiak was given one bird skin parka, a shirt and a pair of boots for her year's work.

In exchange for work and furs, Alutiiq hunters were paid in items that they would normally have made themselves had they not been working for the RAC. For instance, they received birdskin parkas, *kamleikas*, seal skins, and nets. Rarely were they paid in European goods but sometimes received tea, sugar, tobacco, glass beads, metal pots, knives, axes, needles, mirrors, cloth, bracelets, earrings, rings, combs, pipes, bells, buttons, crosses, or items of clothing.[25] Occasionally rum and vodka were given in trade or as part of the workers' rations, but during most of the Russian period company policy forbade using alcohol for trade. Although the RAC outlawed private distilleries, Russians and Natives alike devised ways to make liquor from berries. In fact, Russian laborers so desired liquor that by the end of the Russian period many preferred to be paid in rum or vodka rather than in company money. No information survives about alcohol use or abuse among the Natives of Russian-period Katmai (though observers did note its negative effects during the American period), but alcohol probably caused problems on the Alaska Peninsula as it did in other locations in Russian America. Company, church, and government officials considered alcohol abuse a major problem by the end of the nineteenth century.[26]

Alutiiqs took quickly to utilitarian trade items such as metal pots, axes, knives, and needles. Other commodities such as beads were considered prestige or luxury items for decorating ceremonial clothing and were extremely popular during the early years of the

Child's boots, probably from the Alaska Peninsula, 1838–42. Alutiiq women continued to make skin foot gear for their families into the twentieth century.
National Museum of Natural History, Smithsonian Institution (NMNH 2129)
Photograph by Carl C. Hansen

Russian trade. By the 1860s people preferred objects that could be used in subsistence activities. Still other trade goods, such as cloth clothing, benefited the company more than the people. If Alutiiqs wore wool, linen, or cotton rather than furs, the furbearing animals they would normally have used for their own clothing could be traded to the Russians instead.[27] After about 1816, the RAC also offered as payment a special kind of company money called *marki* which was good only at RAC stores. Most Natives preferred to trade for goods rather than *marki*.[28]

In the early 1800s two Russian travelers to Russian America kept journals describing the Koniag people and the fur trade. The first was a young naval officer named Gavriil Davydov who had impetuously joined the Russian-American Company for what he thought would be a grand adventure. He arrived on Kodiak in November 1802 and spent several months there off and on until 1805. The second Russian visitor was the Orthodox official Hieromonk Gideon who traveled under instructions from the tsar to inspect and report on conditions in Russian America. Gideon stayed in Kodiak between 1804 and 1807.

There is no evidence that either man traveled to the Katmai *artel*, but both learned about it during their stay in Kodiak. Davydov was told that the Katmai *baidarshchik* traded with Natives from the north and the interior of the peninsula, receiving furs in exchange for Russian goods. These northern inland people were likely Severnovtsy (people of the Severnoskie settlements), Aglurmiut and Kiatagmiut; there may also have been Dena'ina trading partners. They took part in the fur trade as free trappers long before trading posts were built in their home areas.

Davydov and Gideon explained that in the early 1800s the "dependent" Alaska Peninsula Alutiiq men formed several hunting parties. The first party consisted of fifty baidarkas. Its members were "Aliaksintsy and Koniags," or peninsula and island men, who hunted sea otters in the waters between Katmai and Sutkhum each spring and early summer. A second group consisted of old or frail men who were forced to hunt birds on the islands near Sutkhum. The third and largest hunting party was made up of between 300 and 800 baidarkas. Besides peninsula Alutiiqs, this party included Koniags, Prince William Sound Alutiiqs, and Dena'ina Athabaskans from the Kenai Peninsula. The men paddled more than 300 miles along the southern coast of Alaska from Cook Inlet to southeastern Alaska, stopping to hunt whenever the Russian overseers demanded. They had to hunt for their own food along the way as well as for furs for the company. The party was gone for five months, returning at the end of August just in time for the late salmon run. Meanwhile, the hunters' wives had been required to gather berries and sarana [edible wild lily bulbs; *lágaq* in Alutiiq] for the Russian-American Company.[29]

1818 to 1867

Shortly after Baranov left Russian America in 1818, the Russian government issued a new charter to the RAC, and company policies changed. Instead of forcing Alutiiq men to hunt for the company, managers were required to hire them to work for an agreed length of time, paying in either *marki* or goods. After 1821 a Native hunter's normal tour of duty with the RAC was three years, longer only if he wanted to continue working. Although on paper the system was voluntary, in fact each village within the dependent areas was still required to send half its male hunters on the company hunt each year. In addition, those men not already in company service had the option of hiring on as hunters. It is probable that all able-bodied Alutiiqs who lived in Katmai signed on as RAC hunters, for they had chosen or grown up in a company town where life revolved around the fur trade. There would have been no other reason to reside in the settlement.

Meanwhile managers continued to trade with the so-called "free Aleuts" who brought furs to the *artels* from far-flung traplines. In practice, even the free Aleuts were dependent on the company to some extent since the RAC had no competitors. If Alutiiq families wanted trade goods, they had no choice but to hunt for and trade with the Russian-American Company. These hunters were encouraged to hunt large numbers of specific animals—often different species from those they would have sought in precontact days. Instead of obtaining just enough furs and meat for his family's clothing and food, each man spent additional time on the trapline to bring in dozens of pelts, decreasing his available time to obtain subsistence food. As a result, he needed money to buy food and goods to help his family subsist throughout the year. Nor did he have time to make his own snares and traps, depending instead on company-owned metal traps issued at the beginning of each season on credit. The "free Aleuts" thus started each year owing a portion of their future catch to the company.

The company paid workers to produce kayaks and outfitted sea otter hunting parties with food and clothing. Some necessities, such as gut parkas, firearms (for obtaining food rather than furs) and fishing gear, were issued without charge to the hunters, but other items—Russian-made boots and cloth garments, for instance—were charged against the value of pelts brought in at the end of the season. In addition, at Katmai as elsewhere, the *baidarshchiks* issued credit to hunters and their families, keeping detailed records of the items bought. At the end of the hunting season a man's fur catch would be tallied against his credit purchases and he would be given the difference in goods. Each sea otter was credited to only one hunter, probably the first to strike it with his detachable dart point. This meant that some hunters were not credited with a single pelt for an entire year. These men were automatically in debt to the company at the end of the season, and they were not the only ones in financial trouble. Since the RAC determined both the value of the furs and the cost of the goods it gave in exchange, hunters often felt they had received too little for a full season's effort. One Russian visitor, Capt. Pavel N. Golovin, computed that in 1860 the average yearly earnings of a sea otter hunter came to only fifty rubles, equivalent to $25 American dollars at the time—the payment for a single otter. This equalled about one-seventh the salary of Russian artisans working in the towns of Russian America.

Golovin had been sent to Russian America in 1860 to investigate the RAC and report back to the imperial government. A primary goal of his investigation was to decide the company's and the colony's future after examining how well it operated and what its future monetary returns were likely to be. An excerpt from his report includes a description of hunting operations:

> According to its statute, the Company has the right to assign Aleuts to the hunt, provided that such individuals are not younger than 15 nor older than 50; also provided that not more than half of the able-bodied hunters from each settlement are sent out. However, this provision is not strictly adhered to. Without the old experienced leaders, the Aleuts will not go out to sea; the younger ones have to be trained to hunt at the age of 11 or 12, for otherwise they would rarely learn to become skillful hunters. The Aleuts are well aware of this, and therefore they begin to train their children in the art of managing a baidarka from the time they are very young; when they

are 11 or 12, they are taken out to hunt under the supervision of the older hunters. Obviously none of these youngsters can take any sea otters at first, but the older hunters always give them a part of the catch regardless.

The colonial administration does not use force to organize these hunting parties. Discussions about the next year's hunt usually begin in December when the elders gather from all areas into the main settlement to deliver the pelts Aleuts have taken, and to buy all their necessary provisions from the colonial warehouses. At that time every elder or toion announces how many baidarkas and how many Aleuts can be sent out from his settlement, and they come to an agreement about the leaders of the hunting party, etc. Then they reach decisions about when they should go and where they should go out to hunt the sea otter, when the archers should be sent out after birds, when the party should go out to kill sea lions, seals and whales, when the hunt for land animals should begin, and how many women and men should be sent to fish and prepare *iukola* [dried fish] for winter use, to provide food for the inhabitants of all the settlements.

In order to outfit the sea otter hunting parties the Company provides the following at no cost: lumber and *lavtaks* [skins] for making baidarkas, whale sinews, sea lion gut and throat [for boots], cordage, two cups of rum per person for the entire period, and one and one-half pounds of tobacco. They also distribute for every 80 to 100 baidarkas a certain amount of weapons, powder and shot to kill birds that are to be used for food, and they also give out a small amount of tea, sugar and flour for persons who become sick while they are out on the hunt.

Since the sea otter hunting parties often have to go out as far as 150 or even 300 versts [100 to 200 miles] from their settlements, they send out a supply of provisions to the area near where the hunt will take place: seven and one-half pounds of flour per person, and whatever amount of *iukola* and blubber is necessary.

Each hunting party is assigned a certain number of women to help build baidarkas, care for the sick, prepare food, etc.; these women receive ten paper rubles from the Company for the entire period of the hunt.

...Generally all the hunting parties are ready and leave for their hunting areas by April 10, and they return

during the first part of July. Meanwhile the Aleuts who
have remained in the settlement go out in their baidarkas
from time to time, also in parties, to hunt birds, sea lions, walruses and whales. All parties return to their
settlements by August 15. Aleuts who stay in the settlement with the women and children prepare weirs to trap
fish in the rivers from the month of May on, and they
also use poles to fish at sea, and from the catch they
prepare *iukola* for their settlement for winter.

...The Aleuts may sell their catch of sea otters only
to the Company, and at a set price. At present they receive 50 paper rubles for a good sea otter.

Aleuts who are constantly involved in hunting or preparing for the hunt have no time for any other activity
from which they could make some profit. As a result their
well-being depends completely on the pay which they
receive for these animal pelts. This is all the more true
since the climate prevents them from developing agri-
culture or raising livestock. Moreover, the Company
charges high prices for all the things the Aleuts need such
as shoes, clothing, bread and other provisions.[30]

In 1860 the RAC's charter with the Russian government was up
for its fourth renewal. Company owners studied operations and proposed a new policy that would do away with obligatory service by
Alutiiq and Unangan men. The policy never went into effect, for the
holdings in Russian America were sold to the United States only seven
years later, before the wording for the new charter had been finalized.

By the end of the Russian period the RAC oversaw hunting and
trading from six regions, each of which was managed from its own
central settlement. The regions were the Kurile Islands (in what is
now Russia); the Atka section in the western Aleutian Islands; the
Unalaska section in the eastern Aleutians and western Alaska Peninsula; the Kodiak section which included the Kenai Peninsula, Prince
William Sound, Katmai and Sutkhum; a section including the Pribilof
Islands and St. Michael near the mouth of the Yukon River; and
the New Archangel or Sitka section in southeastern Alaska. The
managers of the small fortified redoubts and *artels* including Katmai
and Sutkhum sent furs to their various regional centers and received
trade goods from company stores in those settlements.

RUSSIANS ALONG THE KATMAI COAST AND
THE NAKNEK RIVER DRAINAGE

Baidarshchiks

Over the years the Katmai and Sutkhum posts grew and shrank and grew again in both size and economic importance. Sutkhum was never more than a minor outpost of the Russian-American Company. In 1803, Davydov had noted that the Sutkhum *artel* was made up entirely of Kodiak Natives, and that there was no settlement of non-employees nearby.[31] Sutkhum was abandoned for a while during the early 1820s, but by 1824 furs were being harvested there again. An RAC official reported that Sutkhum's population in 1825 was 41.[32] By 1833 the population had dropped to 32, and in 1842 to 38.[33] That seems to have been the last year the RAC operated the Sutkhum post, although an American trading company resurrected it temporarily forty years later.

Although Katmai was an important post within the Kodiak region, and regularly supplied the RAC with skins, it was never home to more than a few Russians at a time. Beginning with Fëdor Kolmakov, who became the company's *baidarshchik* sometime before 1818, RAC managers were married to either Alutiiqs or creoles (who were themselves the children of Russian fathers and Native mothers), and lived in the village with their families. One or two additional Russian, creole, or Alutiiq company workers helped manage the hunting expeditions or livestock, but Katmai's population otherwise consisted entirely of Alutiiq families. For instance, in 1825 Katmai was home to one Russian in active company service, one Russian released from service, ten Alutiiq men and two Alutiiq women working for the company. The rest of the settlement's population consisted of sixty-nine male and sixty-two female Alutiiqs.[34] Most of the Russian and creole company employees lived in sod-covered barabaras like other Katmai inhabitants, and like them wore skin clothing. Cloth and Russian clothing were costly to transport to Russian America from Europe, so the company held much of each shipment in reserve for trade with Native hunters. It is likely that all of the forty-three adult Alutiiq men living in Katmai in 1825 worked for the company in some way, either by hunting sea otters or gathering food for the hunters.

With a few breaks in the record, it is possible to reconstruct a list of Russian-period *baidarshchiks* at Katmai. Several were ancestors to many of today's peninsula Alutiiqs.

Following the eighteenth-century managers Delarov and the slain Maksimov mentioned earlier, the next recorded *baidarshchik* at Katmai was named "Barsanov" or "Barsanaev." He was in charge when the *Phoenix*, carrying Alaska's first bishop, Father Iosaf, shipwrecked in Shelikof Strait and lost all hands. Chief Manager Baranov reported in an 1800 letter that he had told Barsanaev to search for the missing ship.[35]

The record does not indicate how long Barsanaev held the post at Katmai, but Fëdor Kolmakov is the next *baidarshchik* mentioned in Russian correspondence.[36] Originally from Tobol'sk in Siberia, he had traveled to Russian America to work for the RAC in the late 1700s or early 1800s. By 1806 he was married to an Alutiiq woman named Natalia, who was probably from either Kodiak Island or Katmai. Kolmakov became *baidarshchik* at Katmai some time before 1818. That year he was ordered to establish and manage a new post called Novo-Aleksandrovskii (referred to after 1821 as simply the Aleksandrovskii post) at the mouth of the Nushagak River in Bristol Bay. In 1839 he was to begin plans to establish another post on the Kuskokwim River but died before he could carry out the orders. The post, built by others, was named Kolmakovskii Redoubt in Fëdor's honor.[37]

Shortly after Kolmakov died, his widow Natalia asked the company for permission to return to Katmai. Her request was at first denied. As the widow of a long-time and highly placed company employee, she was entitled to services that could not be supplied in the small post of Katmai. In the end, both she and her daughter-in-law Daria, widow of son Pëtr Kolmakov, settled in the village. Daria was told not to expect any help from the Russian-American Company, although her two children were given permission to attend school at New Archangel for up to eight years at company expense.[38] In 1863, eight Kolmakovs were confessed by the priest during his annual visit to Katmai.[39] Many of Fëdor Kolmakov's descendents still live on the Alaska Peninsula and elsewhere in the state, today spelling their surname "Kalmakoff."

The next Katmai *baidarshchik* to be mentioned in Russian records was Iakov Shangin. His name first appears in connection with Katmai in the confessional records of 1831.[40] Shangin had traveled to Kodiak with Shelikhov in 1783 aboard the *Three Saints*. He was married to Irina, who was probably a Koniag Alutiiq.[41] Shangin was *baidarshchik* of Katmai until at least 1837, but some of his descendents remained there until the village was destroyed in the 1912 volcanic eruption.[42] Today Shangin is a common surname on the Alaska Peninsula.

Shangin was replaced at the post by his son-in-law, Ivan Kostylev. In 1834, Kostylev was offered a position at Katmai at a salary of 400 rubles per year, perhaps as assistant manager.[43] At the time Shangin's creole daughter Nadezhda was seventeen years old. It may have been while serving under her father that Kostylev wooed and wed the young woman. He was made head manager in about 1837, the year a disastrous smallpox epidemic swept through Russian America. Worrying that smallpox serum would not arrive in time from Kodiak, Kostylev vaccinated 243 Alaska Peninsula Natives using lymph from other recently vaccinated Alaskans. The inoculations saved all of the Katmai Alutiiqs, with the exception of twenty-seven people who refused vaccination and died of the disease.[44]

In 1848 Kostylev was replaced as manager by the Russian Pëtr Ivanovich Naumov, who served in that position for ten years.[45] His successor was the creole Visarion Brusenin, who was in turn replaced in 1863, likely for pilfering company supplies.[46] The new manager, the creole Vasilii Nikiforov, had been educated in St. Petersburg at company expense, then returned to marry Ekaterina Kolmakova, granddaughter of Fëdor Kolmakov and daughter of Pëtr. Their son was given permission to attend the seminary at Sitka. Nikiforov maintained connections with the Alaska Peninsula long after his duties with the Russian-American Company ended. In 1908 the *Alaska Orthodox Messenger,* a church newsletter, reported that the "Russian" Vasilii Nikiforov had financed a new chapel at Chignik.[47]

Katmai in the Nineteenth Century

Travelers' journals and RAC records give glimpses of nineteenth-century Katmai. Davydov's descriptions of the hunting parties in the first decade of the nineteenth century are described above. The next view of the settlement appears in the journals of explorer Pëtr Korsakovskii, written more than ten years later. In 1818 he was ordered to cross the peninsula to decide whether a new Russian post should be founded in the Bristol Bay area. Korsakovskii stayed in Katmai for two weeks preparing for the journey and getting to know its manager, Fëdor Kolmakov, who was to act as traveling companion and guide. The two did not get along well, however; in fact they had frequent arguments. Nonetheless, Kolmakov remained in the good graces of RAC officials, for not long afterward he founded and became the manager of the new Novo-Aleksandrovskii post at Nushagak.

While on his voyage, Korsakovskii observed some minor differences in clothing between the Katmai and Kodiak Alutiiqs, but otherwise found them similar to each other. He reported that the *artel* itself contained "rather good buildings: a house, barracks, warehouse, shop, barns, etc. Over 20 head of cattle." A census taken that year counted 386 male Aleuts and 451 women under the jurisdiction of Katmai, a figure that included both those resident in the settlement and in smaller villages to the south.[48]

Katmai next appears in RAC records in 1820, shortly before Chief Manager Semën Ianovskii left Alaska for Russia. He proposed that the Sutkhum *artel* be closed, and that Katmai be reduced to an *odinochka*, or small isolated outpost manned by one or two Russians.[49] His recommendation was based on two factors. First, as always, the company was short of money. Ianovskii was looking for ways to lower costs and decided that posts that did not pay their own way should be eliminated or made more efficient. Second, traders from England, Spain, and the United States had begun squeezing the Russians out of the fur trade in southeastern Alaska. The RAC decided to give up its attempts at a monopoly in that part of the territory and instead concentrate on the northern areas. Men and goods were diverted from Alutiiq and Unangan regions and sent to Yup'ik and Athabaskan territory to prepare for the shift.[50]

The RAC experimented with raising cattle at Katmai, and was at first successful, but officials eventually decided to reduce the herd because there were too few men to care for the animals.[51] Three years after Ianovskii's proposal to downsize the post, the Russian buildings at Katmai burned down. Ianovskii's successor, Chief Manager Matvei Muraviev, wrote to the company's main office in St. Petersburg, Russia, "Katmai burned down completely, but it is no great misfortune," implying either that the post was so inconsequential that the loss of buildings hardly affected the company, or that the structures were easily replaced.[52] In fact the disaster did not keep the post from trading for furs. RAC employee Kyril Khlebnikov reported that in 1825, two years after the fire, the Katmai post took in 114 fox pelts, 510 beaver pelts, and 27 otters.[53] This tally signals a shift from sea to land mammals, a consequence of the decline in sea otters from years of overhunting.

In 1829, Ensign Ivan Vasiliev passed through Katmai during a journey of exploration, and the next spring spent a week there. He received particular help from two inhabitants of Katmai village, Vasilii Iaki (the surname, shared by a number of peninsula residents today, is now spelled "Yagie") and Vasilii Tonuial, both of whom were later rewarded with suits of cloth clothing for their efforts. While at the post during the fall of 1829, Vasiliev had waited for a boat that was to deliver Chief Manager Chistiakov's orders to him. The boat was destroyed on its way across Shelikof Strait on November 14, one of the many shipwrecks in that hazardous stretch of sea.[54]

Katmai and Sutkhum were not the only Alaska Peninsula locations considered as sites for RAC posts. In 1828, Chief Manager Pëtr Chistiakov suggested a new *artel* in lower Cook Inlet at Kamishak Bay, off the northern coast of the peninsula. He wanted to provide a direct link in the supply line between Kolmakov's ten-year-old fortified post, Aleksandrovskii Redoubt, and the Kodiak regional headquarters.[55] Nothing came of the idea.

During the nineteenth century the Russians also researched the Alaska Peninsula's geological potential. Baranov reported that coal had been found at Sutkhum in 1818, though no other available documents mention this discovery, perhaps because the coal was of low grade.[56] The Russians also noted the curative value of the hot springs near Katmai, springs heated by volcanic fires far beneath the earth's surface. In 1843, Chief Manager Arvid Etholen discussed replacing New Archangel with Katmai as the hot springs treatment center of Russian America. The idea was abandoned because new buildings and more employees would have been required at Katmai at a time when company funds were needed elsewhere.[57] Finally, in 1861, only six years before the sale of Russian America to the United States, the creole explorer and naval officer Aleksandr Kashevarov reported that he had been told of oil lakes near Katmai.[58] In spite of these attempts at diversifying the economy of Katmai, in the end the settlement and the Pacific side of the Alaska Peninsula were important to the Russians only for what they could offer the fur trade.

Woman's sewing bag from Katmai, 1879–1882. Although this bag was made long after Langsdorff's stop on the Katmai coast, it represents a continuation of the art of sewing with sea mammal intestines that he reported.
National Museum of Natural History, Smithsonian Institution (NMNH 72495)
Photograph by Carl C. Hansen

RUSSIAN PERIOD ALUTIIQ SETTLEMENTS

Although Katmai and Sutkhum were the only two Russian posts within the territory occupied by Alaska Peninsula Alutiiqs, they were not the only settlements, nor were their residents the only Alutiiqs engaged in the fur trade. Davydov reported that by the early 1800s residents of the village of Ugashik on Bristol Bay had broken an earlier trade agreement with the Russians. Like Unangan and other Alutiiq hunters, they had agreed to hunt for and trade with the Russians only because family members had been taken as hostages. The trade agreement was apparently so unsatisfactory that the Ugashentsy decided to forfeit the hostages rather than continue. However, within thirty years they were once again involved in the fur trade, selling their pelts to the Katmai and Aleksandrovskii posts.[59]

In 1806 the naturalist Georg von Langsdorff visited another Alaska Peninsula Alutiiq village, the settlement of "Toujoujak," which lay twenty-five miles northeast of Katmai in Kukak Bay. The explorer relied on what he termed "Alaksan"—that is, Alaska Peninsula—interpreters on board his ship to communicate with the people of Toujoujak. Langsdorff's short visit yielded some objects bought for European museums and a brief description of the village and the people:

> Early the next morning we were visited by several of our acquaintance of the evening before. Every one brought his wife with him, to treat her with a sight of such very unusual guests, and a European ship. Two young girls had got into the inside of a two-seated baidarka, and when we thought it quite empty, we saw their heads on a sudden popped out at the holes to stare at us. Both the men and women upon our invitation came on board without any apprehension, and brought us fresh fish, with many trifling objects, such as bags made out of the windpipes of birds and sea-dogs [sea lions], or of fish-skin, thread and slings for arrows made of the tendons of whales and rein-deer [sic], very neat baskets, caps of weasel-skins, ornaments for the lips and ears, etc. etc. which they bartered for tobacco, glass-beads, and needles. The traffic [trade] was carried on without the least difficulty, and seemed to give entire satisfaction to both parties....

[W]e resolved to make use of our baidarkas for visiting the summer-huts of the natives on the northeast shore of the bay, not far from the promontory of Amawack, at the distance of about a sea-mile.

We were received by the inhabitants in the most kind-hearted and friendly manner. Their habitation was small, and covered with earth grown over with grass: the entrance was so low, that we could only get in crawling upon our hands and knees. The family were all seated round a fire, which was burning in the midst of the hut, and on which hung a kettle [note: obtained by trade from Europeans], where they were cooking fish. Some small salmon were spitted upon a little stick, which was stuck into the ground near the fire, and by this means they were roasted; we were regaled with some of these cookeries, and saranna root; the latter had to us a disagreeable taste, a sort of mixture of sweet and bitter. Opposite to the door the floor was strewed with chips and hay, over which was laid some clean sea-dogs skins, and here we were invited to sit down. The habitation was upon the whole much cleaner than any we had seen at Kodiak. In our conversation we learnt that the place had been much more populous, but that the population had decreased in the last ten years, most of the young people having been carried away to Sitcha [Sitka] to hunt sea-otters: indeed, we observed that here, as at Kodiak, we saw chiefly old men, women, and children....

The customs, the manners, and in a great degree the clothing and language of the Alaksans, are the same as those of the people of Kodiak. The object in which they diverge the most from each other is in their food. The Alaksans joining on to the continent catch a great many rein-deer [caribou] and wild sheep; these constitute a principal part of their food and clothing; they are taken chiefly in the autumn.... The physiognomy of some of the girls was really not unpleasing, though very much deformed by the lip-ornaments and by the tattooing of the chin.[60]

Kukak Bay, the location of the village Langsdorff visited, continued to be the site of an Alutiiq village until the early 1890s.[61]

A number of Russian reports and letters refer to a group of settlements collectively called "Severnovskie" (meaning "northern" in Russian), modified to "Savonoski" during the American era. The designation first appears in a record of an 1807 marriage between a Severnovskoe settlement inhabitant named Semën Danilov and Anis'ia, a woman from one of the Aleutian Islands.[62] The Severnovtsy were also mentioned in explorer Pëtr Korsakovskii's travel journal. While Korsakovskii was in Katmai preparing for his trip across the Alaska Peninsula in 1818, he was told that Severnovskie men were plotting his murder. The rumor was apparently false and Severnovtsy later served as his interpreters.[63] Severnovtsy traded at nearby Katmai from a fairly early time, as shown by an 1832 order from the RAC headquarters in New Archangel to Katmai's *baidarshchik*. This order told the manager to send "two Katmaitsy and four Severnovtsy" to help his fellow manager Fëdor Kolmakov at the Aleksandrovskii Redoubt on the Nushagak River, indicating both that Severnovtsy were well known and that they could be expected to serve the company reliably. The task was accomplished with the help of the Severnovskii *toion*.[64]

When Russians first met the Severnovtsy in the early 1800s, part or all of their number had recently—probably within a generation—been pushed to the upper Naknek River area from its mouth by a warring group of Yup'ik speakers who called themselves "Aglurmiut" ("Aglegmiut" or similar spellings in Russian and other sources).[65] The Russians called the displaced people, along with those who may have been already present in the interior of the peninsula, the "Severnovskie Aleuty" [northern Aleuts]. This designation as Aleuts provides some evidence that the people were Alutiiq, rather than Yup'ik speakers, for Russian observers were well aware of language differences among the people with whom they traded and called Yup'ik speakers by tribal names such as Kiatagmiut and Aglegmiut.[66]

Throughout the Russian and early American periods there were several Severnovskie villages, variously called Alinnak, Ikak or Ikagmiut, Nunamiut, and Kanigmiut. Whether these names represent distinct settlements, renamed villages, or successive habitations in different locations is unclear. At least by the early 1900s, Alutiiq residents of Douglas recalled two extant villages which they called Savonoski, located at the eastern tip of Iliuk Arm (Naknek Lake) and today known as Old Savonoski, and Upper Savonoski, located up the Savonoski River.[67] The villages lay along a portage route which began at Katmai, crossed the coastal mountains, then descended the Naknek Lake drainage. Severnovtsy often visited the post at Katmai, traveling over the pass by dogsled. When the 1912 eruption of Katmai volcano destroyed their villages, the inhabitants resettled in South Naknek and a place they dubbed "New Savonoski" on the Naknek River. New Savonoski has since been abandoned.[68]

Like their Katmai neighbors (see below), the Severnovtsy were early converts to Christianity. In 1841, forty-six people were baptized into the Russian Orthodox church.[69] By 1864, three years before the United States purchased Alaska, all Severnovtsy had been baptized.[70]

Other peninsula villages were mentioned in the notes of RAC employee Vasilii Kashevarov. As manager of the RAC's Kodiak region during the 1830s, he was responsible for gathering furs taken on the peninsula as well as Kodiak Island. He knew of two other settlements in the Katmai area, one which he called "Naugikaksoe," probably the now-abandoned Nauklak, and the other which he called "Alikhanovskoe," probably either the Severnovskoe settlement of Alinnak or a location called Alagnak in the interior of the peninsula between Lake Iliamna and Dillingham.[71]

Finally, two mid-nineteenth-century atlases show a settlement named "Kaliak" ("Kayayak" by Pinart) located between Cape Douglas and Kukak Bay.[72] This village is not described in Russian documents, so it must have been quite small or short lived.

RUSSIAN ORTHODOXY AND THE ALUTIIQS

Alaska Peninsula Alutiiqs were introduced to Christianity during their first encounters with Russians. If the Russian overseers visiting the peninsula followed the common practice of the day, as soon as they established *artels* they baptized Alutiiq hunters and their families. When a Russian baptized an Alutiiq, he often gave the new convert his own last name and the two sometimes became hunting or trading partners. This relationship between the economic activities of the fur trade and Christianity continued throughout the Russian period.

In Orthodox practice, baptism, often performed by a layman, was followed by a formal chrizmatism administered by a priest. This sacrament was available to Alutiiqs once a year from 1841 until the beginning of the twentieth century when parish priests resident at Kodiak, Afognak, or Nushagak traveled to settlements on the peninsula. Even after chrizmatism, believers could not take Holy Communion until they had undergone religious instruction and showed the priest some understanding of the dogma.

Orthodox missionaries first visited Russian America in 1794, in the beginning concentrating their efforts on Kodiak Island, Prince William Sound, the Kenai Peninsula, and the Aleutian Islands. Archimandrite Ioasaf Bolotov reported that 6,740 Natives from Kodiak, the neighboring islands, and the Alaska Peninsula were baptized in 1795, and 1,573 others had wed in the church.[73] The rate of conversion greatly increased during the years of the Russian-American Company's Second Charter of 1821, under which the company was required to undertake an organized effort to missionize the Natives within its jurisdiction. Paragraph 37 of the charter states that the company "will see that there is always a sufficient number of priests and church employees in the colonies, so that the churches or places for religious services are established wherever there are sufficient inhabitants, and are kept in proper order."

Although, in theory, independent of the RAC, the church also served as a quasi-governmental institution. It received financial support from the RAC in the form of funds to build chapels and churches, pay the salaries of priests, and operate schools, most of which were conducted by priests under contract to the company. Priests also helped carry out company policies; for instance, when they visited the communities in their parishes, they regularly conferred with the company-appointed *toions*, who were sometimes church elders as well, and in some cases encouraged the removal of leaders they felt were unsuitable.[74] On the other hand, priests felt free to criticize company management when they saw the workers being abused, and they were considered champions of the Alutiiq hunters in later years under American rule in demanding that workers be allowed to rest during feast and holy days.[75]

Before the church undertook organized missionary efforts, the Alutiiqs' relationship with Christianity was marked by haphazard and infrequent encounters. When Langsdorff visited the village of Toujoujak in 1806, he found that the local Alutiiqs knew how to give the sign of the cross, but he believed that they did not understand anything of the religion itself.[76] His judgment accords with the conversion experiences described for other colonized populations throughout the world. Conversion is often a gradual process, its first visible manifestations being the new believers' adherence to new rituals, accompanied by public self-identifications as Christians. This stage may be succeeded by a growing understanding of the dogma or beliefs attached to the religion, but the level of understanding ultimately achieved varies from individual to individual, depending on personal interest, internal and external motivations for change, and the availability of instruction in the new religion. Meanwhile, as converts learn about their new faith, they commonly maintain a world view and relationship with the supernatural based on their former spiritual beliefs; in other words, in translating from one belief system to another, converts unconsciously incorporate elements, practices, and concepts from their first religion into the second. Conversion may begin with one or two individuals within a community, but at some point, if the new religion is to take hold, a critical mass must convert and carry most of the remaining people with the tide.[77]

The process played out on the Alaska Peninsula in this manner. Partly under the impetus of the perceived economic benefits of adopting Russian Orthodoxy, at first hunters and their families agreed to be baptized individually. Once the Katmai settlement had been established and Alutiiqs had begun to live there, two conditions facilitated additional conversions: Potential converts were a captive audience, available for proselytizing whenever the *baidarshchik* or visiting priest chose, and tutors in the new religion, in the person of the *baidarshchik* and, once a year, the priest, instructed initiates in the dogma. The critical moment of conversion, that point when nearly all within reach of the settlement agreed to convert, was reached when *baidarshchik* Kostylev successfully treated inhabitants for smallpox in 1837. Shortly afterward the confession lists swelled to incorporate virtually the entire community of Katmai.

Other factors undoubtedly attracted Alaska Peninsula Alutiiqs to Russian Orthodoxy. The church's relationship with the economic system and the company that ran it was not lost on the hunters. It was obvious to them that the people with economic and social power followed the Christian God, and that incorporation into the system could bring similar benefits to them. Another factor in the ready adoption of Christianity may have been a perceived decrease in individual responsibility for success in hunting and good health. Whereas in the past hunters and their families had to adhere strictly to taboos and rules associated with the supernatural *sua* of animals, Russian Orthodoxy taught that much of this responsibility was shouldered by the priest alone. Through the sacraments of baptism, confession, and Holy Communion, he took responsibility for ensuring proper behavior and achieving absolution in case of a lapse. Through careful ritual observation he could prevent the famine, illness, or death that had been ever-present dangers under the old religious system.

Finally, two church policies invited Alutiiqs into the Orthodox fold: the willingness of the clergy to preach in

Russian Orthodox peg calendar used to keep track of feast and fast days, from the Alaska Peninsula, 1883.
National Museum of Natural History, Smithsonian Institution (NMNH 90435) Photograph by Carl C. Hansen

Alutiiq and the church's role in promoting social and economic mobility for Natives through its practice of educating creoles and, later, Natives to become priests.

On the Alaska Peninsula, the conversion process is described in oral tradition and contemporary practice. Both make it clear that the Alutiiq brand of Russian Orthodoxy is syncretic or additive— that is, Christianity is considered compatible with elements of the old belief system and operates as an overlay rather than replacement for it. Even today people often tell of encounters between humans and supernatural beings whose characteristics can be traced to precontact entities, and who still exert power over humans. In most cases, these beings can be placated, or, even better, made to disappear with the judicious use of holy water, the sign of the cross, or a prayer.[78]

The process of conversion itself is portrayed in a peninsula story (transcribed below, p. 91ff) about a famous shaman who is transformed from traditional practitioner to Christian believer. He is initially reluctant to accept Christianity, for his spiritual powers are at their peak, his good reputation solid within the community, and his future assured. Then one day he has a religious epiphany. He suddenly *sees*—not intellectually, but emotionally and morally—that Christianity is the better path to follow. He (and the storyteller, Perryville elder Ignatius Kosbruk) perceives that the two religions operate on the same plane; in fact, their respective spiritual beings are aware of each other. The shaman is convinced to convert by the negative example of his Alutiiq spirit helpers. This story suggests that Alutiiqs who converted to Russian Orthodoxy during the nineteenth century considered both belief systems effective means for communicating with the supernatural powers that control the world.

Much of the specific history of the conversion among Alaska Peninsula Alutiiqs is recorded in church confession, communion, and baptism records. Katmai Alutiiqs received their first visits from Russian Orthodox priests in the 1830s, the Severnovtsy in the 1840s. The earliest surviving confessional records for the settlement of Katmai date to 1831, but the only Native to be confessed at that time was Irina Shangin, the Aleut or Alutiiq wife of *baidarshchik* Shangin. In fact, only two families, a total of four males and seven females, took confession. Both families were listed as "Russian" rather than "Aleut."[79]

According to visiting priests from Kodiak Island, by the mid-nineteenth century most Alaska Peninsula Alutiiqs professed the Russian Orthodox faith. Several times during the 1830s and every year after 1843 until the destruction of Katmai the parish priest made a summertime visit from his seat at Kodiak or Afognak to the Alutiiq settlements along the Pacific coast of the Alaska Peninsula. After 1844, the Severnovtsy and Ugashentsy were similarly visited by the resident priest of Nushagak (Aleksandrovskii Redoubt).[80]

The Kodiak priests traveled in a party made up of at least two three-hole baidarkas. As a passenger confined to the middle hatch of one of the kayaks, the priest depended entirely on the Alutiiqs who guided him. Besides navigating the kayaks across dangerous Shelikof Strait, these Alutiiq men also hunted for the party's food, set up camp for tea breaks, and found shelter if the group had to wait out bad weather in small bays along the way. The priest stayed in each village for one or two nights, longer if weather detained him, before being paddled to the next village. Priests' reports to their Kodiak bishops included descriptions of the church or chapel, an accounting of church funds, summaries of the sermons given and sacraments performed, recognition of local Alutiiqs who served as readers or interpreters, and lists of the people who made confession and took holy communion.[81]

The *baidarshchik* Kostylev built the first chapel in Katmai a few years after he had averted the smallpox epidemic described above.[82] Record numbers of local Alutiiqs began confessing and taking holy communion, likely attracted to the church by the seemingly miraculous prevention of the disease, an outcome they may have contrasted with the ineffectiveness of traditional shamanic remedies. By 1845, a total of ninety-nine males and ninety-six females were confessed during the priest's annual visit to Katmai.[83]

In 1850, local residents built a second village chapel to replace the old one. Soon afterward Kodiak's new parish priest, Father Pëtr Filipovich Kashevarov (younger brother of the creole naval officer Aleksandr Kashevarov mentioned earlier), began visiting his Pacific coast chapels.[84] As the son of a Russian father and Koniag mother, Father Pëtr was the first of several priests who spoke the Alutiiq language of his parishioners. As important as the priests in the maintenance of a level of faith among the peninsula Alutiiqs were the *baidarshchiks*, who often served as church readers and religious instructors. Church history records the particular contributions of Shangin, Kostylev, Naumov, and Nikiforov.[85]

The widespread religious conversions on the Alaska Peninsula occurred at a time when life had already changed immensely from the pre-Russian days: Economic activities were now determined by Russians; leadership within the community was decided by the Russians, while the former status of battle leader had been outlawed; epidemics and harsh working conditions had killed many people still in their youth, leaving gaping holes in the leadership and family structures; former villages had been abandoned as people moved to Katmai, where new alliances had to be established among people who had formerly been enemies; and people could no longer hunt and fish as their needs demanded, being now restricted by the company's hunting calendar.

Given these changes, a new religious orientation may not have seemed as vast a change to Alutiiqs as might appear to a modern reader. Some tenets of the old beliefs had already come under assault: the smallpox epidemic, only the worst of many to befall the peninsula, had shown the ineffectiveness of traditional shamanic medicine against diseases brought by Russians. Probably even more fundamental was the attack on an entire belief system that had been based on the idea that human survival was only possible through a respectful relationship with the rest of creation. It must have been profoundly disturbing for Alutiiqs to observe that animals did not retaliate in the expected manner in response to the breaking of taboos against waste of meat, careless disposal of bones, and failure to perform rituals to placate their souls. Indeed, the eventual shortages and near extinctions of these animals and continued high incidences of sickness and death among Alutiiqs were taken by many as evidence that some of the old beliefs were reliable and contributed to the continuation of clandestine shamanism. But Alutiiqs also saw clear evidence that the Russians could break Alutiiq taboos without repercussions; in fact, they could thrive, in defiance of the most strongly held Alutiiq beliefs.

As in all societies, some people had benefited more than others under the shamanic system, and those who had felt victimized were undoubtedly glad to rid themselves of its authority. People had both respected and feared the powers of the *kalagalget*; those for whom fear was the primary reaction must have embraced the relief Russian Orthodoxy afforded. Not only did they hope to be freed of the tyranny of unscrupulous *kalagalget* (a vain hope, as it turned out, since the shamans continued to operate, both openly and secretly, until well into the twentieth century); they were also able to relinquish some of their personal spiritual responsibilities. Under the old system each individual had to carry out many practices and taboos to maintain the delicate balance between herself and the rest of the natural world. In the past, breaking a single rule—for instance, sleeping with one's husband on the night before a hunt—could result in immediate or eventual difficulties in finding game, bearing children, safe travel, and successful trade and warfare. Under Russian Orthodoxy the priest, and through him Christ, took on the responsibility for maintaining balance between good and evil, natural and supernatural.

An indication of the psychological stress that accompanied conversion, symbolized here by physical pain, is communicated through the *unigkuaq* presented below, originally recorded in Perryville by Ignatius Kosbruk in 1992. It is the story of the conversion to Russian Orthodoxy of the *kalagalek* Puglálria (his name means "the one who came up to the surface"). The shaman was said to have lived during the last days of Katmai and had been the hunting partner of Simeon Takak, the last chief of Katmai and first chief of Perryville.

The following English version of Puglálria's story was translated with the assistance of Ignatius Kosbruk, Ralph Phillips, and Dr. Jeff Leer. Italicized portions were originally spoken in English.

> I used to hear this story in the past from that old man, *his name was Wasco Sanook. He used to tell me stories.* He used to tell me stories there in the trapping grounds. Then I didn't understand what he

told me. He was really talking about a shaman. Later, when I thoroughly understood it, he made me tell that story back to him.

From Naknek to Katmai, a maternal uncle went down to see two old people. They had only one son—one. Then that uncle made that son into a shaman—but the uncle didn't tell the nephew's two parents anything.

When he was about to go home, he took that boy out, the one he had made into a shaman, and he put him into a garbage pit. *It was about in the fall, in September, I guess or October, whatever.* So he made him stay there the whole winter, through the entire winter, in the back of the pit. *We call it a garbage hole.* He was there the whole winter. Then when spring came, that uncle went down from Naknek to Katmai. Then he asked the two parents, "Where on earth is your son?" Then his mother got all excited, not having known where he was since the fall; she had lost him, her *boy.* Then that uncle told her to look for him out there in the garbage hole. *In the pit—the garbage pit.* His mother did as she was told, she went down to that pit. Then she saw him there in the pit, in the process of leisurely cleaning his teeth, taking fish eggs out from his teeth. She took him down to his father, to his dad.

Now that boy knew every last thing in the world. He knew what was on everyone's minds. He knew how people would live in the future. He was a person who knew things. Now that uncle was just beginning to make him a shaman.

From then on, being a shaman, he didn't hurt his fellow humans, he just helped his fellow humans. He became a shaman. People in those villages didn't know what kind of person he was. That Puglálria, *he knows everything what was going on.* He killed only his uncle. He killed him because of the fact that he had made his parents cry. *The only person he killed, that was the only one.* When he was just leaving, when that uncle got ready to go home again, Puglálria tied a hair around his neck. That uncle didn't know it, *he didn't know he tied a hair around his neck. He didn't know. So he went back, back to Naknek, and that same year, one year after that, he went back. He went back to Naknek, and looked at him. He was almost cut by the hair what he put around his neck.* As a shaman, the only person he killed was his uncle. On the way, he helped people out.

Then again one time when people were hunting for sea otters in the sea, when they were way out in kayaqs, in three-man baidarkas, there were lots of them hunting sea otters. The wind came up, it blew really hard, and they had absolutely nowhere to go. Then that Puglál̲ria, he called those who were hunting sea otters, *the ones that went out for sea otters. And all of a sudden* suddenly all the kayaqs went towards each other, they gathered without anyone doing anything. *Nobody touched them.*

They were out in the storm. They didn't know. And they all gathered in one place and made a path for them to go up to—back to Katmai.

There was no human agent—*nobody touch them and they didn't know what happened. They all go through that one path—right up to Qayihwik* [Katmai], *right where they live. And when they landed, Father,* Apawak [the Russian priest told him not to do that any more].

Then he, that shaman, lived among the people. He was kind and nice to the people. He only helped those people. He used that magic.

Now, once, unexpectedly, this couple's child got a fish bone stuck in his throat—in the village—a bone got stuck in his throat. His parents asked shamans to come help. That Puglál̲ria watched all those shamans from somewhere or other, *in their home. They couldn't do nothing to him. And Puglál̲ria was watching them from his home— and wondering what kind of kal̲agalek are they.*

At last, finally they think of him. They call Puglál̲ria down. And he went out. And when he entered the house he told them, "What are you shamans good for anyway? You just torture people in their minds, you're just killing people instead of helping. Is this child suffering here? You can't seem to help him." *So he just take the child and put him on his lap. I don't know what he did. And he take the bone out and show it to them kal̲agaleks every one of them.* "Was this hard?" *He take the bone out and show it to them—every one of 'em.* Then he told them to look, that "A person who pays attention to himself can be a shaman. He helps people, doesn't do anything bad to them." *And they said some of 'em were real criminal, in that group. He seen them, their mind.*

And then after that then the shaman lived there helping people.

This chief there, *the one I told you about* [Simeon Takak], *the chief, he never hire nobody, only Puglálria for partner. He say he never carry no gun. And fall of the year when they watch for bears at night, he let the bear come right close to them, up to them right there. He had no gun. That's something amazing. He never let the bear see him.*

Then he used his shamanism as a means of helping people out. He helped people out with his shamanism. Then he lived and just helped people.

Then once he started to ponder, "Am I doing the right thing?" Then, then when he started to think about it, he started to think he wanted to quit it, what he was doing, being a shaman. Then he started to become sick. He was sick then. Then one time, once, all of a sudden his shaman helpers came back to him. They broke his joints. *Arms and legs were broken up without nobody touching 'em. And he hollered, "Whoa! I wouldn't come with you guys!" And his arms and legs started to break up without nobody touching them.*

And he hollered, "I wouldn't come with you guys, because I think that we are doing something that is wrong." He screamed that it wasn't right. *"It's not right. It's all devil's work." And it got worse and worse and worse. His legs start to break without nobody touching them.* Then it got worse and worse. *His arms and legs start to break without nobody touching them.* Then he screamed, saying he will not go with his spirit helpers, they're not doing right. He said he would follow only the true God.

Then the poor thing died. He just vomited blood until Good Friday. I heard this, that the poor creature died on Good Friday, vomiting blood.

That's the end, it's all done[86]

In this *unigkuaq*, Puglálria became a *kalagalek* in a way that was typical for Alutiiq shamans: his mother's brother—the male relative most responsible for the education of a young man—who was a shaman, initiated Puglálria through a strenuous ordeal.[87] At the end of a year of initiation spent in a hole in the ground, nowadays called a "stink-head pit" because it contained fermenting fish heads ripening for a feast, Puglálria emerged a clairvoyant, healer, and controller of weather. He is shown as a model Alutiiq man in performing deeds for the good of the people, in contrast to the work of other shamans who benefited themselves or harmed people. The story veers from precontact mores and merges with Christian motifs and values when it tells of Puglálria's deathbed realization that shamanism was essentially evil and that his spirit helpers were agents of the devil. He threw them off, dying in excruciating pain. As with Yup'ik shamans, his spiritual power was located in his joints, which burst open when he expelled his spirit helpers.[88] He died on Good Friday, which, according to Orthodox tradition, assured that he would go straight to Heaven.[89]

This story indicates the belief that shamans could benefit the people, but did not always do so. It also shows Christianity incorporating and eventually overpowering—but not erasing—the beliefs that existed in precontact days. As Ignatius Kosbruk tells it, Puglálria's story symbolizes not just one shaman's conversion, but the conversion of all Alutiiqs. Kosbruk portrays Puglálria in a Christ-like manner, and just as Christ is a model for future generations throughout the world, so Puglálria is a model for Alaska Peninsula Alutiiqs.

CREOLES

Several priests and *baidarshchiks* who served or worked on the Alaska Peninsula were not Russians, but creoles, a special class within the Russian social and legal system. Most were children of Russian fathers and Native mothers—usually Unangan or Alutiiq, though some Natives were also accorded the rank of creole.[90] Second generation creoles might be children of two creole parents, or of one creole parent and one Native parent, or of a Russian father and a creole mother. Children were usually assigned the class of their fathers, so that, for instance, a child with an Alutiiq father and a creole mother was generally considered an Alutiiq.

By 1817 the Russian-American Company was worried about the increase in the number of children born to Native mothers and Russian fathers.[91] The group was rapidly increasing because there were only a handful of Russian women in Russian America, all of whom were married to Russian men. The company saw two causes for concern. First, few priests were available to perform marriages and therefore many of the children of unions between Russians and Natives were illegitimate. Second, as children of Russian men these youngsters should have been enrolled in their fathers' taxation districts in Russia, requiring both paperwork and payment of taxes.

At the same time, the company saw an advantage to the growth of the creole population. On the one hand, from their Russian fathers these people learned the Russian language, heard stories about Russia and their fathers' childhoods and families, and were baptized into the Russian Orthodox church. Some were taught to read by their fathers. In other words, they were potentially loyal Russian subjects. From their Native mothers, aunts, uncles, and grandparents they learned the Native language and how to live off the land and sea near their home villages. They were likely to stay in Alaska, unlike many of the company's imported Russian workers, and so could become a stable workforce for the RAC.[92]

The Second Charter of 1821 spoke directly to the status, rights, and responsibilities of the creoles. The company was to provide priests to perform marriage ceremonies throughout the colony to legitimize the children. The company also agreed to give creoles a free education in exchange for future work for the company. The government freed the creoles of taxation and of compulsory company service, unless they were educated at company expense.[93]

Not every creole was able to take advantage of the offer of a free education, since schools were located only in larger settlements. The Russian schools of longest standing were in Unalaska (the Aleutian Islands), New Archangel (Sitka), and Pavlovskaia [Paul] Harbor (the location of the current town of Kodiak) on Kodiak Island. Schools opened in various other small settlements from time to time as well.[94] However, Katmai, like most *artels* and *odinochki*, had no school. The creole sons (few girls were educated at this time) of the *baidarshchiks* learned to read, write, and do sums at home from their fathers, but this was the only education many of them received. Some creoles, including Stepan Shangin, son of *baidarshchik* Iakov Shangin, chose to stay in Katmai and work as hunters. Others, Pëtr Kolmakov and Vasilii Nikiforov among them, were sent to Sitka or Russia for specialized training in navigation, shipbuilding, accounting, the priesthood, or other jobs that would prepare them to work for the RAC.[95] By the 1860s the company's dream of a local workforce had been realized and day-to-day company operations throughout the colony were largely in the hands of creoles.

EFFECTS OF COMPANY AND CHURCH ON ALASKA PENINSULA ALUTIIQS

Life had changed for the Alutiiqs in many ways by the 1867 sale of Alaska to the United States. Decisions regarding residence, travel, and hunting were no longer in the hands of the Alutiiqs, but rather determined by company needs and policies. New systems of leadership were in place.[96] The emphasis in hunting had shifted from meat to furbearing animals. People depended on purchased food and clothing to supplement what they could obtain by hunting and trapping. Trade was carried out in a new language and under the auspices of distant leaders. The very name people called themselves had changed. But the most immediately noticeable transformation, both a result and cause of other changes, was a drastic population decline.

Population Decline

When Europeans came to Alaska, they unwittingly brought diseases that the Native people had never before experienced. Because they had not been exposed to such ailments as measles, smallpox, influenza or even the common cold, Alaska Natives had not built up protective antibodies and hence immunities. Many indigenous people died with each wave of each new illness. There is little information about epidemics at Katmai itself, but some of the diseases affecting Kodiak were undoubtedly carried to the Alaska Peninsula aboard company ships and baidarkas. A list of epidemics recorded on Kodiak Island, compiled by physician and historian Robert Fortuine, illustrates the devastation this unexpected weapon caused the Alutiiq population:

- By the end of the 1700s tuberculosis was common among Aleuts of the Aleutian Islands and Kodiak.

- In 1791 a severe respiratory disease struck Kodiak.

- By the early 1800s venereal disease was reported on Kodiak.

- In 1802 a Russian ship transported a deadly fever from Siberia to Kodiak.

- In 1804 another respiratory epidemic killed off many of the shamans on Kodiak Island.

- In 1806 and 1808 a fever swept throughout all of Russian America.

- In 1810 an epidemic of diarrhea weakened over a hundred people and took two lives on Kodiak.

- In 1819 an illness, probably some type of flu, struck Kodiak and killed its victims within three days of falling ill. This illness left so many orphans that Father Herman established an orphanage and school to care for them.

- In 1824–28 a respiratory illness, again probably influenza, killed 158 Alutiiqs and creoles on Kodiak Island.

- In 1830–31 the Alaska Peninsula itself saw an epidemic of coughing and chest congestion that killed 30 people.

- Although most Katmai Alutiiqs were spared the scourge of smallpox during the 1837 epidemic, hundreds of Koniags died.

- During the 1840s the visiting Russian lieutenant Lavrentiy Zagoskin reported that tuberculosis was so common that it was rare for a man not to cough blood by the time he was 20.

- In 1848 a measles epidemic claimed many lives on the Alaska Peninsula.

- In 1852 pneumonia struck at Kodiak and at Aleksandrovskii redoubt in Bristol Bay.

- In 1853 the Lake Naknek villages (including the Severnovskie settlements) were stricken by epidemics of cough and stabbing pains, resulting in 163 deaths.

- In 1860 a similar ailment in the same region claimed 116 lives. That year measles and typhus struck Afognak Island north of Kodiak.

- In 1865 a scarlet fever outbreak occurred at Kodiak.[97]

The Russians were able to control smallpox and venereal disease using medicines available at the time, but they had no cures for influenza and other respiratory diseases, for the mumps, measles, or tuberculosis. As a result the population of Alaska Peninsula Alutiiqs dropped sharply during the Russian period.

As disruptive as the fact that there were far fewer Alutiiqs after contact than before was the loss of primary caregivers and educators, the mothers, family leaders, and elders. This meant that knowledge was lost, some children grew up as unwanted foster children, boys lost the trainers who would have traditionally prepared them for manhood—in short, the traditional ways of transferring knowledge, status, authority, and power smoothly from one person to another, and one generation to another, were interrupted. The situation allowed people who might not normally have been afforded leadership roles to gain power. For instance, a man of a small and powerless family but with a valued skill, such as fluency in Russian or ability in guiding expeditions across mountain passes, could cooperate with the Russian traders, gain their trust, and be afforded prestigious gifts or, perhaps, elevated to the status of *toion*.[98]

Changes in Warfare and Trading Practices

Another change during Russian times was in the Alutiiqs' practice of traveling broadly in search of food, to wage war, or cement political alliances. Between 1786 and 1818 the so-called dependent Natives like those at Katmai could relocate only under orders from the RAC, not by their own choice. Men were sent far from their home villages to hunt and, according to written company policy, were to be allowed to return home at the end of the season. However, many died in accidents or from illness while working for the company. Meanwhile, the hunting party system left few able-bodied men in the villages at any one time. Without the support of hunters and protectors, many families moved from outlying villages into the *artel* settlements where store-bought food was available. In other cases, whole villages relocated to be closer to the posts. Even outlying Native villages eventually were brought into the Russian fur trade through the *toions'* persuasion or through trade by free Aleuts.

Gradually the populations of the small Alutiiq villages on the peninsula shrank as people converged at Katmai, Ugashik, and the Severnovskie villages.

Wars ceased under pressure from the Russian government and because work for the company left men with no time for battle. At the same time, thanks to the Russian fur trade, Yup'ik and Alutiiq people came to know, work, and intermarry with each other more than ever before. This was especially true between 1786 and 1818 when Katmai was the only trading center serving the Alaska Peninsula and Bristol Bay, before the opening of the Aleksandrovskii post.

Subsistence

Despite the presence of the RAC posts at Katmai and Sutkhum, some parts of Alutiiq life remained insulated from company control. People continued to speak the Alutiiq language. Some became bilingual, but many remained monolingual speakers of their ancestral language. They continued to pass on knowledge and lore from generations past.

In addition, many subsistence practices and the cosmology that underlay them continued throughout the Russian period. The RAC's Second Charter of 1821 ensured that there were always some adult hunters in the villages to feed the people through the winters. Peninsula Alutiiqs hunted big game animals such as caribou, sheep, and bear during the fall after sea otter season. Some spent the winter trapping land mammals such as lynx, beaver, mink, and fox for trade at the Katmai post. Ducks and geese added variety to the diet, but the most important subsistence activity continued to be salmon fishing during the summer and fall. In fact, Peninsula Alutiiqs had no choice but to subsist from the animals and plants of the land and sea, for the RAC could not supply enough food or clothing for either its Russian or Native workers.

Still, the subsistence practiced during Russian days was different in important ways from pre-contact days. The most obvious change was in the amount of time spent obtaining fur for trade as opposed to getting meat and furs for food and clothing. In precontact days all animals had been taken for what they could directly provide

Goose snares collected at Ugashik, 1885–86. The snares were set near the bank of a pond. Geese became caught in baleen loops attached to the wooden stakes. *National Museum of Natural History, Smithsonian Institution (NMNH 127778)*. *Photograph by Carl C. Hansen*

the people, but beginning in Russian days the Alutiiqs only ate or wore a fraction of what the men hunted. Most of the furs were traded away and the meat was discarded or left to rot.

The first generation of RAC hunters must have been horrified at the waste of meat, expecting the *suas*, or souls, of the wasted animals to wreak vengeance at any moment, as tradition dictated it would. A horror of waste, profligacy, and greed persists. Ignatius Kosbruk told an *unigkuaq* about a *piculi* (or "great hunter") who lived in Katmai some time after Russian goods had become available. It is these goods and the man's greed for them that cause the *piculi's* problems; the new shoes and clean clothes he so values are not the traditional sealskin or fishskin boots and gut or fur parka, but European-style clothes. In this story the man blasphemes the Christian God, not a precontact *lam sua*, but the result is the same.

Piculi is reproduced here in English translation, written with the assistance of Kosbruk and Ralph Phillips.

There's another story.... There used to live at Katmai an expert hunter. I don't know his name. He was a great hunter. But I don't know his name. Anyway, this guy was a real good hunter and—great hunter. He used to hunt year-round. Fill all his garages [caches] up for the winter, with whatever they had. I guess, I don't know how they were made, made out of grass or wood. He let his servants make him three big warehouses for winter. Dry up meat. All the meat he put away.

So I think it must been in the fall. Finally he came back from his hunting. When he came back, they were putting up fish, he saw them down at the river. The Alutiiqs were putting up fish. There used to be lots of fish in the past.

Then he said to his wife, "My new shoes. I've never used them." He put them on and went for a walk. He put on clean clothes, and went to visit. He went to the village by way of the river.

While—the sun was shining; it was fine weather and that man had on clean clothes; he went to the ones who were fishing at this river. While he was going along the road, he stepped on some fish—you know—they were exposed to the sun.

Then he splashed his shoes with the rotting fish. Boy then he cursed. He cursed about the fish, even though it hadn't done anything to him. He cursed God. For no reason, "Why did you send fish here?" Because it just dirty his shoes when he stepped that fish, rotten fish. And he splash it on his new shoes. Boy, then he cursed God. He cursed God for no reason. And then He [God] answer him from the air without nobody. Nobody around. And answered. The word came out from the air. All the people that were along the creek listened to it. Every one of 'em. And listened to Him and stopped....

And then He said, God tells him Himself, "I sent this food, fish, down so the kids wouldn't go hungry. I sent it down due to the people that will go hungry, so they wouldn't go hungry."

And this guy, he answered Him right back and told Him, even if he doesn't eat any fish, he will make it through the winter.

And then God gave him the best of luck. All the game he wanted—came. And he dried all the meat he can, and put away three big warehouses, just full of dried meat. He went out and God gave him all the luck he wanted. He didn't punish him. But at the end he was punished.

And then he—he filled all his warehouses full. When time to quit, then he quit. And then winter came. Winter came. Oh, I don't know how big those warehouses were!

Then it became fall, it was snowing and cold, and he quit hunting. These caches were full to the top.

Then he must have had a wife. He said to his wife, I don't know how many times, to open that first warehouse. He sent his wife to open that first warehouse. She opened it as she was advised to from her husband. She opened it but nothing but sod. All the meat: All dirt! And then he send her to the other one. Same thing: It was all sod. All that work he did. And then the third one, it was same thing: Nothing happened. No meat, all dirt. That's when God punish him.

And then she ate in the table with him, tried to feed him, and couldn't. She feed him out of her own plate and put it in his mouth and it turn into mud. And everything what he tried to put in his mouth turned into mud. He died from starvation.

He hollered. Three times he answer Him [God]. God told him that He sent the fish down so the children wouldn't go hungry, that's why He sent the fish to the earth.

Then that one answered Him, "Even if I don't eat fish I will survive the winter." He died from starvation.

That's why they always tell us not to step on the fish, when we're around the creek. Because it is just like bread—bread and butter. That's what they call it, how big the fish is. That's the meaning of it.

That's all.[99]

The story illustrates the importance of the old Alutiiq virtues long after first contact with Russians. In fact, this *unigkuaq* merges a common precontact Sugpiaq/Alutiiq theme with a Christian message: mocking or showing disrespect to an animal or food will eventually cause trouble or even death to the perpetrator. Phrased from a Christian perspective, the message extends to an illustration of the sins of pride, love of material objects, greed, and blasphemy.

Kayaks and fish rack at Egegik, 1917.
  MSCUA, University of Washington Cobb Collection, 4179

Beginning of an Alutiiq Identity

One of the most lasting effects that close contact with Russian economics and religion had on the Alaska Peninsula Alutiiqs was the adoption of a Sugpiaq or Alutiiq identity that encompassed an entire region, far beyond the precontact village-wide sense of identity. Through the Russian-American Company and the Russian Orthodox church, peninsula Natives were in regular and frequent contact with Alutiiqs from other parts of the colony as well as Yup'ik, Dena'ina, Unangan, and Tlingit Natives and Russian immigrants. They recognized a common language and culture with other Sugtestun speakers in contrast with those of the other peoples, particularly the Russians. Treated as members of a collective group, they began to see themselves as such. This was the beginning of an Alutiiq identity that was to be strengthened and solidified during the twentieth century.

NOTES

1. Steller 1988: 97.

2. Tikhmenev 1978: 10; Fedorova 1973:3; Pierce 1990: 41; Alekseev 1990:50.

3. Efimov 1967: 140.

4. Efimov 1967: 165.

5. Litke 1835: 269–70.

6. Efimov 1964: 180.

7. Petroff 1882: 145.

8. Alekseev 1996 [1970]: 85; Pierce 1990: 483.

9. Arndt and Pierce 1990b: #8: February 17, 1981, #89: April 22, 1832; and Arndt and Pierce 1990: #29: February 16, 1832.

10. Arndt and Pierce 1990b: #197: April 30, 1831.

11. Tikhmenev 1978: 185; Pierce 1990: 533.

12. Polonskii n.d.

13. Tikhmenev 1979: 7.

14. Shelikhov 1981: 47.

15. Izmailov 1787: Folios 16 and 20.

16. Khlebnikov 1979: 24.

17. Tikhmenev 1979: 32, 33, 35.

18. Tikhmenev 1979: 95, 98. The location of Sutkhum is problematic. Although most modern sources place the *artel* on Sutwik Island (e.g., Crowell 1992: 29), evidence points to its having been located instead on the mainland of the peninsula. Baranov did not indicate the Sutkhum establishment's location in those letters and reports that remain extant (cf. Tikhmenev 1979). Gideon's references to Sutkhum lacked the word "island." He explained, for instance, "They hunt sea otters along the south coast of Aliaksa [the Alaska Peninsula], between Kenai Bay and Sutkhum" (Gideon 1989: 64). Davydov, who never visited the *artel*, was the first to locate it on Sutwik Island (Davydov 1977: 192). Khlebnikov specifically stated that Sutkhum was located on "Aliaska" (Khlebnikov 1979: 42–3; 65). Vasilii Kashevarov's reports from the 1830s agree; he stated, "The Sutkhum *odinochka* is located on the east side of the Aliaksa Peninsula, to the south of Katmai Bay" (Kashevarov ms.). Alphonse L. Pinart, who traveled up the Alaska Peninsula's Pacific coast from the Aleutian Islands, actually visited the site and located it on the mainland as had most of the

earlier sources (Pinart 1872; 1873a: 14–15). In the 1880 census report Petroff similarly stated that "Sutkhoon" was located on the "Aliaska Peninsula" (Petroff 1900: 89). Further, Bureau of Indian Affairs archaeologists conducted a site survey on Sutwik Island in 1990 and were unable to locate any Russian structures. Nor, unfortunately, did they locate the site of the Russian-American Company's *artel* at Kujulik Bay where Pinart had landed (O'Leary, pers. comm. 1993). To local residents, the locale "Sutkhum" refers to an old village site on Kujulik Bay.

19. See, for instance, Davydov 1977: 196.

20. Davydov 1977: 193; Gideon 1989: 6; Arndt and Pierce 1990b: #74: February 27, 1823.

21. Cf. VanStone 1967: 54–5 for a discussion of the methods by which RAC officials chose *toions* in the Nushagak area, just north of the Alaska Peninsula.

22. Cf. Khlebnikov 1994: 60, 360–361; Golovin 1979: 25.

23. Cf. Gideon 1989: 191–193; Davydov 1977: 193.

24. Davydov 1977: 196.

25. Davydov 1977: 193.

26. Fortuine 1989.

27. Veniaminov 1984: 181–182; Golovin 1979: 37–38.

28. Pierce 1990a: 145 ff.

29. Davydov 1977: 194, 195; Gideon 1989: 62.

30. Golovin 1979: 76–78.

31. Davydov 1977: 192–3.

32. Khlebnikov 1979: 31, 32.

33. RAC 1842: 41.

34. Khlebnikov 1979: 31, 32.

35. Tikhmenev 1979: 105.

36. VanStone 1988: 20.

37. Pierce 1990: 248–250.

38. Pierce ms: #121: April 16, 1843; #173: April 27, 1844.

39. ARCA Reel 176.

40. ARCA Reel 175, 176.

41. Shelikhov 1981: 116.

42. Arndt and Pierce 1990b: #324:July 10, 1832, #12: January 21, 1833; Pierce
    ms.:#200: May 3, 1837.

43. Arndt and Pierce 1990b: #342: August 1834.

44. Fortuine 1989: 233.

45. ARCA: Reel 175.

46. ARCA: Reel 176; Pierce ms.: #158: 1863.

47. ARCA: Reel 176; Pierce 1990: 251, 386; Pierce ms.: #211:September
    23, 1866; AOM 1908: 65.

48. VanStone 1988: 20.

49. Arndt and Pierce 1990b: #60:April 15, 1820.

50. Tikhmenev 1978: 174, 180ff.

51. Khlebnikov 1979: 46–47.

52. Arndt and Pierce 1990b: #197: May 10, 1823.

53. Khlebnikov 1979: 31.

54. Arndt and Pierce 1990b: #257: October 5, 1830, #283: May 4, 1831,
    #82: May 4, 1830.

55. Arndt and Pierce 1990b:#171: May 16, 1828.

56. Pierce 1984: 58, 85.

57. Pierce ms:#129: April 16, 1843.

58. Pierce 1990: 216.

59. Davydov 1977: 197.

60. Langsdorff 1968: 234, 235.

61. AOM 1896: 119.

62. Gideon 1989: 141.

63. VanStone 1988: 19.

64. Arndt and Pierce 1990b: #324:July 10, 1832.

65. Wrangell 1980: 64.

66. Dumond and VanStone 1995: 4.

67. Kaiakokonok 1975a.

68. Vick 1983: 238; Mary Jane Nielsen, personal correspondence 1998.

69. ARCA Reel 175, 176.

70. Dumond and VanStone 1995: 9.

71. Kashevarov ms.

72. Teben'kov 1981 [1852]: Chart XXII, Pinart 1972.

73. Cited in Kan 1988: 507.

74. AOM 1902: 432.

75. Afonsky 1977: 32–8; Stepanoff 1969.

76. Langsdorff 1968: 64.

77. Cf. Hefner 1993: 25ff. on the importance of the "reference group" in self-identity formation.

78. This additive tendency in the conversion to Christianity is a common response to missionizing attempts throughout the world. Cf. Hefner 1993: 23.

79. ARCA Reel 175.

80. ARCA Reel 175, 176.

81. See, for instance, Veniaminov 1993, AOM 1898, 1899.

82. AOM 1898: 508.

83. ARCA Reel 175.

84. AOM 1898 :509.

85. During the American period, some post managers (notably Aleksandr Petelin) continued to perform dual roles as temporal and spiritual leaders in the communities. In addition, most religious instruction, as well as elementary education in reading and math, was conducted by parents in their homes.

86. Ignatius Kosbruk 1992.

87. *Puglálria* contains many interesting motifs, most of which are beyond the scope of this book. For instance, shamanistic contests are common themes in Eskimo lore (Lantis 1953: 156). Further, the story contains information about Alutiiq social structure: Davydov had noted in the early nineteenth century that among the Koniag Alutiiqs, heredity passed from [maternal] uncle to nephew, precisely as among the Tlingits (Davydov 1977: 190). The story of *Puglálria* shows a similar hereditary system (though there is no indication that this was the only route by which a person became a shaman). Golder (1903) reported the motif of the cruel uncle in Kodiak folklore (1903: 90ff.), and Boas (1919) compared it with similar Northwest Coast stories (1919: 796ff. and 951ff.). Lantis (1938) saw the motif as an indication of close cultural contact between Koniag and Tlingit peoples (1938: 128, 154).

88. Although people claim to know little about shamanism nowadays, the bone-breaking episode at the end of the story indicates that portions of the previous belief system are remembered. It is likely

that the Alaska Peninsula Alutiiqs, like the Yupiit about whom we have more information, broke the bones of a shaman when he died to ensure that he would not come back to life (Mather, pers. comm. 1992; Fienup-Riordan 1990: 54).

89. According to a Russian Orthodox folk belief, one who dies on Good Friday will go straight to heaven (Leer 1993, pers. comm.). For parallels elsewhere in Alaska, see Mousalimas (1992: 240ff.) for a discussion of the relationship between shamanism and Christianity, particularly as exhibited among Kodiak and Prince William Sound Alutiiqs. See also Fienup-Riordan (1988) for a story of the death of a Yup'ik Christian during Holy Week.

90. Oleksa 1990: 185.

91. Black 1990: 143.

92. Fedorova quoted Russian archival sources on the issue of creoles as company workers: "The lack of Russian people in the colonies can be compensated for.... Creoles, brought up and educated at the Company's cost and effort, thereafter employed in various capacities, or carrying on its business, can obtain food and livelihood" (1973: 210–1).

93. RAC Second Charter, Paragraph 41; RAC Third Charter, #243.

94. Partnow 1990.

95. Pierce 1990:250, 386.

96. See Fall 1987 for a discussion of the effects of the Russian *toion* system on indigenous Dena'ina leadership roles and intergroup social relationships.

97. Fortuine 1989.

98. Reports of disruptions in traditional social structure following contact with colonial powers are common in the ethnographic literature. For instance, Drucker (1966) and others have written much about the development of competition in Northwest Coast potlatches. He noted, "At one time there were twelve Eagle titles at Fort Rupert. Investigation has revealed that most of these Eagles were not chiefs at all, but were men of intermediate or even common status who through industry and clever trading amassed great quantities of material wealth" (1966: 106). See also a short discussion of the power of Indian interpreters and translators in Kawashima 1988: 252–3 and the effects of gifts in Prucha 1988.

99. Ignatius Kosbruk 1992b.

4

THE AMERICAN PERIOD, 1867 TO 1912

THE AMERICAN FUR TRADE

Alaska became an American territory in 1867 with its purchase from Russia. Surprisingly, for many years the change in ownership hardly affected Alaska Peninsula Alutiiqs. Language, religion, economy, and social life continued much as they had during Russian days. It was only as the fur trade declined that an American influence became obvious.

Hutchinson, Kohl and Company, a San Francisco business that was later to become the Alaska Commercial Company (ACC), bought Katmai and other RAC posts in 1867.[1] Katmai remained the center of the Alaska Peninsula fur trade for many years afterward. When the Frenchman Alphonse L. Pinart stopped there on an 1871 voyage along the peninsula coast, he reported that the settlement had a population of about 150 "Koniags," with one white man, the trader. He wrote that the post did "a fairly large fur business with the villages in the interior and on Bristol Bay."[2]

Six years later, Katmai's ACC trader, A. B. Francis, received instructions from company headquarters for outfitting sea otter hunting crews. His orders demonstrate that the fur trade had changed little since the Russian days; the outlines of the relationship between company and hunters were the same, the details differing only in an

Chirikof Island sea otter hunters, probably early twentieth century.
University of Alaska Fairbanks Rasmuson Library Archives, Accession Number 74-175-72

expectation of quick repayment for provisions provided at the beginning of the season. Francis was told that for each hunter he was to package one pound of tea, five pounds of sugar, two pounds of leaf tobacco, and a peck of flour. He was to give the provisions to the chief of the party who would sell them to the hunters. Francis was then to take pelts in payment for the provisions.[3]

The system whereby traders issued orders to Native hunters through *toions* and crew chiefs and required them to buy provisions for hunting trips from the company sent some families into debt they could not overcome. If the furs delivered to the manager at the end of the season did not equal the money owed the post, there was no way to make up the difference except with proceeds from the next year's hunt—yet families needed supplies for the following year, and these could only be purchased on credit at the company store. A second year of poor hunting would add to the previous year's debt. One visiting priest reported that by the time the Katmai post closed for good in 1902 some families had had a debit on the company books for 50 years.[4]

Not only was the fur trade as a system virtually unchanged from Russian days, some of the same traders and officials continued to represent the economic structure. For instance, the ACC trader at Katmai between 1878 and 1890 was a creole named Nikolai Romanov

Fomin (referred to in Douglas log books as "Fomka").[5] Similarly, Vladimir Stafeev, a Russian who had married a Dena'ina woman, stayed in Alaska after the sale and in 1889 became manager of the ACC Douglas post north of Katmai. The creole priest Pëtr Kashevarov continued to visit the peninsula chapels and churches as he had before the sale of Alaska. In fact, the Russian language was still used to carry out most business in the smaller settlements of southwestern Alaska until well into the twentieth century. Alfred B. Shanz, who gathered information on the Nushagak district for the 1890 U. S. Census, reported,

> The fact that the territory is now owned by the United States cuts no figure and many of the native members of the church are not even aware of that fact. The natives of the north peninsula villages divide mankind into two classes, Russians and non-Russians, and to all of the latter class they apply the generic term Americanski, no matter whether the individual specimen be a German, a Scandinavian, a Finlander, or a Kanaka [Hawaiian]. One unable to speak any Russian whatever is looked upon as pitifully ignorant and is treated with contempt.[6]

Father Harry Kaiakokonok of Perryville explained in a 1972 interview how a particular American businessman adapted to the preference for the Russian language in the 1910s:

> [Foster, the owner of the Kaflia Bay saltery in 1912] speak a little Russian too! All those people that lives in Kodiak speak little Russian. That the language Kodiak used to use—even the Kodiak natives hardly speak their dialect, mostly in Russian. That's why this Foster guy speak a little Russian too, so the people can understand whenever they inquire for something.[7]

Thus for many years after Alaska's sale, Alutiiqs had no need to learn English. In fact, it would have been difficult for them to do so even had they wanted to, for there was no American school on the Pacific coast of the Alaska Peninsula until the 1920s.

Throughout the nineteenth century the ACC maintained the Katmai post while opening new trading posts in other parts of the Alaska Peninsula. By 1876, people from Katmai and Savonoski had formed a new village at Cape Douglas north of Katmai that they called "Ashivak." At about the same time the Alaska Commercial Company opened a post there and at Ugashik, though the Ugassarmiut continued their centuries-long practice of seasonal travel to the Pacific coast for trade and hunting.[8] The old RAC Sutkhum post was reopened and operated between 1882 and 1887 as an ACC post.[9] At Wrangel Bay (also spelled "Wrangell" and sometimes called "Port Wrangell") a store operated from about 1884 until 1900.[10] The company also opened stores at Kukak in 1891 and Wide Bay in 1897.[11]

Although the Alaska Commercial Company was the most successful trading company in the Shelikof Strait area, there were others. In the 1880s the Western Fur and Trading Company (WFT) operated a post at Douglas for a short time, and the North American Company was rumored to be contemplating the establishment of a post there in 1893.[12] In addition, freelance schooners sailed the shores of the Alaska Peninsula with wares to trade and money to spend on furs. While it lasted, the competition afforded by the various traders, coupled with an ever-growing shortage of sea otters, allowed Alutiiq hunters to ask higher prices for their furs than formerly. The hunters could also demand cash rather than goods in exchange for their furs. As an example of the prices paid during the years of competition, in May 1893 the Douglas trader bought the following from Alutiiq hunters:

- Sea otter: three at $100.00 each
- Land otter: two at $3.75 each
- Red fox: eighty-six at $1.87 each
- Lynx: six at $1.00 each
- Mink: one hundred at $.49 each

In contrast, in 1850, shortly after a rise in rates instigated by dwindling furs, the Russian-American Company paid fifty rubles ($25) per sea otter pelt, six rubles per land otter, three rubles per red fox, five rubles per lynx, and fifty kopeks per mink. Thus in forty-three years the prices paid for each item except lynx increased, and the value of the overall assemblage of furs more than tripled.[13]

The hunters' good fortune did not last long, however. All fur trading posts on the Pacific side of the peninsula had closed by 1902 due to shortage of furs.[14]

While the posts were in operation, managers recorded information about local social and economic activities in day books and log books. These volumes also list daily weather reports and catch statistics and occasionally give personal glimpses into residents' lives. For instance, in a log book entry in April 1887 the Douglas trader tells a tragic tale while showing how isolated from the Kodiak base the posts were:

> This day schooner *Kodiak* arrived and discharged and left for Kodiak. Also heard that the Schooner *Flying Scud* [*Scot*] had not arrived at Kodiak since leaving here November 14, 1886 with my wife and five children on board.[15]

The entries report deaths and sicknesses in the settlements. On May 5, 1888, for instance, the Douglas trader wrote, "People all sick here." They also provide a clue to intervillage relationships, as in this 1893 entry: "2 men arrivet [sic] from Inland Village for Douglas men partners."[16] The fact that Douglas men had hunting or trading partners who lived in distant villages—likely one of the Savonoski settlements—was a change from Russian days when each hunter's route and schedule had been determined by the company.

Finally, the log books list the home villages of the hunters and trappers who did business at the post, revealing the immense distances people traveled during the latter part of the nineteenth century in order to make a living. Twelve settlements, representing speakers of three languages and ranging over an area of nearly 20,000 square miles, appear in the 1890s Katmai and Douglas log books alone. Locations cited include Cold [Puale] Bay, Egegik, Kukak, "Pahliak" [Paugvik, at the mouth of Naknek River on its northern shore], "Aio" [Hallo] Bay, Afognak, Ikuk Island (this probably refers to the village of Ekuk, on the shore of Nushagak Bay), Savonoski, Ekwok (a village

Two young women of Chignik, 1909. Note the cotton clothing sewn in
Euro-American style.
Alaska State Library, Flamen Ball collection, PCA 24–106

on the Nushagak River), Kamishak Bay, Nushagak, and Iliamna. A
group of Aglurmiut also came to trade, but their home village is not
named.[17]

The goods available at the posts remained similar to those in
stock during Russian days: metal pots, traps, knives, and other uten-
sils; cloth goods; sugar, tea, tobacco, and flour; rifles and ammunition;
and personal items such as combs, beads, and mirrors. Although not
available at company stores, alcohol continued to be sold by boot-
leggers who sailed up and down the coasts of Alaska. Traders and
traveling priests reported that almost everyone knew how to make
homebrew from flour, sugar, and berries, which were readily available at company stores and the surrounding land.[18]

Because of the reliance on the fur trade and company store, the
typical nineteenth-century Alaska Peninsula or Kodiak Alutiiq
household contained many Russian and European goods. While on
the outside the dwelling resembled a precontact sod house, on the

Meshik children, 1910, in front of a sod barabara. Note the combination of skin and cloth clothing.
MSCUA, University of Washington Elkinton Collection, NA 3177

inside its style showed a unique blend of eras and cultures. The entry tunnel, locally called a "callidor," was the storage area for outer garments and barrels of berries, bear oil, and dried fish. Prominently displayed in a corner of the main room was a family icon and candle suspended on a filigree chain. Members of the household wore manufactured clothing for special occasions, but traditional fur and gut clothing for everyday work, particularly in the winter.

Spiridon Stepanoff, one-time Mitrofania and Chignik Bay resident, born on Kodiak Island in 1883, recalled that his father Ivan, a sea otter hunter in the employ of the Alaska Commercial Company, was especially fond of tea. The family samovar, a large brass urn for brewing the beverage, had a central place in the house. It offered not just refreshment but also served as a social locus around which the old men of the village told stories and passed on lore. Stepanoff recalled,

> That's the kind of sugar—we used to get sugar before like that, you know. Black. Comes in big chunks. Cooked one lump, you know, the smallest one about the size of a saucer....

We used to buy sugar in Kodiak like that before. Black like that. When you melt it out, they take it and melt it in hot water, it melts. Then they skim it off of the top, you know, it's like hair—sugar. Was from the tree [sugar cane]. Skim it out like long strings.

And then it had a thick layer, then they cook it up in a saucer full of tin. Next time, then they cut it up about an inch square. Maybe half inch square, cut it up like that and break it off, you know.

When they go down to drink tea, they have samovar, you know, tea boiling. And the charcoal inside.

And two old fellas would sit together, telling stories, and they break off one of those little chunks [of sugar], put it in their mouth, they fill it full of tea, they start to drink it, sweat! Took their shirts off, still telling stories. And drinking that tea! I used to watch 'em. All day....

My old man used to have one like that. That's how they used to drink plenty up here. They loved that samovar, you know. Sit down at table, and just lump of sugar in the mouth, [until] that kettle's empty.[19]

Another carryover from Russian days was a pervasive feeling of exploitation at the hands of the white traders. In Alutiiq oral tradition the trader may be either Russian or American; his power and stinginess rather than nationality are his crucial characteristics. Indeed, from the Alutiiq point of view there was little difference between the RAC and ACC employers. One particular trader, in this case an American but characterized as a "Russian king," is remembered in legend as the quintessential example of the type. Although his fellow countrymen considered the man fair, generous, and kind, Alutiiq oral tradition paints a different picture. His life story follows the trajectory of a traditional Alutiiq morality tale in which greediness is punished. This man, a Vermonter named Benjamin McIntyre, was the ACC's chief trader for the Kodiak region. He was shot in the head through an open window on November 1, 1886, allegedly by a Russian drifter. The murderer was never apprehended, but his body was found many years later by a man he had wounded in the assault.

Alutiiq baidarka at Chignik with a trader in the center hatch.
Anchorage Museum of History and Art B81.64.26

The story about the death of McIntyre, or "Macintine," as he is remembered on the peninsula, is still told as a lesson about stinginess, arrogance, meddling outsiders, the company system, and the ultimate victory of the Alutiiq spirit over Western capitalism. Spiridon Stepanoff recorded the tale in Chignik Lake in 1969. He had been a three-year-old toddler living in the small village of Eagle Harbor (the former site of an RAC post, called "Orlova" during the Russian period) on Kodiak Island when the murder occurred.

In introducing this story, Stepanoff explained that during the nineteenth century the village of Mitrofania on the Pacific coast of the peninsula had been the site of a major sea otter hunt. The interviewer commented, "Yeah, used to make a lot of money?" and Stepanoff had answered, "Yeah, not *people*! *People* for nothing! But they say company made a lot of money. They could get two thousand dollars for the skin, they pay sixty dollars." For him the Macintine story was an example of the inequities of the company system.

In the following transcription, "SS" refers to Stepanoff and "DK" to Don Kinsey, the Chignik Lake teacher who conducted the interview.

SS: Oh yeah, long time ago. The first, like, the Kodiak king, he get killed, you know. And it always used to be bishop come up all the time, you know. In Kodiak. All the villages, you know. And that, that superintendent of the AC Company, he don't like that priest come [unclear], and he stop the people gonna hunt. That's what he did. So they don't hunt when the priest's around, you know. So the priest went along. They had big schooner *Kodiak*, you know. They used to go to the Bristol Bay with that schooner, to, around Nushagak. And it was first when they started that Nushagak. And that priest went along up there. They had a Russian church up there. And they throw them overboard.

DK: They threw the priest over, huh?

SS: Yeah. Priest overboard. They [unclear] to the priest, they will come back with him. And there was two Indians from up there, Bristol Bay, you know, they pulling along out in the bay. And they see the sea gulls. Fine weather. All they see, are the sea gulls starting just flying, just sea gulls flying. They pull off with those, with them fellas' line, you know. Sea gulls. Just flying around up in, like long pole. Sea gulls all together like that, even at dark. And they get up there, there was a man floating. That bishop, you know. And they don't know much about the priests, them fellas, you know. And they haul it up [unclear] of some type. They they got somewheres down—and got hold of 'em in Kodiak. Some of them send a letter down there, they found him dead up in Bristol Bay.

Had to wait long, that fellow name been Macintine. Macintine was the superintendent's name, you now. Yeah. That priest never come back.

Same fall, there was a little boat, little economy boat, you know. Coming from outside. Sailing. One man. And he was Russian. They had black sails, come to Mitrofan. He wouldn't do nothing! He just stay around there, and that superintendent went down, that fella stayed in Kodiak. So they stayed around, well they always climb up that big high mountain, you know. Back there by the Kodiak town. See that mountain? Sharp [Pillar] mountain?

So they had a big cross up on top there. So they always walked up to there all the time. And he stayed around, all summer stay around.

So Macintine get tired of him. "What are you sticking around for?" Well, that fella didn't never say nothing. In the fall, when he was gonna ready to go down [to Seattle], loading the schooner up for fall, big boxes full of nothing but otter, sea otter skins. And they load 'em up the schooner. Just for to bring 'em down. He and his gang go down, they used to go down the wintertime, you know. They were—only summertime they used to come up. Stay all summer, Kodiak.

They killed a cow. This fella was right there alongside the work. And they ration out chunks, you know. So many pounds for that people, so many pounds for everybody in his gang, you know. So this fella he come up too. "Won't you give me a little piece for my supper?" Macintine says, "Ah! You! You're not my man. You're not working man. You don't do nothing! You don't get nothing from me! You get home!" "All right," that man, he said, "Thank you very much!"

He went aboard to his schooner. Everybody seen him, onto his schooner. In dark, in the fall of the year, you know. Windows open like this, you know.

They start to eat supper, the fresh meat.

So they get down to this fella. He put some [gun]powder and he's waiting in there. And he went to show. But [Macintine] was eating supper, and he watch him through the window, you know. But he shot. Buckshot. Back, shot him, bang, bang, two shots. One fella fall down. All three of them fall down. Stunned 'em. One fella get up. "Somebody playing here? Somebody playing here?" They light a lamp, he was found over there, his head all messed up, Macintine. He killed. This fella [who had also been shot], this fella, he was howling, "Who's playing around here?", and he got this big scar, buckshot. Just missed him. He would have killed two of 'em.

DK: This guy shot 'em then, huh?

SS: Uh huh. Reported it right away, that somebody shoot. Went down to his boat, to blame it right away. Sure enough, all full of powder....

And they went round, looking 'round, when the trail goes up to that big high mountain [Pillar Mountain]. They follow the trail up to the mountain. They know they used to go up there all the time. All night. When they got about halfway, he left his waist-coat right in the road, rolled 'em. They went up a little ways, he took his cap off, and left 'em in the road. They climbed up the mountain. Way up on top. Pitch dark night. Everybody went up on top. They couldn't see any—course, they didn't have no flash-light. They didn't see nothing. They had lanterns. Couldn't see nothing, they come back.

And there was [unclear] right on the post, "Anybody seen some-body walking strange places, and you get $10." They went down below [to the continental United States], them fellows. Took the Macintine along with them, along. Lots of people made the money for nothing. Once in a while they'd say, "There he is, up there! See the man up on the hill!" One of the bosses would go, go find him, they find nothing. Never find him, all over the Kodiak and they're climbing mountains, look for that man. Never find him. Never find him.

So [unclear], they see the ship come up to, to behind that Kodiak. Everybody seen him go up to that, to [unclear] Harbor up there. Next morning, he was gone....

DK: And they went out. They never did see him after that?

SS: Never did see him, no, after that. He left his boat in Kodiak west coast.

DK: I'll be darned. Well, then he had that all planned out, didn't he?

SS: Yeah, he had it all planned out, yeah.[20]

This story tells much about Alutiiq involvement in and attitudes about the fur trade in the nineteenth century. First, "Macintine" is called a "king," an indication that he, and by extension other trad-ers, was seen to have had absolute power over the Alutiiqs. Second, the priest who represented the Russian Orthodox church is seen to be at once the champion of the Alutiiq people and a thorn in the trader-king's side. His death is reported to have been suspicious. In fact Bishop Nestor did die in 1882 under circumstances similar to those narrated in this story, but there is no indication in the historical record that his death was related to company operations.[21] Nonetheless, the animosity of American traders, teachers, missionaries, and other settlers toward Russian Ortho- dox priests is well documented in the record (discussed below), a fact reflected in this ominous opening to the Macintine story.[22]

Benjamin McIntyre (1846–1886). *Photo courtesy of Mr. and Mrs. Hugh H. McIntyre, Waitsfield, Vermont, great nephew of Benjamin McIntyre*

The Macintine story also collapses Russian with American elements, the Russian era with the American era, evidence that for the Alutiiqs the relationships to traders, the economics of trading, and the company system were equivalent despite a change in nationality. Finally, the story shows that Macintine lacked one of the most basic Alutiiq attributes, gen- erosity, and this shortcoming warranted the harshest of punishments.

Twenty-three years after Stepanoff recorded the Macintine story in the presence of a small audience at the Chignik Lake school, Ignatius Kosbruk retold it at his Perryville kitchen table. The pass- ing of nearly a quarter century—a period when profound political, economic, and social changes had occurred on the Alaska Penin- sula—coupled with the personal interests of the storyteller, had changed the tale in three ways. First, Kosbruk accentuated the harsh treatment the Alutiiqs received at the hands of the "king," Macintine:

> He tortured Alutiiqs, the ones that went sea otter hunt- ing. He gave them for their sea otter catch only one pound of tea. He made them go out hunting, the Kodiak Alutiiqs, out to sea. He made fun of them. A little flour, a little sugar was all he gave them.

Second, Kosbruk noted that the murderer had sailed to Alaska from Seattle at the request of the Alutiiqs who had hired him as a shaman-hitman to kill the trader:

> Well, they made a plan from down there: Someone would kill him. Their minds were made up, all the Alaskan Alutiiqs. Then the one who would kill came from Seattle, from down there, the government from the Lower 48 sent him to Kodiak.

Third, Kosbruk portrays this man not as a lazy worker, as had Stepanoff, but rather an outsider with strong spiritual power:

> Then that assassin got to Kodiak. He walked among the people, and they didn't see him. He was invisible. He was some kind of man, I guess. People touched him, not knowing it.[23]

These changes in the narrative strengthen its moral message by painting the actors in the drama in sharply contrasting colors. The Alutiiqs are completely powerless and downtrodden. The Russian merchants are merciless and exploitive. The killer illustrates the victory of Alutiiq spiritual power over European love for money and temporal power.

Like all events, Macintine's death was remembered and depicted differently by different people. While Stepanoff's and Kosbruk's narratives represent similar versions of the remembered Alutiiq reaction to the events of 1886, contemporary printed accounts in newspapers and other publications written by and for a white American audience emphasize other messages. The first published chronicle appeared in an 1887 travelogue by Heywood W. Seton-Karr, who had been a member of the *New York Times* expedition to Alaska during the previous summer, and, coincidentally, McIntyre's dinner companion during the shooting. Witnesses Ivan Petroff, the deputy customs agent at Kodiak, and Wesley Ernest Roscoe, Kodiak's recently arrived Baptist missionary and school teacher, also left written reports of the incident.[24]

Seton-Karr's eyewitness account illustrates a mainstream American orientation, empathy with McIntyre and his family, and emphasizes the pointless tragedy of the murder. His narrative is reprinted here for comparison:

St. Paul, Kodiak Island, Alaska,
November 3d, 1886

The night before last I was the eye-witness to a shocking murder—none other than that of the general agent, whose corpse is on board. We start at noon for California, nearly two thousand miles distant.

We were seated at supper at six o'clock in the evening—McIntyre at the head of the table, and Woche, a storekeeper, at the foot. Ivan Petroff was by my side. The meal was nearly over, and McIntyre had half-turned to get up from his chair, when a terrible explosion suddenly occurred, filling the room with smoke and covering the table with fragments of plates and glasses.

McIntyre never moved, for he was killed stone-dead in a moment. Woche fell under the table, and then rushed out streaming with blood in torrents, for he was shot through the lower part of the head. The double glass window was smashed to atoms, for a cowardly fellow had fired through it, from just outside, with a spreading charge of slugs, presumably aiming at McIntyre, who received the main part of it in his back. Meantime the murderer who had thus shot into a group of unarmed and unsuspecting persons had time to escape.

I succeeded in stopping the bleeding from Woche's wounds, every one appearing paralysed!

The suspected man, Peter Anderson, a Cossack of the Don, cannot be found. He had, we found, attempted to fire his sloop, lying at anchor near the wharf; and had refused employment at cod-fishing, in order, as he said, to be present at the departure of the schooner. He had also been seen loitering with a gun behind the house. He owed money to McIntyre, who had twice fitted him out for sea-otter hunting, but both times he was unsuccessful.

We have been scouring the woods with rifles, but the natives are frightened to death. Not a light can be seen in any house after dark for fear of its being shot into by this madman, who is still at large if he has not

Erskine House, site of McIntyre's murder.
Kodiak Historical Society

> committed suicide. Nor can any of them be got to stir
> out at night, or to keep watch like sentries over the sloop,
> in case he should return, unless a white man is with
> them.[25]

The different versions of the McIntyre story demonstrate how
people in different positions and with different interests remember
and report the same incident in widely divergent ways. To Seton-
Karr this was the tale of an uncivilized madman who lived on the
edge of society and who killed the most civilized man there, Benjamin McIntyre. To Stepanoff it was a half-amusing story that shows
the incompetence of the Americans at apprehending a killer, particularly when their success depended on the cooperation of the
Alutiiqs, for whom they had done nothing to warrant positive feel-
ings. To Kosbruk it is, in part, a cautionary tale to other greedy
outsiders and an example of the Alutiiqs' triumph over powerful rich
men. While the facts of the incident remain fairly constant in all
accounts, the messages converge only in the recognition of great
social and economic inequality.

A dozen years after Macintine's death the era of all-powerful fur
industry was in its final throes. The inequities explored in the
Macintine story assumed a different mask.

END OF THE FUR TRADE

During the last decades of the nineteenth century, the sea otter hunt continued to dominate the seasonal round. In Katmai, for instance,

> there were two major hunts each year. The summer hunt (mid-May to late July) focused on Cold Bay (Puale Bay) to the south. Nearly every able-bodied man from Katmai participated, and they were sometimes joined by a few men from the Severnovskie settlements and from the Bristol Bay side of the peninsula. The winter hunt (February to April), which usually had fewer Katmai participants, focused on the Douglas area and Kamishak Bay.[26]

Trader Fomin's ACC Record Book entry for the 1885 summer hunt describes the arduous and often dangerous existence of the otter hunter:

> 18 July 1885: At 7:30 P.M. one baidarka of the Kodiak party arrived. The Aleut [Alutiiq] reports that yesterday morning they went out to sea to drive sea otters. There was fog. Suddenly after several hours a wind came up from the west like a hurricane and they were far from shore. The whole party was dispersed over the sea and was lost [to sight] except one baidarka in view was upset by the wind. This was Creole Roman Shangin with his son and one Aleut. They drowned. He [the narrator] did not have the means to save [them]. He was torn from the shores of Shelikof Strait and was two whole days at sea. He somehow was able to catch Cape Katmai. They were barely alive, emaciated, but he does not know whether the other baidarkas are alive or not. He says that still others were farther [out when the squall hit].
>
> 19 July: Today I am dispatching two baidarkas, one to the cape [at Cold/Puale Bay] and the other to Amalik. Toward evening one two-hatch Katmai party baidarka arrived. It was torn away, carried out to sea from the cape [at Cold/Puale Bay]. It got to Amalik Island at dawn and was at sea 38 hours without water and food. He reports

Aleut or Alutiiq kayakers, early 1900s.
Archives and Manuscripts, Alaska and Polar Regions Department, University of Alaska Fairbanks, Accession #74-175-510

he does not know whether the whole party is saved or not. He saw only one single-hatch baidarka upset at sea, there was no man, and from him four baidarkas were faster than him. He does not know whether they got to shore.

. . . .

22 July: Today the whole party came back to the settlement and the *zakashchik* [crew boss] says that they are ill. Some are spitting blood and others, old men, are not in a condition to be in the party any more. In two and one-half months they got 33 large sea otters in all. All is well. The whole party was saved except for one baidarka, Roman Shangin and his partners. They saved one baidarka, a single-hatch. They let the baidarka go, but they took the man into the hold and took him to shore.[27]

Late in the nineteenth century, the economy of the Alaska Peninsula began to change. American newcomers filtered through the area, some looking for adventure and a new life, others searching for gold, many hoping to escape the economic depression afflicting the rest of the United States. A few stayed in the region to compete with Native hunters for sea otters and furbearing land mammals. By

1890 many of the bays along the coast southwest of Katmai were occupied during the winter by white men hunting otters.[28]

The newly arrived Americans often clashed with long-time Alaskans. Stafeev recalled a visit several newcomers made to Douglas in 1890 during which they ridiculed the Russians still living in Alaska. Stafeev was insulted. He wrote that he felt one of the men "deserves bad luck for it." He also reported that two Americans had come to his store to buy provisions and find women, intending to settle in Kukak. He opined that the settlers were making a mistake, that their venture in Alaska "will soon be worthless."[29]

More upsetting to Alutiiq life than the influx of isolated newcomers, at least in the short run, was the decline of fur-bearing animals. With ever fewer skins to sell to consumers, the Alaska Commercial Company was unable to make a profit on the fur trade alone. Instead, the company turned toward the thousands of Americans trying to reach the gold fields of Nome and the Yukon. Company management decided to concentrate on providing transportation and supplies to gold seekers rather than on the dwindling fur trade. The ACC closed the two Alaska Peninsula posts still in operation, abandoning Douglas in 1901 and Katmai in 1902.[30]

For the Alutiiqs of the area, the collapse of the fur business was nearly catastrophic. In the report of his 1898 summer journey to Alaska Peninsula village chapels, Father Vasilli Martysh wrote,

> This [the ACC] company...in many places removed their stores, and in other places, where stores still exist, stopped distributing to Natives not just goods, but even food on credit or on account against future animal catches. Moreover, for furs on hand, which Natives bring to the store for sale, they are paid, not in money but by company checks, which can be cashed only at the company agents'.... It's not an infrequent occurrence, where even for furs in hand such checks are not issued, but simply the catch added to a half-century-old debt.[31]

During the winter of 1897–1898, most of the villages in the region had suffered starvation. The priest's report continues,

Last summer, the inhabitants of Douglas went to sea on
a hunt and brought in 11 otters, for which, taking them
to the store, they didn't receive a cent and not a pound
of provisions for the winter. They had not been able to
put up fish or berries and other supplies, having been on
the hunt the whole summer long. They supposed that
the store wouldn't deny them provisions. Their hunt's
value, 11 otters, by the most cheap but scrupulous reckoning, stretched to $8000.00. However, their hopes
weren't borne out. In the fall, the manager of the store
at Douglas received from the main office of the Alaska
Commercial Company orders not to give anything from
the store without money from the Aleuts. The manager,
William Rode, an honest German, fulfilled the manage-
rial orders to the letter. Starvation began. Each day the
inhabitants of Douglas went out to the beach and waited
for the tide to go down, so they could have the possibil-
ity of catching shellfish and feeding themselves. Sickness
and death ripped into them. What would have happened
to the poor Douglas people, if it hadn't been for Kodiak
creoles, who came by for the hunt...who, having with
them a fairly good supply of provisions, risking their own
hunger, shared with the dying Aleuts.... The store managers themselves, strictly fulfilling the order of the main
office, seeing the people suffering hunger, were unable
not to offer such help as they could.[32]

Father Vasilii wrote his last published travel reports for Douglas
and Katmai in 1902 and 1904, respectively, describing life at the end
of the fur-trading era:

[In 1901] the settlement of Douglas is composed of 10
barabaras, arranged on the flats, elevated above the sea
shore. All the inhabitants number about 45 people. In
former times, this settlement was famous for the sea otter catch, and the Alaskan [Commercial] Company up to
the present year maintained a store here and only two
weeks before my visit closed it.[33]

This year [1902] no one has died [at Douglas] and
even two sick syphilitics have recovered, probably because, owing to the absence of the store, there was no

convenient way to drink too much. Concerning this, what effect on the Aleuts the closing of the store had, it's difficult to say anything definite. It seems that it brought more good consequences than bad ones. First, drunkenness is undoubtedly less, since obtaining flour and sugar for beer became so difficult. Secondly, the Aleuts returned to their original foods, which are the only ones appropriate to Alaska.[34]

> In both religious and moral attitude, the Katmai inhabitants stand much higher than the other Alaskan Aleuts. Drunkenness and lechery do not rage as strongly here as in other settlements. The Katmai people are also more hardworking, and therefore they live better than the other Aleuts. Almost every Katmai inhabitant has provisions the whole year round. In general, the Katmai Aleuts are far different from their neighbors, blessed with the good influence of...[ACC manager] Aleksandr Ivanovich Petelin. Continuously for nine years, he, without compensation, held the position of psalm reader for the chapel and labored for the spiritual and corporeal benefit of the inhabitants. It's a real shame that this year he leaves Katmai, since the company is closing the store there.[35]

The former ACC posts remained vacant, and in 1907 an agreement was made to sell them to a company owned by Omar J. Humphrey and W. J. Erskine of Kodiak. The Katmai buildings were valued at $150, those at Douglas $25, and all other ACC holdings on the Alaska Peninsula's Pacific coast amounted to a total worth of only $25.

With this sale an era had ended.[36]

SUBSISTENCE

Even before the demise of the fur trade, Alaska Peninsula Alutiiqs had obtained most of their food by hunting and fishing during the American as during the Russian era. Katmai was located on a broad river delta inland from the coast, so mammal hunting focused on caribou and moose rather than the sea mammals more common in other peninsula settlements. Salmon constituted the most important food resource, while waterfowl was also plentiful. Now deceased, Father Harry Kaiakokonok of Katmai, later of Perryville, was five years old at the time of the 1912 eruption that caused the village's destruction. In 1972 he recalled an area that had been rich in natural resources:

> And this creek was so clean, crystal clear water—oh, summertime, and thousands and thousands salmon go into that river. Every kind of a species of salmon; dogs, humpies, silvers, reds, mix up. Then springtime they say...our rivers used to be plugged with those [candlefish].... Springtime, front of that village, the flat used to be all black with geese, many kind of ducks, swans.... There was moose all the time, and caribou.[37]

Sea lions and seals were (and are) commonly hunted throughout the peninsula. Archaeological sites contain few whale bones, but residents reported harvesting beached whales. Spiridon Stepanoff of Chignik Bay spent his early years not on the Alaska Peninsula but on Kodiak Island, where he observed a turn-of-the-century whale hunt in Ugak Bay outside Eagle Harbor. Alaska Peninsula Alutiiqs who lived at locations on the Pacific coast other than Katmai also likely hunted whales as Stepanoff described in this 1969 interview.

In the transcript that follows, "SS" refers to Spiridon Stepanoff; "DK" to Don Kinsey, the teacher who conducted the interview, and "BL" to Chignik Lake resident Bill Lind, who was also present at the interview:

> SS: [Eagle Harbor was] just a small village. Not like this here. Smaller than this place now. They didn't have no electric lights or nothing. No lamps, just candles, that's all for lights. Very few of them had the gas—the standing lamps, you know, coal oil lamp....
>
> Lots of them brought in the seal oil for the lamp. The whale oil....
>
> Catch the whale with their baidarkis, you know. They had a harpoon, rock harpoon, oh about that long. They go alongside the whale, you know. Not the old ones. When the whales come in

there was a young one behind, you know. And they're after the young one. Course when they come up, go right along side of them, and you put the harpoon NOW! The harpoon broke off of the pick [the harpoon shaft], you know. Then the rock [harpoon head] was in there and when the whale started moving, he'd crush it up.

Black slate, they look like, you know.

And he stay with his mother for a long time, you know. When he start to get sick, then they wouldn't dive no more. Still following, trying to follow his mother. Then he lay down. Then mother watch him for a long time. Sometimes mothers dove down, whole day, never come up. And when they didn't expect [her], [she'd] come up again. Alongside [her] young one. It was pretty dangerous. Lots of fellows get drowned. Going like this, you know. [She'd] come up, flopping, [she'd] churn 'em all up, you know.

DK: Flap their baidarka?

SS: Yeah. Turn 'em over.

When they killed him, he floated up, till his mother goes away, and they call all the rest of the baidarkis. But there would be a hundred baidarkis, you know. Go out there. Tow that big whale inside. All the food for the winter for the whole village.

And they got the rope tied up, they stand up like this, close together, you know, and stood to one side like this, you know, right down. They started peeling blubber from the top. I guess that's how they get pieces like that....

BL: What you do with the inside of the whale? The guts? You used them too?

SS: They used them too, yeah. Whale guts, they make a kamleiky [gutskin parka] out of 'em....

I seen one time at the village where I was born, you know, at the village everybody was going to church in the morning. There's two whales, a whale coming in [with] a young one, you know. Three brothers, whale hunters, you know, they all got in the three-hatch baidarki. Went after those whales. And they harpooned the young one right away, go right to the front of the village in the bay, in Eagle Harbor. And the mother swing around, you know. Mother hit them with the tail. Dumped them overboard. Some kids come in and they start hollering, you know, "They turned over!"

Seen 'em out there in the harbor, three men. So far away, you know, that the fellas was [lost]. But then they get out there, tired out, sunk, right there, three of them....

Get too late. The whale went away. Left the young one....

And then the young one, he was diving around there, once in a while he'd come up, diving around. Pretty soon he don't dive no more. He died right in the bay. And that mother went right away.

And when they skinned the whale, left-hand side, was a man's hand mark in his side.... Red. Red marks from a hand....

Hand print. They drag him ashore and then they eat him, some of 'em eat him. But they get the left-hand side, they never find that rock [harpoon point].... Right hand side, right side fat was all right. But the left-hand side, the people eating it died right away.

That hand print. Left side. That was real funny 'cause one side of the whale was poisoned. Right side fine....

Lots of people died there. And they find it out, and throw the whole thing away. If they keep on hold of that meat, you know, whale blubber, they would have killed the whole village.[38]

This Eagle Harbor whale hunt was conducted by people whose livelihoods had been dependent for generations on European and American economic networks, first in the fur trade through a nearby RAC *odinochka*, and later in the salmon fishery through a saltery on the north shore of Ugak Bay. Despite decades of association with the cash economy and Western trade goods, Eagle Harbor Alutiiqs were expert whale hunters who followed ancient practices. Stepanoff did not explicate the meaning of the hand print on the whale's left side, except to remark that the print appeared at the site where a poisoned harpoon had pierced the animal's skin. Those who avoided meat on that side of the animal survived, while those who ignored it died. Stepanoff's unspoken message may have been that the presence of poison marked the work of members of a dangerous secret society who were heavily involved in esoteric and spiritually powerful practices. Corroboration of the significance of ancient knowledge as late as the 1930s was provided by Chignik Lake elder Doris Lind, who explained that she was to have been betrothed to such a whale hunter from Kodiak Island. Her grandmother had called her into the living room in the Peninsula village of Kanatak and said, "That man wants you to be his wife." "What do I want a husband for? What would I do?" young Doris had asked, and walked out of the house. That was the end of the discussion at the time, but years later Mrs. Lind learned that the man had been a shaman who conducted the whale ceremony, and had threatened and harmed a number of people with his powers.[39]

Ugashik fish cleaning, 1900, part of a subsistence catch.
National Archives, Record Group 22-FFA-2552

As these anecdotes and others described in the following chapter indicate, peninsula Alutiiqs continued to depend on hunting, fishing, and gathering for much of their food throughout the nineteenth century and early in the twentieth, especially once the ACC posts closed for good. Along with the technological knowledge and skills required to obtain food and clothing, the people maintained

Andersonville (Chignik Bay) barabaras, 1909, before Alutiiqs were involved in commercal fisheries on a large scale.
Alaska State Library, Flamen Ball Collection, PCA 24–106

many elements of the precontact spiritual relationship with the animals who provided sustenance. Though they were practicing Russian Orthodox Christians, they saw no contradiction in continuing to perform rituals that showed appreciation and respect for the animals on which they depended.

COMMERCIAL FISHING AND OTHER ECONOMIC OPPORTUNITIES ON THE ALASKA PENINSULA

Just as the economic situation looked bleakest, a new industry came to the peninsula. The first salmon cannery was built at Chignik in 1888. It was followed the next year by three additional nearby canneries, one in Anchorage Bay and two in Chignik Lagoon. Others later sprang up in various bays along the coast. The Ugashik River on the Bristol Bay side saw fish processors in the late 1880s as well, and they arrived at Naknek River with the establishment of salteries in 1890. Additional salteries and canneries were built on the peninsula throughout the next decade.[40]

Commercial fishing at first affected resident Alutiiqs only indirectly, through the hundreds of newcomers it brought seasonally to the peninsula. Even this effect was mitigated during the nineteenth century, particularly on the Pacific coast, since most Alutiiqs lived not in the cannery town of Chignik but far to the northeast in Katmai, Douglas, or other small villages. Even had they lived in Chignik, they would not have been hired to work or fish for the canneries. Management imported fishermen and laborers from foreign countries and the United States. In 1890 the Chignik cannery employed 60 white men and 120 Chinese laborers, but no Natives.[41] By 1900, only six percent of the fishermen and cannery workers from the two canneries on the Naknek River were Natives. The vast majority, 271 men, were Chinese.[42]

Like many late nineteenth-century American businesses, the Chignik area canneries treated people of various races and ethnicities differently. For instance, Scandinavian fishermen (called the "white crew") were preferred, and were paid the most. Italian and Greek fishermen (called "Dagos") were paid less for the same work.

Chignik cannery, 1900s.
Anchorage Museum of History and Art B82.389

Chinese, Japanese, and Filipino cannery workers, brought north from San Francisco or Seattle for the summer and then shipped back in the fall, were paid the least.[43]

Spiridon Stepanoff, who witnessed the early days of commercial fishing in the Chignik area, remembered the schooners that brought workers and supplies to the canneries from San Francisco.

> It could be smoking. Put the reefs on the sails, the schooner go. Smoking wind. As long as they don't tear up the sails. They reef 'em now, you know, make 'em smaller, sails, so they're slow now....
>
> There was no pilot houses in them. There was one man in the stern, with a rope around his waist, made fast to [the wheel]. He's under water, his feet are on top! He went around twice. He went clean over! Those people crazy. Some of them young fellas, if they take the gas engines away, put 'em in a sailing schooner, they'd say they're crazy!...
>
> And [when] the weather's blowing, the sailors, they go up, way up top of the mast. And they lower the sails down. Tie 'em up, you know, to the boom. They're walking around way up there,

ship is rolling, blowing, just like flies. Only they have good rope where they're standing, on top of that wire. Holding on to make the sails fast. Way up on top there. Gee!

I went halfway one of those ship masts. I looked down. Jeez! Ship was rolling, I could hardly get down! Never been up since!

...[They would stay on them] all summer, you know. But you couldn't sleep on them. We could hardly sleep. And the riggings, you know, just whistling. The ropes, so many ropes, you know, when the wind blowing northwest. Just whistling out there....

1911, one ship come up from Down Below. Tacking up. Northwest [wind] blowin' up. And they started dragging anchors. Gets outside the Northwestern cannery, and they landed [stern] first. High water, landed stern first to anchor, falling like that, you know. When the tide fall he broke in two.[44]

Stepanoff also remembered the ill treatment the Chinese workers regularly received as part of cannery company policy. He explained,

SS: Long tail [braided queue], they go dragging down to their feet. Later on, now, they cut 'em all off.... [Treated] like the dogs! And the Chinamen, they don't care about them, because they couldn't speak English, you know. They couldn't understand nothing. They take 'em, grab 'em by the tail and drag 'em around, to go to work. Yeah, that's the bad thing, I never see. Poor Chinamens—they be at the bunkhouse, or they be inside, they could see daylight all over.

DK: Cold, too, I suppose, you know.

SS: The poor Chinamens, they make themselves a little room, sometimes six of 'em together. Little—like a cupboard, they put their bedding in the bottom. And rice sacks, you know. They used lots of rice, that guy, you know. And they sleep there. Lie there upon the rice. Trying to keep together, warm. I used to walk that way, a bunch of 'em up there, when I stay with my brother-in-law summertime. And they'd lay down, you know, all six of 'em in one bed.[45]

Alaska was a huge territory with few government officials to po-
lice its businesses. In this atmosphere of laissez-faire government
and economy, cannery owners could run their companies largely as
they wanted without concern about government intervention. As a
result, the canneries, like the fur trading companies before them,
operated entirely for profit, paying little attention to the well-being
of their employees or the natural resources on which they depended.
For this reason, in 1899 Capt. Charles P. Elliott of the United States
Army was sent to investigate the fishing industry in Bristol Bay and
the Chignik areas. His report pointedly criticized the industry. He
described the huge fish traps that were set at the entrances of bays
and rivers, catching nearly all the salmon before they could spawn.
He predicted that in a short time the areas would be completely
fished out. Elliott wrote,

> The special fish commissioner, during the summer of
> 1899, ordered that certain traps, placed clearly in viola-
> tion of law, should not be used. The boat of the special
> fish commissioner was hardly out of sight before a load
> of fish from these same traps was brought to the canner-
> ies and packed.[46]

Fish traps continued to be used in the Chignik area for more than a half
a century after Elliott's report. They were finally outlawed in 1959.

Chignik Bay resident Walter Stepanoff, Sr. (nephew of Spiridon
Stepanoff) remembers the days of fish traps. He recalled that before World War II there were traps inside Chignik Lagoon at Hume
Point and opposite Chignik Island, nearly blocking the salmon run
up Chignik River. There was another just outside Chignik Lagoon
spit, and one at a site called "Waterfall" at the entrance to Anchorage Bay. Hook Bay had a trap, and Aniakchak Bay had two. During a
1990 interview Stepanoff explained how the fish traps worked:

> They'd bring a scow alongside with a big square brailer pipe, that
> heavy pipe on the top and the bottom and they'd lower that thing
> under the fish and the big bag in there, and then they'd pull the
> wires, start pulling, and the fish...come get lifted up and it would
> fall right into the [scow]....

Fish trap with a small skiff alonside.
Anchorage Museum of History and Art, WWS 2006-13

They used to have a big pile rack over there where my brother's at, they put different ones in different places. They had piles where they pull 'em up after the season, roll 'em out and have big stacks of logs, there piled up. They were anywhere from 60 to 70 foot....

They'd take pile drivers like in the spring and drive the piling and then the web crew would go out to the scows and put the webbing on the leads and then in the pot and spiller, and then their traps were ready. On the tunnel where the fish go in they'd close it until the season opened and they'd send somebody out to open it and then they start fishing....

The last time I worked on them traps was just before I got in the service in '44. '43, I guess. They might have been a year or two after that, after we got in the service, but that was about it and then they did away with them. The seiners took over then. Big seiners.[47]

Mike Sam of Chignik Lagoon and Anchorage also remembered the fish traps in the lagoon. He explained to interviewer Lisa Scarbrough of the Alaska Department of Fish and Game:

LS: So you worked with the fish traps themselves?

MS: No, I never worked it, they had their own trap gang, you know, from around here, some of them, and some of them from Outside [of Alaska]. Most of them from Outside, you know. A trap gang was eight men to each trap. Ten with the deck hand and tug boat and scow. They load them scows.... [They'd] just drive the pilings so far down and put a wire web....

The one place they used to call the "horse bar," it was the heart of the trap. And from there [the fish] go different ways and...there's no way they can get out.

LS: And then how would they get 'em out of the pot?

Mike Sam of Chignik Lagoon and Anchorage.
Lisa Scarbrough

MS: Scow tied up, scow had a big winch and a boom, lower to the web, tie the scow.... No time at all they fill the scow. Maybe two, three thousand at a time, you know....

They outlawed [fish traps], you know. They outlawed 'em [be-cause they were] killing not only fish, and all kinds of bottom fish, codfish and halibut, and flounders, sculpin, all get in there.... And halibut and codfish, overboard, you know, all dead.[48]

Other opportunities besides commercial fishing had drawn new-comers to the peninsula by the end of the nineteenth century. American shopkeepers opened stores in villages or set up camps in abandoned sites to serve newly arrived miners of gold, quartz, and coal. Despite Stafeev's complaints about the immigrants, some of the fishermen, entrepreneurs and adventurers settled down on the peninsula. They married local Alutiiq women and built homes in cannery towns, founding the families that today make up most of the populations of Chignik Bay and Chignik Lagoon. In 1898, the *American Orthodox Messenger* described the influx of newcomers in this way:

> From this time [1867] the dying out of Russians and the influx of all sorts of nationalities, chiefly Swedes and Finns, began.
> Displaced from their places of birth, cheated in the states, unemployed, hungry, thirsty, these knights of woe-ful countenance found, and up to now find, a warm and hospitable corner in cold Alaska; having set aside all sorts of dreams about family life, they unexpectedly find a warm family hearth, by marrying local creoles or Aleuts— and start with their progeny a new generation of Orthodox creoles while they themselves remain hetero-dox: Lutheran, Episcopal, Catholic, and other erring Christians. However, they are for the most part indifferent in the matters of belief and therefore don't have their own temples.[49]

The new "Scandinavian-Aleut" families, as they came to be called, settled into a life on the peninsula that was a mixture of Alutiiq, Russian, and American practices. The children were baptized into the Russian Orthodox church and worked and played with their Alutiiq cousins, but many spoke English at home. Their fathers learned winter hunting practices and other customs from their Alutiiq relatives, but their main occupation was summer fishing and tending fish traps, and, later in the twentieth century, fox farming or trapping.[50]

Anthropologists Craig Mishler and Rachel Mason explain that these families constituted

> a new social and economic class…[that] may have arisen at least in part due to the lack of obligation to share subsistence resources, labor, and cash income with the father's side of the family, which was far off somewhere in Europe. All else being equal, less sharing allowed a few families to accumulate capital and wealth.
>
> Another aspect of the "Scandinavian effect" is the Protestant work ethic embraced by the Norwegians, Swedes, Danes, and Finns who settled in Alaska. These immigrants eschewed conspicuous consumption and lavish displays of wealth.[51]

Although first-generation Scandinavian-Aleuts had local kin only on the mother's side, succeeding generations made up for this scarcity. Families tended to be large, resulting in a proliferation of cousins, aunts, and uncles with similar responsibilities for reciprocal sharing and involvement to those of local creoles and Alutiiqs.

CREOLES IN THE AMERICAN PERIOD

During the American period the term "creole" disappeared, replaced by the pejorative "half-breed" or "mixed-blood," or the more neutral "Russian." The word's demise was due partly to differences between the Russian and American social systems, partly to American boosterism that saw non-Americans as un-American, and partly to the sheer numbers of white immigrants who flooded the territory thirty years after the sale.

The creoles had belonged to a relatively privileged legal estate in Russian America in recognition of their value to the company as a potentially stable workforce with no desire to be sent back to Russia. Furthermore, many had received formal education unavailable to their indigenous cousins. All nineteenth-century Russians had been members of a hereditary rank under a fourteen-level system established by Peter the Great in the previous century. Each status was afforded distinct economic, educational, social, and professional rights and responsibilities. The United States recognized no similar hereditary ranks or statuses, and its social system did not accommodate noncitizens such as Native Americans, African-Americans, or recent immigrants. Thus, with the sale of Alaska the status of creoles plummeted from favored children to invisible savages.

In contrast to the view taken by American immigrants to the territory, on the Alaska Peninsula people favored honorable titles for the former creoles. The terms "Russians" and "Russian Aleuts" communicated culture, intelligence, and nonforeignness unattainable by newcomer Americans. Ironically, after 1867 those who had previously been considered outsiders—the Russian immigrants—were now afforded the highest status within the society. The newly labeled "Russians" had been baptized into the Russian Orthodox church, spoke both Russian and Alutiiq (many of them later learned to speak English as well), had Alutiiq relatives, and had lived all their lives in the region hunting, trapping, fishing, and gathering. They differed from their Alutiiq cousins not genetically, for nearly all Alutiiqs had Russian ancestors, but culturally, in their educational levels and the roles they assumed as go-betweens or cultural brokers between Alutiiqs and Americans.

From 1880 until the 1930s one group of these newly termed "Russians" lived in the village of Mitrofania, on the Pacific coast between Chignik and Perryville. Spiridon Stepanoff's father, Ivan, moved his family there from the tiny village of Eagle Harbor on Kodiak Island in about 1895 when his son was twelve years old. Ivan Stepanoff was church *starosta* or elder at Mitrofania for many years. Other well-known and respected "Russians" such as Nikolai and Innokenty Kalmakoff lived in Katmai, Douglas, and other Pacific coast villages.

ALASKA PENINSULA VILLAGES
IN THE NINETEENTH CENTURY

A number of descriptions of nineteenth-century Katmai were recorded by visiting adventurers and government agents (refer to map, p. 20). In the 1880 U.S. census report, customs agent Ivan Petroff of Kodiak wrote,

> The Katmai people have timber at their command, such as poplar and birch, which grows in fair abundance along the Katmai River, reaching up a little way on the hill sides. They have an abundance of fish, plenty of water fowl, and in the mountains, which rise abruptly around them, bear, deer, land otter, among the animals, and the ptarmigan (*S. albus*) and ruffled grouse (*Bonasa sabinii*) are found. At this point excellent cranberries are gathered abundantly by the people.[52]

> The settlement of Katmai, in this vicinity, was once the central point of transit for travel and traffic across the peninsula.... Now Katmai's commercial glory has departed and its population, consisting of less than 200 creoles and Innuits [Alutiiqs], depend upon the sea otter alone for existence.[53]

In January or February 1889 a British nobleman, Hugh Cecil Lowther, fifth Earl of Lonsdale, traveled across Canada and through Alaska. He stayed in Katmai for several weeks waiting for passage to Kodiak. Unfortunately, his diary, which would undoubtedly provide a fascinating picture of life in Katmai, has never been published.

An American named Frank Lowell, who later ran a trading post in Chiginagak or Wrangel Bay, took the Katmai census in 1890. His report appeared in the Eleventh Census report as follows:

> The village, consisting of sod huts surrounding the "store" and a small log chapel, was built upon a swampy flat along the banks of a salmon stream, and owing to the scarcity of dry ground about them their dead have been buried indiscriminately among the dwellings until the whole settlement presents the appearance of a graveyard. The

summer visitor is impressed with an idea of what winter must mean in this desolate spot when he notices the heavy chains and ropes which are laid over the roof of the trading store and securely anchored in the ground as protection against the furious gales that sweep down the steep mountain sides but a few miles beyond.

The river, small as it is, furnishes the Katmai people an abundance of salmon, the valleys and swamps abound in berries, oil is obtained from seals and occasionally from a stranded whale, and the more enterprising hunters kill cariboo [sic] in the mountains, while their traps yield them skins of foxes and land otters.[54]

The following year, E. H. Wells, working for the popular magazine *Frank Leslie's Illustrated Weekly Newsletter,* described his trip through the territory of Alaska. The journey ended with a portage eastward across the Alaska Peninsula and a wild sled ride down the mountains into Katmai. Wells stayed in the village for two months waiting for a return ship to Kodiak and Seattle. He reported that a trader by the name of Smith was cordial to him, and that "the village was of good size, containing some 200 souls, mostly Aleuts, who eked out a living by fishing and hunting the sea otter."[55]

When in 1896 gold was found on the Klondike in Canada, thousands of Americans rushed to cash in on what they thought would be instant wealth. Some of them traveled north by a route that took them through the Katmai portage. More important to the Alaska Peninsula's ultimate destiny, the gold finds awoke United States government interest in Alaska. In 1898 government geologist Josiah Edwin Spurr traveled up the Naknek River, over the Katmai portage, and into the village, describing the geology and terrain along the way. From the creole trader Aleksandr Ivanovich Petelin, he learned,

the natives have a tradition of the time when the whole flat where the village [Katmai] stands was bay, and there were villages on both sides of the bay which no longer exist. He does not believe their tradition goes back more than 200 years.[56]

In Spurr's official government report, he described what he perceived to be the physical characteristics of the Katmai people. He wrote,

> The Katmai people, [unlike the Naknek and Savonoski Natives], on the other hand, show differences in their stature and physiognomy which indicate an important admixture of other blood, probably Aleutian. The typical Eskimo, as seen from Nushagak to the the Yukon, has very scanty beard, while some of these Katmai natives have profuse bushy growths. They are also a stronger and in every way finer race than most of the natives we had lately seen.... The natives of Savonoski, on the other hand, are a sickly and undersized race.[57]

Spurr's remarks illustrate a common problem in Alaska's change from Russian America to an American territory: most newly arrived Americans knew nothing of the Russian history of the place. Spurr wrongly assumed the Katmai people had intermarried with "Aleutians" (by which he meant Unangan), when in fact the physical characteristics he observed were those of a largely creole population who had lived in contact with Russians and other creoles for a hundred years. His preference for the more European-looking Katmai residents over Eskimos was a common prejudice among Americans at the time.

In 1901 the American author Rex Beach visited Alaska, stopping at Katmai on his way home. He later published an account of the voyage in the book *Personal Exposures* (1940). Beach described Spurr's acquaintance, the trader Petelin, as

> a globular, cross-eyed little half-breed Russian. His name was Petellin and he read our letter of introduction by rubbing his nose back and forth across each line. Petellin's English had almost rusted out from disuse.[58]

In later years Petelin was remembered far differently, with respect rather than disdain. He had been sent to Katmai as manager of the ACC post in 1893, and stayed until the store was closed by the company in 1902. During those nine years, he acted as psalmist for

Chignik man in front of barabara, 1909. Note the traditional sod barabara with a wooden door, western clothing, and sealskin *nalugatut*, or boots. Note also the "bushy beard" as Spurr descirbed in his 1898 report.
Alaska State Library, Flamen Ball Collection, PCA 24–102

the church, served as Russian-Alutiiq interpreter for the visiting priests, kept the church in good physical and economic order, and in 1901 supervised the building of a chapel from shipwrecked lumber. After returning to his home on Kodiak from Katmai, Petelin studied for the priesthood and was ordained in 1905. He was stationed at the Afognak church, where he also had responsibility for the chapels on the Pacific coast of the Alaska Peninsula. In fact, Father Aleksandr had just left Katmai after his yearly visit at the time of the 1912 Katmai eruption.[59]

Barbara Shangin Sanook, who was born in Katmai and spent her adulthood in Perryville and Chignik Lake, remembered that the village was so far inland that the only time people saw the ocean was during extremely high tides. Large sailing ships would travel up the river with goods toward the village, with its the sod-covered barabaras, church, and a few wooden frame houses built with lumber salvaged from shipwrecks. Cargo was usually unloaded onto the spit and carried overland to the store.

Beached *Pilgrim* off Katmai, 1898.
Museum of History and Industry, Seattle, Moran Brothers Collection

Katmai people with Reverend Alexander Petelin (with beard, center of photo on the right), 1912.
   Kodiak Historical Society

The center of village activity after the closing of the ACC store
was its *qasgiq*, or "community house." This was the site of games,
dances, and ceremonies. Like other barabaras of the time, it boasted
a roof-window or smokehole in its ceiling large enough for a person
to fit through. During a recorded interview in 1993, elder Doris Lind
of Chignik Lake described to her niece, Virginia Aleck, Mrs. Sanook's
memories about the *qasgiq*. Mrs. Sanook is called "old gramma" to
differentiate her from Mrs. Aleck's other grandmother, who was Mrs.
Lind's mother-in-law.

> They used to have big dancing place there. Like a barabary, big,
> huge thing. Then they have window, I mean a hole in the top.
> Your old gramma used to tell me she didn't have no shoes. They
> go up and they'd be dancing away, the *yuwaqing* [Native dancing],
> you know, having fun, then they'd look down from that hole up
> there. Once in a while she tells me, "I've got no shoes on, no
> stockings, barefooted!"

> They were looking down there, *yuwaq* dancing, watching those
> dancings. Said they used to have fun watching them from up
> there.[60]

Northeast of Katmai, trader Vladimir Stafeev recorded in his
diary daily life in the village of Douglas between 1889 and 1895. Stafeev
wrote of the accidents, disappointments, marriages, and general go-
ings-on of the settlement. He comes across as a cranky man who
repeatedly complains about small inconveniences, aches and pains.
His unhappiness was no doubt caused in part by the fact that he had
left his family in Kodiak while he lived alone in Douglas. But beyond
his own lonely life, he described tragic social conditions in the Douglas settlement itself. For instance, he reported frequent drunkenness.
In 1890 he stated, "just as the Americans consider the dollar their
God, so on Douglas it is Vodka that is both God and chapel." Fur
catches were declining drastically. In April 1893 he wrote, "Nowhere
are there any catches; at Aleksandrovsk, Seldovia, Kaguiak and
Aiakhtalik not a single otter [was taken]. On Afognak, Lesnoi,
Nuchek and Kad'iak the catches are extremely small." He felt that
the American fishermen new to the Pacific coast of the peninsula

Starring is still part of life in Chignik Lake (1992). Doris Lind is on the far right.
   Patricia Partnow

had an evil influence on the Alutiiqs. He reported that one had fatally beaten his wife.

Stafeev also noted some bright spots in Douglas life. He reported that people were largely self-sufficient in obtaining food, putting up winter supplies of fish each year. They went to church regularly and each year "starred" during Russian Christmas in their own and neighboring villages. At least one person from each household could read and write. Stafeev praised the local "dugouts" (barabaras) as being warmer than the wood-frame houses supplied by the ACC. He obviously liked some aspects of living in Douglas, for once while on a vacation visiting his family in Kodiak he wrote in his diary, "I, the hermit, became bored immediately and wished myself back in Douglas."[61]

Published descriptions of the Savonoski villages during this period are limited to brief paragraphs in the census reports. In 1890, the village of Ikak was described as follows:

> The only inland settlement of the Aglemiut [*sic*] is the
> village of Igiak, on Lake Walker or Naknek, and here,
> within reach of the spruce timber which partially covers
> the northern slope of the Alaska range of mountains, we
> find them in dwellings much more comfortable and ris-
> ing higher from the ground, with wooden floor and
> platforms for sleeping. In this village a dwelling is rarely
> occupied by more than one family.[62]

The author's designation of Ikak as Aglurmiut rather than Sugpiaq continues Petroff's mistake of the previous decade and ignores both Russian records and linguistic and familial evidence. Local house types, described as "more comfortable" than the semisubterranean dwellings of the rest of the Nushagak district, were probably a re-flection of both abundance of timber and longstanding contact with Russian and American traders.

A number of new villages appeared along the Pacific coast of the peninsula during the American period. Table 1, based on U.S. census information, lists the Alaska Peninsula settlements with sizable Alutiiq populations, along with their respective populations over a period of thirty years. The Pacific coast villages are arranged geo-graphically from northeast (Ashivak near Cape Douglas) to southwest (Mitrofania), followed by Bristol Bay and interior villages. In several cases the names of settlements changed from one census to the next, either because American government officials preferred English over Native or Russian names, or were ignorant of the old names. As the shifts in population show, this was a time of great movement and change.

The seven settlements with sizable Alutiiq populations on the peninsula's Pacific coast included Ashivak (near Cape Douglas), Kukak, Katmai, Kuyukak, Sutkhoon (Sutkhum), Kaluiak (near the present town of Chignik Bay), and Mitrofania. On the Bering Sea side three villages, whose populations were said to be made up of either "Aleuts," "Eskimo-Aleuts," or "Eskimo-Aglegmiuts," included Mashikh (the present-day Meshik at Port Heiden), Oogashik (Ugashik), and Oonaugashuk (Unangashik, just south of Port Heiden). Finally, the census reports listed the population of the inland village

Population Figures (based on the U.S. Census) for Selected Alaska Peninsula Settlements: 1880 to 1910

1880	Pop.	1890	Pop	1900	Pop.	1910	Pop.
Ashivak	46	Cape Douglas	85	Douglas	72	Douglas	45
Kukak	37						
Katmai	218	Katmai	132	Katmai	81	Katmai	62
						Cold Bay [Puale]	11
		Kanatak	26	Portage Bay	27	Kanatak	23
Kuyukak	18	Wrangell Bay	62	Port Wrangell	57		
Sutkhoon	25						
Kaluiak	30	Chignik Bay	193	Chignik Bay	329	Chignik Bay	565
				Chignik River	195		
Mitrofania	22	Mitrofania	48			Mitrofania	27
Mashikh	40					Port Heiden	54
Oogashik	177						
Oonaugashuk	37						
Ikkaghmut	162	Kinuyak	51	Savonoski	100	Nunamute/ Savonoski	32
Total	812		1015		1252		896

of Ik-khagmute (or Ikak, also called "Kinuyak," "Nunamute," and "Savonoski").

Short sketches of the changes that took place in some of these villages show how transient people were at this time. For instance, Kukak Bay on the Pacific coast is the site of a large prehistoric site. A settlement in the bay had first been described in Langsdorff's 1806 mention of the village of Toujoujak. It was inhabited without a break throughout the Russian period. In 1880 a village called "Kukak" boasted a population of 37 and had its own ACC store by 1891.[63] In 1893 Kukak was rumored to be the future location of a new store to be run by the rival North American Company.[64] The store was never built, and the village was abandoned in 1895. That summer Father Tikhon Shalamov traveled from Kodiak, only to learn on his arrival that all the villagers had moved to Douglas.[65]

Sutkhum had been a nearly abandoned site when Pinart visited it in 1871.[66] Although he could see the remains of a large village and a church, he found the church in ruins and only five barabaras inhabited. In 1880, twenty-five Sutkhum inhabitants were counted. For a brief time from 1882 until 1887, the Alaska Commercial Company operated a post at Sutkhum, but the village had become only a summer hunting camp for Wrangel Bay Natives by 1890.[67]

Mike Sam of Chignik Lagoon and Anchorage recalled being told about hunting sea otters near Sutkhum, especially off Sutwik Island. His grandfather, Innokenty Kalmakoff, used to tell Mike about the old days. In the following transcript, MO refers to Bureau of Indian Affairs interviewer Matthew O'Leary, MS to Mike Sam.

> MO: We heard you know a story about Sutwik. Like, about the Russians.

> MS: I don't know about Russians. I know about Natives, used to sea otter hunt in there. A whole bunch of 'em, kayaks. They got stuck for days out there sometimes, storms, you know. They used to—get [stuck] so damn long—they used to make bow and arrows. They used bow and arrows for rifles that time.... They camp with the gear, with the furs they caught there, sea otters and all. Sometimes they'd be stuck for months. [They'd] have to go out there and eat, you know, clams, seal, sea lion and stuff. Then they

116.

F. Chignik. Alask

Alutiiqs on Chignik Dock, early 1900s.
Anchorage Museum of History and Art B91.9.46

played bets, my grandpa used to tell me and some of those guys go home, lose everything that they had, even their wives! Those guys start gambling, start losing. Go home and got nothing. And some of them more like just playing, take everything they give, but when he gets home give everything back, even his wife back too. [Grandpa] used to make me laugh telling stories.

MO: You never heard about any battles out there or fighting?

MS: No, I never heard of any. They used to go out there for sea otters, you know them days good price on sea otters. Double ended kayaks they used to go out there with. They got that [gut shirt] around you, water splashing, no water gets in there, in the kayak. Kneeling down....

I got in one of them one time, had no place to sit down. I had to go underneath the deck. Real spooky, I [was] a little fella then, you know. No light, kneel down. After that my grandpa says, "you want to go again?" I said "Oh no!"[68]

The village of Kaluiak, located near the present-day Chignik, was home to only thirty people in 1880. Within the next decade the population of Chignik Bay had ballooned to 193, after the opening of the fish processing plant in 1888.[69] Most of the people counted in

1900 and 1910 were seasonal workers who returned to the lower United States for the winter. Today the area is the population center for the entire Pacific coast of the peninsula.

Mitrofania, the southernmost of the Alutiiq villages reported in the 1880 census, had been founded that year by Kodiak immigrants. United States Navy Lt. Z. L. Tanner reported, "Sea-otter hunting is their chief occupation, but cod, halibut, and salmon are also taken for home consumption."[70] The 1880 census listed the entire population of twenty-two as creole. In 1889, Mitrofania's first chapel was built, and by the next year's census the population had grown to forty-eight.[71] The chapel was repaired in 1904.[72]

Father Harry Kaiakokonok remembered a legend he had heard about the Mitrofania area. Apparently the region was populated long ago not by creoles or Alutiiqs but by Unangan, until a bear attack forced everyone to leave the village. In the following transcript, HK refers to Father Harry Kaiakokonok, HS to National Park Service interviewer Harvey Shields.

HK: This little creek runs [into] this river, Humpback Creek right here. From here, I always think when that bears attacked this village [a now abandoned village near Mitrofania], they claim they came alone. And then landed through Mitrofania, along that long beach. According to the legend I always hear, the stories, there was so many kayaks there, they landed and almost covered the whole beach. There's quite a length of beach there.

HS: Yep, in Mitrofania there. And what's that, the west shore?

HK: Yeah, that's where they first landed when they escaped from that bear attack. And from there I always think since there was no protection here, it was too open for the soldiers, the warriors, they decided to live in this two islands [Spitz Island and a small islet off Mitrofania Island]. So they split up and let half the village maybe or so, live here, and then the other part live in the smaller flat-top [island].

HS: So some lived in the fortified place on Spitz Island and some lived on the flatter island to the south.

HK: Yes, that's what I think always. And this story we heard
from these people, Mitrofania village, that's an old village right
there, these people know it because they live there a long time.
They know all about these westward Aleuts [Unangan].... They
tell us all about this village which have been attacked by bear.
And for that reason they moved....

That's where we heard the story about this people who [were]
attacked by bear. See that kind of a little bite here [on the map].
Here is a creek. Summertime this creek is full of fish. Easy to
catch them, that's why we live here. They make lots of dried fish.
See that kind of a little bite right here? Right above that, there
lots of old locations there. We heard about this people from
them—Mitrofania people....

And the first escape landed right here. The whole beach was almost covered by kayaks, 1-, 2-, 3-hole kayaks. And I always think,
"Where could they be gone from then?" There's no location or
site anywhere that we can see. The only way I always think, even
I don't tell nobody, they maybe had no protection there; they
decided to move here in these two islands after their exploring
around these places they don't know. [That's] why—they didn't
find no locations there for protection, then they go to islands.[73]

Kuyukak (called "Kuyuyukak" by its Alutiiq inhabitants) was located in Chiginagak Bay, just around the point from Wrangel Bay
south of Katmai. The nearby settlement of Wrangel, established in
1882, was the site of an Alaska Commercial Company post and store
by at least 1884.[74] William J. Fisher, who collected Alutiiq and Eskimo objects for the Smithsonian Institution, was the ACC trader
at Wrangel between 1884 and 1889. He had married Anna Nikiforova,
daughter of the former Katmai trader Vasilii Nikiforov and great-
granddaughter of Fëdor Kolmakov. Wrangel's first chapel was built
in 1884, followed by a second in 1895.[75]

By 1890 more changes had occurred in Alutiiq peninsula settlements. A new village called Kanatak, located at the Pacific end of
the Ugashik River portage across the Alaska Peninsula, had been
founded by "resettled people from the interior of [the] Alaska
[Peninsula], namely from the Nushagak parish."[76] These interior

Kanatak, pre-1912.
Capps Collection 83-148-2240, Archives and Manuscripts, Alaska and Polar Regions Department, University of Alaska Fairbanks

people were most likely from Ugashik, with camps at Lake Becharof. Alutiiq elders today recall the yearly trips they made each spring from Kanatak to two cannery towns on the Bristol Bay side, Ugashik and its northern neighbor Egegik, to take part in their rich fisheries.

In 1890 the ethnic background of the people of Ugashik puzzled the census takers. The people were described as

> Aleut half-bred type..., a people who speak a language with marked dialectic differences from the Eskimo, and who show the peculiar domestic traits which character-ize the inhabitants of the Aleutian Islands.[77]

In fact, Ugashik had already experienced a long history as an Alutiiq settlement by 1890. Its makeup changed during the early part of the twentieth century when the community population grew to include Iñupiat reindeer herders transported south to tend the newly ar-rived herds. Other Iñupiat followed to work in canneries.

Unangashik, to the south of Ugashik, was entirely Alutiiq, ac-cording to former Port Heiden resident Aleck Constantine, until the 1918 flu epidemic killed so many people that the rest abandoned the village. In the 1930s an Eskimo (Iñupiat) family settled in the long-abandoned village.

The Savonoski settlements are represented in the 1880 U.S. Census records only by Ikkaghmute, called "Igiak" in the 1890 census narrative but "Kinuyak on Lake Walker [Naknek]" in the table of villages for the same year. The population is greatly decreased in the 1890 count, perhaps because the people were fishing in Bristol Bay or seeking work at one of the newly opened salteries on the Naknek River when the census-takers visited the village.

Two other areas on the Pacific coast were settled during the 1890s. The first, Cold [Puale] Bay, was a hunting area for local and Iliamna Natives (Kiatagmiut or Dena'ina).[78] When Father Tikhon Shalamov visited the bay in 1895, he reported that it was used as a hunting camp for Katmai Natives in both summer and winter.[79] By 1902, Cold Bay had been taken over by American oil prospectors. Father Vasilii Martysh reported that these men regularly bought fish from Kanatak villagers. Cold Bay prospectors gave the priest provisions so he could continue his voyage down the coast.[80] Later a store was built there.

The second new settlement, Wide Bay, lasted less than a decade. Like Kanatak, it had been settled in 1890 by people from across the Alaska Peninsula.[81] In 1897, twenty-nine men and nineteen women in Wide Bay, all "Aleuts," took confession.[82] There was an ACC "Wide Bay Station" in 1897.[83] However, when Father Vasilii Martysh arrived on his yearly trip in the summer of 1902, the village was abandoned. He reported, "when otter hunting ceased, the inhabitants, abandoning their barabaras and the chapel, headed north."[84] An American named Jack Lee opened a store in Wide Bay sometime during the twentieth century, and for a time it again became a gathering place on the coast.[85]

RELIGION

Russian Orthodox priests continued to make yearly trips to the villages during the American period. The creole Pëtr Kashevarov, Katmai's second traveling priest, died in 1879 and was replaced by the creole Nikolai Rysev, who served at least through 1883.[86] Another creole, Pëtr Dobrovolskii, ministered to Katmai and other villages along the peninsula during part of the 1880s.[87] These three were followed by a Pole, Aleksandr Martysh.[88] Douglas trader Stafeev was furious at new policies Martysh instituted. He wrote,

> Here is news, he has forbidden us to sing the burial service over the dead.... Also [he ordered] the psalm reader not to put on the stikharion without [his] blessing and not to read the Gospels. Well, who will come or who will want to come to the Temple of God to hear the Hours conducted by a person wearing an ordinary coat? After all, there is someone literate in every household and he can read the Hours at home![89]

Other priests who traveled to the Pacific coast villages during the nineteenth century were, in order, Tikhon Shalamov, Nikolai Kashevarov, and Vasilii Martysh. During the 1890s and the first decade of the twentieth century, the priests tried to visit peninsula chapels each year, although weather sometimes prevented them from completing their rounds.[90]

The Nushagak parish was similarly ministered by a traveling priest. In the 1890 census report, Alfred Shanz wrote,

> With very few exceptions all the coast Eskimo of the entire district are Greek Catholics [Orthodox], at least as far as adherence to the ritual can make them Greek Catholics. Those who live near enough go to the church with commendable regularity. Some have even acquired a knowledge of the texts and chants, so that in a pinch they could conduct the services themselves.... About twice a year...Father Shishkin, in spite of his advanced age, undergoes the hardships of Alaskan travel and makes a trip over the entire district, his travels each time occupying nearly two months and covering a distance from 300 to 800 miles.... On his trips he baptizes the children, marries young couples or ratifies marriages already informally entered into, and gives the last blessing to those who have died since his last visit.[91]

Three Chignik Lake youngsters dressed as *makalataqs*, January 1992.
Patricia Partnow

During the American period Orthodox chapels were built in several Alaska Peninsula villages. For instance, in 1876 the first chapel in the settlement of Douglas was built, and a new one was completed sometime between 1890 and 1893. In 1877, a third chapel was built at Katmai, following the first built by Kostylev in the 1830s or 1840s and the second constructed in 1850. Another was built in 1901, then refurbished in 1904. Chapels were also built or repaired at Kukak before 1880, at Wrangel in 1884, 1895, and 1905, Mitrofania in 1889 and 1904, and Kanatak in 1890 and 1910.[92] After 1896, the seat for the parish that included the Pacific coast villages of the Alaska Peninsula was relocated to Afognak, north of Kodiak.

As discussed in the previous chapter, the Russian Orthodoxy practiced on the Alaska Peninsula incorporated elements from the precontact religion, especially in the winter ceremonies. While the starring, masking, and New Year's celebrations were now performed with the understanding that they were Christian

A *maskalataq* at Chignik Lake, January 1992.
Patricia Partnow

ceremonies, parts were carryovers from bygone days. For instance, the hilarious midwinter masking festival lasted many days and allowed people to dance from house to house in costumes. The custom likely derived from both Russian traditional masquerades and from the precontact midwinter masking festival that was held to thank the *suas* of past prey (represented in masks) for giving themselves up to the hunters, and to ask them to do the same in the future.[93]

Similarly, Vladimir Stafeev described the New Year celebration that occurred in 1892–93. His use of the term "savage" indicates both his patronizing attitude toward local Alutiiqs and creoles and a supposition that the New Year celebration the Katmai Alutiiqs practiced had elements of a traditional, non-Christian culture.

> In the evening went to watch the ball and the New Year's Eve celebrations among the savages, it is truly savage, a devil without horns was dressed in a parka, the old year in a kamleika [gut parka], the new year completed the attraction appearing all in white, the face pale and holding a lighted candle in his hand. He looked like a living corpse. He proclaimed the new year, and everyone started to kiss him. Exactly at midnight I went home, prayed to God, and having drunk some cider, returned to watch the savages. I am surprised that neither [Father] N. N. Rysev nor G. A. Chechenev had taught them how to mark the Russian New Year.[94]

Virginia Aleck was told by her grandmother, Barbara Shangin Sanook, about similar New Year celebrations at Katmai. Virginia explained,

> This day [New Year's eve], I remember, she used to tell me they used to get together, must be same barabary [*qasgiq*]. They bring the masquerades together. They have the old year and the new year. And the old year is all tattered, and I guess they had a gut or something. A stomach from probably a seal or some animal, that they filled up with something, look like blood. And they had sticks and the new year would pull this guy all uphill, he punctured that thing [the stomach] and by the time they were through with him he was just a heap on the floor. And the new year would have a big victory. The new year was dressed all in white, she used to tell me. And she said it was a big occasion.[95]

Ralph Phillips of Perryville also remembered hearing about the unique New Year's masking celebration that used to take place each year in Perryville. The practice stopped shortly after he was born in the 1920s. This is how it was explained to him:

> One *maskalataq* [masquerader] was dressed as the New Year (*nutawaq uksuq*) in clean nice clothes and mask. This one used to hook the Old Year (*uksulek*) with a long hook and throw it out a window. Suddenly, one year, the church bells started to ring. One or two guys went to the church to check, and saw that no one was ringing them. The people knew that this meant they were doing something wrong. The people started holding *molieben* [prayer] services every year, and they never had any other troubles.[96]

Although Russian Orthodoxy remained the only organized church on the Alaska Peninsula, American protestant missionaries also came to Alaska during the nineteenth century. They had three goals: To convert the Natives to Protestantism—even those who were already Orthodox Christians; to teach the Natives English; and to guide the people away from Native and Russian ways and toward

Perryville's Orthodox Church, 1990.
  Patricia Partnow

American culture. Because of these goals, which conflicted with established custom on the Alaska Peninsula and Kodiak, relations between the newly arrived Americans and the Russians who had stayed in Alaska were strained. Baptist missionaries Ernest and Ida Roscoe of Kodiak resented the Russian Orthodox priests who hampered their attempts to establish a mission and orphanage on Kodiak. In 1887 Ida wrote,

> The old [Russian Orthodox] priest...is very much displeased with the American school. He told some of the men that as soon as the children learn to read English they would leave the Greek [Russian Orthodox] church, so he does all he can to make them go to the Russian school which they started two days after E[rnest] commenced his. They even went so far as to send a man around to gather the children up in the morning, when they first commenced, but I think we will come out best in the end.[97]

Several years later another missionary, C. C. Currant, worried, "The Greek [Orthodox] priest here is doing what he can to oppose. Pray God that he may not harm us."[98] Census takers in 1890 observed that it was not only the priests who objected to religious instruction by newly arrived American school teachers. The census report states,

> The requirement that the teachers of schools thus subsidized by the government abstain from sectarian teaching must of course...be only a dead letter, and may remain such in nine-tenths of the territory brought within reach of educational facilities without causing harm or offense to anybody. At a few points, however, the system interferes seriously with the progress of the public schools. I refer to places where Russian parish churches have been in existence for nearly a century of which every native inhabitant is a member. In these places the fact that the teacher is also a missionary of some other denomination interferes very much with his usefulness though he be instructed not to teach religion during school hours. The people in these communities, who have been christians [*sic*] so long, resent the presence of a missionary of another sect among them by not sending their children to his school.[99]

Following his 1899 survey of the fishing industry in southcentral and southwestern Alaska, Capt. Charles P. Elliott showed a distrust for the Orthodox church shared by many Americans:

> The Indians [*sic*] under the domination of the Russian church, and the personality of the priest in charge determines to a considerable extent the condition of the Indians. The priest at Kadiak preaches sedition against the United States, his influence being distinctly for evil.[100]

The Orthodox priests' point of view was very different. An 1898 article in the *American Orthodox Messenger* entitled "Short Historical Description of the Kodiak Parish" summarizes the attitude of the established church:

> Only this year on Woody Island the Baptists, weaving a
> nest for impertinently taking Orthodox children, are
> building a prayer house, and, it seems, not so much for
> vagrants without pastors of the heterodox, as much as
> for the seduction and luring of Orthodox Aleuts.[101]

As bitter as the religious rivalry was on Kodiak, the Alaska Peninsula Alutiiqs were hardly aware of it, for the missionaries did not
travel beyond Shelikof Strait. Protestant missionaries had no effect
on the peninsula until the midtwentieth century.

GAMBLING AS CONTROL: THE GAME OF KÁTAQ

Gambling had been a favorite pastime for Alutiiq men since before
the coming of Russians. Lisiansky described a game called *kroogeki*
played in 1805 that involved throwing sticks at a mark on a skin.[102]
By the American period, the most popular game was called *kátaq*
(from the Dena'ina *kadaq*). It apparently originated among Native
Americans in California where it was learned by Alaskans stationed
at the RAC agricultural post at Fort Ross north of San Francisco
Bay. Established in 1812 to supply food for the Alaska colony, Fort
Ross was operated by Russian, Dena'ina, Alutiiq, and Unangan men
and women sent to tend fields and hunt sea otters. When they returned north they carried the game with them.[103] *Kátaq's* popularity
was widespread and often unrestrained, perhaps because of the combination of skill and luck—neither of which involved the meddling
of outside bosses—it required.

For years Russian Orthodox priests warned their parishioners
that *kátaq* was the work of the devil. Their reproofs drove the game
underground, and eventually led to its almost complete disappear-
ance. As a young girl in the early 1900s, Polly Shangin witnessed
many games of *kátaq* played in a large barabara in Egegik. The men
had come from different villages miles away just to play the game.
Ralph Phillips explained how *kátaq* was played:

> They had two sticks; one stick was burned on both ends,
> the other only on one end. The two opponents, facing

Mary Peterson (left) and Rena Peterson (right) play *kátaq* at the newly built community barabara in Akhiok, Kodiak Island, 1989.
  Courtesy of the Alutiiq Museum

each other, sang in Alutiiq during the play. The opponent would point to the side where he thought the two-burnt stick was. Sometimes fighting broke out when one person won too much.

They were told it was evil, leading them toward Hell. They stopped under the influence of the priests. About the same time, *kaḻagaleks* stopped practicing too.[104]

Ignatius Kosbruk was told a story in which people lost their lives because of *kátaq*.

[That's] the meaning of the whale killer [killer whale]. It's a true story, too. You see those whale killers? Are human like we. They are. But there are some evil spirits. Evil spirits help them.

And their power is from evil spirits. That's how the *arwahsuḻḥít* [killer whales] [did it].

[Killer whales lived in a lake at the summit of Smokey Mountain.] One day they dress up just like we, today. Humans. Just like humans. In Smokey Mountain, inside of Smokey Mountain. They dress up and their commander say, "What are you guys gonna do?" "We're gonna go hunting."

And the water was bubbling on Smokey Mountain. Big lake! And they grabbed behind their bed and bring out whale killer skin. They just put that on and go dive right down to that boiling water. Every one of 'em.

And these two was left over in the Smokey Mountain. Two, just two of 'em. And their commander told them, "How come you guys don't go? All the rest of 'em are going." "How are we gonna get out? We got no clothes." He just grab behind 'em and bring out that whale killer skin. So they get that on and dive right down. And they come out in front of the village [Katmai].

And they all spread out from there and went hunting. And when they came out, they float out as a whale killer.

That's where evil spirit. And they all gathered together and float out. There were two groups floating out. And their commander say—tell them, "Which way are you guys going?" Some were going west, some going east. They went out hunting.

[This was] about in Katmai too, I guess. There was a bunch [of men]. All they used to do is *kátaq*. *Kátaq* in that *qasgiq* all the time. That's all they do, they play games. And then one time when they were *kátaqing* in that *qasgiq*, the mens came in. Them people didn't know who they were. Where they were *kátaqing*, all bunch of mens came in where they were *kátaqing*. And them people didn't know who they were. They were from Smokey Mountain. *Puyulek*.

And they would call them whale killers. And they (the ones who came in) win them. They didn't even let 'em win or nothing. Cause there were all evil spirit, worship of evil spirit.

[When the Katmai humans lost the *kátaq* game, they were told to climb up to the top of the Smokey Mountain. They said,] "We can't climb up the mountain. We can't get up there."

[The killer whales answered,] "We'll get you, then, we'll get everybody up there."

They got 'em all out, [all] confused. They didn't know who to follow. So they went up to the mountain, every one of 'em. And when they get up to the top of the mountain, the [killer whales] pull them up by their ropes, the humans. All, every one of 'em excepting two old couples. They left them to tell the story. And they killed every one of 'em. Every one in the whole village.

They took the whole village, excepting that two old couples. And their commander told the [two old people], "You two must go home and stay home. We'll take all the rest of 'em to the mountains."[106]

Told as both a morality tale and a historic episode, this *unigkuaq* is also evidence for the spiritual power of the world's nonhuman people, or *suas*, in this case killer whales. Like many traditional narratives, it is said to have been passed down only because two survivors were left to tell the tale.

The moral lessons from *unigkuat* such as this and from Russian Orthodox priests were not lost on Alutiiqs who came of age in the early twentieth century. Innokenty Kalmakoff told his grandson Mike Sam about hunters who lost everything at *kátaq*:

My grandpa used to tell me he used to go sea otter hunting.

You know, in kayaks. There would be storms, and they stay for weeks for a time up there. And they used to have bow and arrows, and they built a mudbank this high, the two of 'em, and [they'd shoot at it.] It was a long ways to shoot. And they play games, to bet for the things they caught, sea otters and stuff. Some guys lose, lose all, nothing left. They got no kayak. Somebody else win it.

And they got kids and wife at home. They bet those too. And lose 'em. That was a long time ago.

Then their houses, where they live, houses, everything. To lose, some of them. Some of them just keep taking, but when they go home they give everything back to them, just make them worry. And they told 'em, when he gave everything like that back to them, "You should never gamble like that." He said, "You'll never have nothing if you do that."[105]

Doris Lind remembers witnessing *kátaq* on springtime hunting trips when her family had traveled from Kanatak to Egegik. She says she can picture the inside of a tent in Egegik, where men, including her grandfather Nikolai Kalmakoff, sat in a circle playing the game. One man would hide a stick behind his back, as Ralph Phillips described. The players and spectators danced with their upper bodies and sang a song. Once, Doris remembers, she and her friend Figley knelt behind the men, mimicking their motions. Later the two girls were playing together, singing the same song. Doris's grandmother overheard them and scolded them harshly, telling them that the song was the devil's song. They never sang it again.

Despite admonitions coming from all sides, Alutiiqs continued to enjoy the thrill of the game. As late as 1997 Old Harbor elder Larry Matfay was able to demonstrate both the song and moves. He performed with joy, skill, and confidence, winning every game against his equally elderly opponents. Ironically, a game of chance provided Alutiiqs with precisely the autonomy that was lacking in lives controlled by fur traders, cannery owners, and priests. A game that was known for the power it held over those who were addicted to it became the means of power to those who mastered it.

HEALTH

Disease persisted with no respite during the nineteenth century. Tuberculosis was so widespread that the census taker responsible for the 1880 enumeration in the area, Ivan Petroff, remarked, "Consumption is...the simple and comprehensive title for that disease which destroys the greatest number throughout Alaska." A form of tuberculosis, scrofula, was so common that Petroff wrote, "it is hard to find a settlement in the whole country where at least one or more of the families therein have not got the singularly prominent scars [on the neck] peculiar to the disease."[107]

Specific epidemics also continued to plague the Alaska Peninsula and Kodiak during the American period as they had during Russian days. Fortuine reported the following epidemics:

- In 1868 the mumps raged throughout Kodiak Island.

- In 1874–75 an outbreak of measles occurred in the same district.

- In 1880 venereal disease was reported to be common in Unga and soon in nearby Alaska Peninsula locations. Although the Russians had controlled the disease, it spread again after Caucasian fishermen moved into the area.

- Almost every year during the 1880s pneumonia and respiratory epidemics struck the Nushagak and Kodiak areas.

- In 1888 the Douglas trader reported that people were "all sick."

- In 1889 there was an outbreak of influenza on Kodiak.

- In 1891 there were many deaths at Egegik and Katmai from a respiratory ailment.

- In 1893 the Katmai trader reported many deaths from an unnamed epidemic.[108]

DAWNING OF THE TWENTIETH CENTURY

As the century began, the people of Katmai, Douglas, Savonoski, and the other villages on the peninsula were searching for a new way to make a living. The fur trade in its old form was dying. Its replacement was a system whereby traveling fur buyers appraised and purchased furs trapped during the preceding winter. The buyers dealt not with *toyons* or *baidarshchiks*, but with individual trappers. Each man worked his own trapline, generally with a partner, so each pair bargained separately with the buyers to achieve the best price for furs.

Meanwhile, the new industries of mining and fishing were, for the moment, reserved for white immigrants and Chinese itinerant workers. The only sure method of surviving left to Alutiiqs was subsistence hunting and fishing, but even those pursuits required cash for transportation, ammunition, clothing, and staple food items such as flour, sugar, and tea.

The turn of the century thus marked the first time in a hundred years that Alutiiqs not only had choices, but needed to make them.

They traveled, adapted, and used social and economic skills honed during a century of dealing with outsiders. By the decade following 1910, they had begun to break down barriers that had prevented their involvement in commercial fishing and processing.

In the process of altering their economic patterns, Alutiiqs' relationship with the land and each other changed. No longer able to make a living as sedentary village-dwellers dependent on a single industry, they diversified, supplementing trapping and subsistence hunting with fish processing, guiding, and handiwork. Some opened stores or restaurants. All became far more mobile than had been allowed or necessary during the previous century. One result was that village fragmentation increased. Those villages that remained intact did so not because of pressure from outside entrepreneurs, but through kinship ties, customary attachment to specific parts of the land, and the church. Yet these forces were constantly battling the needs of individuals to earn money.

This period of economic unrest saw a splintering not just of settlements, but of the Alaska Peninsula Alutiiq social structure itself. The family, rather than the village, became the primary economic unit and the main focus of loyalty and membership. The sense of belonging to a larger group, nurtured during Russian days, was overshadowed by an orientation back toward kin group. The forces of family and village, sometimes conflicting and sometimes complementary, have continued to alternate in strength throughout the twentieth century.

Ignatius Kosbruk described the beginnings of this new pattern of social interaction, marked by individual initiative followed by group benefit, in the following *quliyanguaq*. The story is about two young men from Katmai who, probably sometime around 1910, journeyed more than 300 miles in search of work.

> There's another one from the grandfather—his name was Wasco. I used to trap with him many many times and he tells all kinds of stories. In this one, he was one of two people from Katmai who were told to portage to Naknek by their chief. From Naknek, they went by way of Ugashik, from Ugashik to Pilot Point. They were looking for work.

Well, once at Pilot Point, I don't know how long it take, they must have really walk! All the way to Pilot Point. They call it *Aisaq* in Alutiiq, is what they call Pilot Point. They got to Aisaq.

Now the Pilot Point people were also Alutiiqs. They were also looking for work. So the leaders of the Pilot Point people showed the route to the two Katmai people. They showed the two how to get to Port Moller by walking along the beach. It was in the spring, in the summer, when the days got long.

So they went as they were shown, those two, and they got another partner, a man from Pilot Point.

So they started the journey, walking from up there at Bristol Bay. At Bear River, only at Bear River was there a big river that they couldn't go over. Their guide went across to the other side by skiff. He knew that they can't cross it [by foot], no way. And they get to other side and they continue on, on their long journey, all the way down to Port Moller, by walk, by foot. And it took them, I don't know, three, four days I guess from Pilot Point to Port Moller.

Then when they got there those Katmai people went to look for work together. They went to look for work by boat. They must have had a boat them days.

Then their boss brought the two back to where they came from, Pilot Point. To Pilot Point the Port Moller boss took the two back. I used to see Port Moller. They say they used to have a big cannery in the spit. Now it's almost gone....They said that whole spit used to be full of canneries. Now they're all [destroyed] by the weather.

Then while they were at Port Moller, Katmai and Douglas people both worked for that boss, both villages found jobs. And [the boss] brought them back with a boat, whatever the boat they must have had, back to Pilot Point, and they were really proud.

Then the people were waiting at Pilot Point for word from them when they would return, what answers they will get when they get back to Pilot Point. Boy then they all gathered together. They were rejoicing.

Then they returned to Katmai. [The rest of the Katmai people] portaged back the same way, same road. With their kayaks and dogs and everything. They went back and flowed through that Naknek River, to Naknek and from there they proceed on down to Port Moller. Days and days and days; I don't know how long it take them. And when they looked for work at Port Moller, they stayed with [the boss]. They stay back because the place was so good. And the people were nice and kind. And a year after that they want them back again, that's how they found their jobs. And they continued to work in Port Moller and on to Pilot Point.

That's how people got scattered in the past. They liked that workplace. They stayed, spent the winter.

That's how I see relatives I didn't used to know all over Alaska. They liked the land, they were happy staying there with them.

That's how Wasco told the story. He told of returning here through that portage above Sand Point. I don't know where that, how they call that. It's on this south side. They came by boat back on this side.

And that's how in the past people used to live. How they looked for the best, like today. People used to live looking for the best, how they will survive, what will be the best.... They just spent the winter on the land....

When they were walking on the beach, the two partners wore out their feet. They wear their feet out walking. Bare-footed all the way down, just wear their feet out. And they didn't have no boots in those days. Only skin boots. I've seen them. They called their boots *naluwat*, leather boots. That's all they used. And I also saw them use *aciqanguat* [another kind of skin boots].

That's all.[109]

Although oral tradition describes ancient wars between Alutiiqs and the people of Port Moller, these age-old animosities were long forgotten by the twentieth century, and, as this narrative explains, Alutiiqs and Unangan began to inhabit the same communities as a result of increased mobility at the beginning of the century.[110]

Despite seasonal jobs in the south, most Alutiiqs stayed in the northern tier of the peninsula until 1912. By that summer, a saltery near Katmai was providing work for nearly all residents of both Katmai and Douglas, who lived in temporary tents or houses in Kaflia Bay, halfway between the two villages. Father Harry Kaiakokonok recalled the work at the saltery. In the following transcript, HK refers to Father Harry, MT to National Park Service interviewer Michael Tollefson:

> HK: [Foster was the one the people worked for in the] summertime—salt salmon, the bellies; smoke the backs. He was one of the fishermen us kids know.
>
> MT: Like, George [Kosbruk] would have been fishing, the women would have been cutting the fish and salting them?
>
> HK: No, no women, all men. Men cutting—salting—men fishing. They fish in that Kaflia Bay inside that inner harbor. And they make the hauls, there, pull them up to the beach. See that big hill, there's a narrow, narrow break between. And in that narrow spot—inside part—that's where they used to splitting the fish on the beach....
>
> How far from Katmai to Kaflia? Oh maybe four hours. In kayak you have three people in kayak, it go fast. One time several kayak had a race.[III]

Katmai was to figure in the destiny of Alaska Peninsula Alutiiqs one more time, with its spectacular volcanic eruption during the summer of 1912. This single event was the catalyst for a new set of choices and decisions of momentous proportions, which provided yet another opportunity for Alutiiqs to make history.

NOTES

1. Kitchener 1954: 32. Kitchener implies that other peninsula posts were operating at the time of the sale as well: "From Kodiak, Alaska Commercial continued the fur trading headquarters and substations which included...Douglas, Kugac Bay,...Katmai" (1954: 138). Neither Douglas nor Kugac [Kukak] is mentioned in Russian-American Company records, so it is almost certain that those two trading posts were

established by the Hutchinson, Kohl and Company several years after the initial purchase.

2.   Pinart 1873a: 16.

3.   ACC 1868–1891: August 7, 1877.

4.   AOM 1899: 91.

5.   Arndt 1999.

6.   Shanz 1893: 96.

7.   George Kosbruk 1975b and Kaiakokonok 1975a.

8.   AOM 1898: 508.

9.   Oswalt 1967: 24.

10.   AOM 1898: 508; Oswalt 1967: 27; ACC/Wrangell.

11.   ACC/Katmai: February 19, 1891; Oswalt 1967: 26.

12.   Oswalt 1967: 30; Stafeev 1893, January.

13.   Tikhmenev 1978: 201–204. Equivalencies derive from a conversion rate of 1 ruble=50 cents, in effect throughout the nineteenth century (Pierce 1997:Personal communication).

14.   AOM 1902: 432; AOM 1904: 32.

15.   ACC/Douglas: April 16, 1887.

16.   ACC/Douglas: May 5 and 8, 1893.

17.   ACC/Katmai: May 5, July 18,1891; ACC/Katmai: August 9, 1891; ACC/Douglas: July 9, 16, 1892; ACC/Douglas: July 4, 6, 8, 10, 19, 1892; ACC/Douglas: July 16, 18, 27, 1892; ACC/Douglas: August 2, 1892; ACC/Douglas: November 7, 1892; ACC/Douglas: May 14, 1893.

18.   Fortuine 1992: 291.

19.   Stepanoff 1969.

20.   Stepanoff 1969.

21.   The bishop in question is undoubtedly Bishop Nestor, who died in 1882 during McIntyre's tenure at Kodiak while on a visit to the west coast of Alaska (on the Alaska Commercial Company ship *Saint Paul*, not the *Kodiak* as in Spiridon's story; cf. Portelli 1991: 20–1 for a discussion of chronological shifts in oral narrative). Almost a century later the *American Orthodox Messenger* described his death as follows:

In 1882 he was in the far north, at Mikhailovsky Redoubt [St. Michael]. On the return trip to San Francisco, Bishop Nestor unexpectedly disappeared. Apparently he was washed completely overboard off the little steamship on which he was traveling. After some time, Aleut fishermen from Michailovsky Redoubt found

Bishop Nestor's cassocked body. Over him circled a seagull. The body was taken to Unalaska for burial (AOM 1972: 113).

To my knowledge, there was no suspicion of foul play at the time of Bishop Nestor's death. Spiridon's motif of discord between the economic activity of hunting and the religious observance of holidays also comes up in the memoirs of Baptist missionary Fred Roscoe (1992:50–1).

22. See, for instance, Roscoe 1992: 10, 124; Elliott 1900: 741; AOM 1898: 266.

23. Ignatius Kosbruk 1992.

24. Seton-Karr 1887; Petroff (under the penname Lanin) ms.; Roscoe, Fred 1992: 6–9.

25. Seton-Karr 1887: 231–32.

26. Arndt 1999.

27. ACC/Katmai, Box 19, folder 245, as reported in Arndt 1999.

28. U.S. Census, Roll 1750; Porter 1893: 73.

29. Stafeev 1890, April, May.

30. AOM 1902: 432; AOM 1904: 32.

31. AOM 1899: 91.

32. AOM 1899: 91.

33. AOM 1902: 432.

34. AOM 1904: 14.

35. AOM 1904: 32.

36. ACC Directors' Meeting Minutes, Dec. 26, 1906.

37. Kaiakokonok 1975.

38. Stepanoff 1969.

39. Doris Lind 1992.

40. Moser 1902: 209–11.

41. Cf. Porter 1893: 73.

42. Moser 1902: 210–11.

43. Davis 1986: 93.

44. Stepanoff 1969.

45. Stepanoff 1969.

46. Elliott 1899: 738.

47. Walter Stepanoff 1990b.

48. Sam 1990.
49. AOM 1898: 266.
50. Cf. Mishler and Mason 1996.
51. Mishler and Mason 1996: 267.
52. Petroff 1900: 33.
53. Petroff 1900: 84.
54. Porter 1893: 199.
55. Wells 1891: 106.
56. Spurr 1898: 38.
57. Spurr 1900: 92.
58. Beach 1940: 63.
59. Stafeev 1893: August 6, 1893 [old style, July 25]; AOM 1896: 57; AOM 1902: 433; AOM 1916: 572–3.
60. Lind 1993.
61. Stafeev 1892: August 14 [old style, August 2].
62. Porter 1893: 169.
63. ACC/Katmai: February 19, 1891.
64. Stafeev 1893, January.
65. AOM 1896: 119.
66. Pinart 1873: 14.
67. Oswalt 1967: 24.
68. Sam 1991.
69. Moser 1899: 165.
70. Tanner 1888: 36–7.
71. ARCA: Reel 132.
72. AOM 1926: 119.
73. Kaiakokonok 1975a.
74. AOM 1898: 508; Oswalt 1967: 27.
75. AOM 1898: 508, ARCA: Reel 180.
76. AOM 1898: 508.
77. Shanz 1893: 93.
78. ACC/Katmai:May 5, July 18, 1891.
79. AOM 1896: 57.
80. AOM 1904: 32.

81. AOM 1898: 508.

82. ARCA: Reel 180.

83. Oswalt 1967: 26.

84. AOM 1904: 33.

85. Partnow field notes.

86. Pierce 1990: 220; AOM 1898: 509; ARCA: Reel 181.

87. ACC/Douglas: August 15, 1885.

88. ARCA: Reel 181.

89. Stafeev 1892, July 12.

90. E.g., AOM 1896: 119.

91. Shanz 1893: 96.

92. AOM 1898: 508; ARCA: Reel 180; AOM 1902: 433; ARCA: Reel 132; Stafeev ms.: December 11, 1889.

93. For a more complete discussion of the topic, see Partnow 1993: 280ff.

94. Stafeev 1893, December 31, 1893; new calendar, January 12, 1894.

95. Aleck 1993.

96. Phillips 1992.

97. Roscoe 1992: 10.

98. Roscoe 1992: 124.

99. Porter 1893: 187.

100. Elliott 1900: 741.

101. AOM 1898: 266.

102. Lisiansky 1968: 210.

103. Bergsland 1994: 657.

104. Phillips 1992.

105. Sam 1990.

106. Ignatius Kosbruk 1992d.

107. Petroff 1900: 43.

108. Fortuine 1989.

109. Ignatius Kosbruk 1992a.

110. It was journeys such as this one that brought the Alutiiq ancestors of today's inhabitants of the village of Nelson Lagoon down the peninsula, just beyond Port Moller, to their new home.

111. Kaiakokonok 1975a.

5

KATMAI, 1912

THE KATMAI ERUPTION

Disruptive as they were, the changes brought about by the demise of the trading posts and introduction of new industries were dwarfed by a cataclysmic event that occurred on June 6, 1912. That day Novarupta volcano near Katmai erupted with such force that its ashfall completely destroyed the Alutiiq villages on the northeastern coast of the Alaska Peninsula and inland along the Savonoski River. People were forced to find new homes and new occupations farther south.

The Katmai eruption was one of the largest volcanic eruptions in the history of the world, and the largest to date in this century. Ash and pumice buried the villages of Savonoski and Upper Savonoski, Katmai and Douglas, and the saltery at Kaflia Bay. Ash fell two feet deep on Kodiak 115 miles away. The explosion created thunder and lightning and buried the region in darkness for more than forty-eight hours. Its roar was heard as far away as Juneau, 750 miles distant. Six days after the explosion the Katmai and Douglas villagers were rescued by U.S. Revenue Cutter Service (USRCS) ships. Later that summer they were taken to a location far to the southwest, where they established the new village of Perryville.

Many people, Native and non-Native, locals and visitors, recorded their experiences during those few days in the summer of 1912.[1] Their accounts give a valuable picture of life on the Alaska Peninsula at

Two women and two children of Chignik, 1909, wearing clothing as described by
Barbara Shangin Sanook.
   Alaska State Library, Flamen Ball Collection PCA 24–103

the time. They also show very different—sometimes opposite—views of the same event.

By 1994, no Alutiiq survivors of the Katmai eruption remained. For two generations the children of Perryville had grown up hearing stories about the terrifying event from the participants, but now they learn about it second-hand or in books. Chignik Lake's "Old Gramma," Barbara Shangin Sanook, described her ordeal to her grandchildren many times before she died in the 1970s. In 1968 she recorded some of her memories for the Chignik Lake school teachers. The following is a transcript of a session in which her granddaughter, Virginia Aleck (VA), and Chignik Lake resident Doris Lind (DL) translated the 1968 recording for me (PP).

VA: She said they used to dress with regular [cloth] clothes. Long dresses. She said they used to even have shoes.

DL: My gramma used to have really long [dresses]. They used to put 'em on the holidays.

VA: She said they had barabaries [sod houses], some of 'em, and then the other people had regular houses. She said there was a boat wreck on the beach, and they took lumber from the boat and made houses with the boat.

They had a beautiful church.

Lots of fish. They used to stay inside of that creek. There was no caribou, just moose.

PP: Did they used to hunt whales?

VA: Gramma said no. But I know that one time when she told me about the volcano that there was whales floating in the bay. She probably seen them when they left. Because where they lived they were way inland inside of this big river.

She said they used to eat fish, had two stores. Didn't need nothing. She used to talk a little bit [Russian]. She used to sing in Russian.

DL: Anyway, you guys' grampa [Elia Shangin, Barbara's first husband] was a Russian.

VA: She said she don't remember them too well, when the first white men came to the village. She said they used to come wintertime, go sledding.

She said they couldn't see from where they were to out to the ocean so they couldn't tell about the big ships. She said if they do come in with the ships they would have to come in to the river.

She came from Katmai when she was sixteen. She said the land was big, Katmai.

DL: That's what she means, there was a big town there.

VA: There was two of 'em [villages; at] Kaflia Bay. She said the volcano blew up when they were there. She's telling Uncle [Bill Lind who was present when the 1968 tape was recorded] that they were from Katmai and the other one was another [village— Douglas], they were at Kaflia. There was a lot of people, she said, in both.

She said they could see the volcano when it ruptured. Rocks were flying all over. She said the volcano was not very far. Two mountains. Rocks and fire were all over. Three feet high, ashes.

They [young men in baidarkas] had to go to [Afognak]. Went over and told them people about what was happening over on Katmai. She said the government [rescued] them.

They had two schools there in Afognak. She said they filled two of 'em, chuck full. The people from the village.

They thought it was the end of the world, she used to tell me. They had a molieben service, and then finally they got okay.

In July they went to Ivanof [Bay]. In August maybe they went to Perryville. Gramma's telling Uncle that's why Perryville's called Perryville, because captain's name was Perry. And then Gramma says she knew all the captains.

She said when the volcano blew up she had her first son, Nick Shangin.... I remember when I was younger that she used to tell me stories about how she carried the baby with her.

They lived in tents for a while [when they first got to Perryville]. She said there was people from two villages, from Katmai [and Douglas], and they put 'em all in Perryville, and she said now they're finishing. She means they're dying off.[2]

Other former Katmai residents also recorded their memories of the eruption and the terrible days afterward. Some have been published elsewhere. For instance, an interview with George Kosbruk was transcribed and published in Kodiak High School's student publication *Elwani*.[3] But the best known and most complete account was written in 1956 by Father Harry Kaiakokonok of Perryville. He wrote the Katmai story for a man named "Aloysius" who worked at the hospital in Sitka where Father Harry had been a patient. Although only five years old when the mountain exploded, Father Harry had vivid memories of the experience, which he supplemented with information from his elders. His 1956 account follows.

Well, yes, I will write something if you wish me to do so. Yes, I came from the small village which they call Perryville. Must be, oh, I'd say roughly between three and four hundred miles southwest of Kodiak Island. The population is about one hundred twenty-five including all the children.

This village of Perryville was established in 1912 during that Katmai Volcano eruption. There was a saltery in Kafluk [Kaflia] Bay in those days. The man by the name of Foster was on that project and in the spring of the year two small villages combined together to work for Mr. Foster of Kodiak salting red salmon bellies and smoking the back part of the salmon for the commercial use. I have no slightest idea how much production they could have put up each season. To my knowledge they could have put up considerable production because in these days people could almost walk on the salmon. I remember when I was a small boy, how thick the salmon used to be when they come in the river. Believe it or not, many times in many creeks people cannot drink water, due to that smell from the dead fish in the creeks. That's when we should have our boats to fish in, huh? Aloysius, we could have make good pay each season.

Oh, yes, I almost go other way, each spring these two small villages would make another procedure to the same location, Kafluk [Kaflia] Bay, to begin their same routine, for their much needed comfortable living and start seining salmon and then bring their catch in to port. Then start splitting and some men salting ready split and washed salmon, barrel them up ready to be shipped to Kodiak by the small schooner, "Alice" of Mr. Foster. From Kodiak, barrels of salmon were shipped on steamers or sailing ships. This continued for several summers and people of these two small villages Katmai and Douglas making very comfortable living with the small amount of money they gladly made. Everything cost just about 1/32 of what they cost today, in them days we didn't go to our refrigerators and dig out whatever we want, like we are doing today. If family carry flour, sugar, tea, he is rich. There was very poor transportation, then a sail schooner comes up from the states with cargo of grocery supplies for various places in Alaska. Many times it took them two or three months before they could complete their one way voyage due to the unsuitable sailing winds. Boy, that must have been a real hard life, eh?...

In the spring of 1912 people of Katmai and Douglas began their same routine as fishermen and saltery, all peppy and happy as usual. Then one afternoon people start getting into an excited mood. They get real lively. They all start saying "Puyulek, puyulek!" (meaning "volcano, volcano!") and too, others start hollering "Tángaci, tángaci!" (meaning for the people to be supplied up heavily with fresh water before the falling of that volcanic ashes over the land). Then all the people start preparing for the eruption. Quite a number of men climb the hill which is located near their camp, in order to get a better view to watch that upcoming mountain. We boys follow up to see what it would be like during the eruption. There we saw the upswelling mountain, west of the Kafluk Bay, the mountain just came up something compare to a fountain, it's quite difficult to make a definite description concerning this erupting mountain. She must rose up something like a bread dough and flow over on all sides with what they might call a pumice stone, a white looking sponge almost weightless. During this period, people work real fast and put their belongings away into wherever they could find to shelter them from the falling ashes. They turned all the boats upside down to prevent the ashes from falling into them and carried all the water supply they could over store. Most every little containers was filled up with fresh water for drinking and cooking convenience, there absolutely wasn't a single empty container by the time the darkness fall. It must have been between four and five PM when it seem to us the whole world start getting dark. I was little too young to pay too much attention to the time, but you can imagine how late the darkness comes up farther north in the month of June. Just previous to the darkness, pumice stone began to fall, some stones fall just as big as the biggest potato you could possibly imagine. Fortunately, no one was reported getting hit with one of those stones on their head. It was then real pitch black, there was no search or flashlight in them days, it was so dark you could not see palm of your hands one inch in front of your face. There was absolutely no breath of wind from any direction, but people manage to go from house to house by wrapping a seal oil soaked piece of cloth or rag onto the tip of a stick for a torch. It was calm all through forty-eight hours and you could have lighted a candle all through the two nights and two days, that's how long the darkness occurred, according to the old people. Noise? Boy, I will never be among such a noise in my life again. I don't wish to, anyway. I don't mind to be among the domestic noise like inside of the cannery among all that noisy machinery or around the carpenters where they are building projects of any kind. But that kind of noise is somewhat sickening or torturing to human ears, so loud, and unlike any noise made by any creature. The shaking seemed to us victims like the whole world was shaking. Earthquakes! Boy, every few minutes! You couldn't even keep your cup on the table without spilling it, due to the unsteady earth. I have no idea how long the earth was steadily moving. Sometimes when she got so bad, people couldn't even stand on their two feet. This is the truth, all this was accompanied with heat. I

can't say how hot it got that time, no one carry ther-
mometer in them days, but I can tell you it was hot. Every
person was naked but still it was too hot, especially when
that red-hot ashes got over where the people was located,
then it was real hot. (I am just lucky to live this long and
tell you this short story, Aloysius, after all that bad time
I had during the ten thousand smokes.) My mom and
myself had to go outside quite a few times during all that
noise, and see all the lightening [sic] and thunder. Boy, it
seemed to me the world was just ending. I can say I was
not alone thinking the world was ending. Even full-grown
people was plenty scared, not very many people acted
very happy. No, there was no bravery anywhere. I am
really glad that the heat never did increase any more just
another few points higher then otherwise we would have
been all dead ducks for soup or steak, eh, Aloysius?

During all that darkness people just stay and wish
for day to break and made a special short prayer service
to the Most Blessed Virgin, Mother of God and several
hours after that prayer service, at last came dawn. It
stayed that way for a considerable time before it broke
to the broad daylight. The elders of these two villages
began to talk about conference or something, whatever
they called it, and decide how many bidarkis or in other
words we say "kayaks," should be sent to Kodiak with a
letter for the evacuation of people from Kafluk Bay. The
place there was not good for any kind of a creature to
live. The ashes were about three feet on level ground
and on slopes as well. There was no drifts anywhere because of the calm weather. When the day got lighter the
land looked just like in wintertime with a coat of snow,
but that coat looked somewhat darker than the snow
itself. The color of ashes is light gray, the first ashes that
came down was real coarse all mixed with pumice stone
just as big as the biggest potatoes, and some smaller down
to the size of a smallest bead. Then down to a powdered
ashes, just like that of unmixed cement. All kinds of birds
got blind from that ashes and could not fly due to their
blindness. Even the porpoises couldn't go down because
of their noses was stuffed with the fine ashes sinking
while he was swimming under the surface of the water.
Tough, eh, Al? But one thing I'm really glad about is,
this terrible action took place before the salmon started

Katmai villagers in their kayaks.
Kodiak Historical Society

to go up the streams, because they would have been all destroyed by the ashes that would have gotten into their gills, no doubt.

I know I left out some items on my story Aloysius, due to my clumsiness, and lack of experience in telling a story, then too, from lack of education.

But anyway, every word of my story is absolutely true. I have seen all this with my two eyes and this was no dream. So, this is the best picture I can really produce right now regarding that eruption. One problem is still a mystery to me, how all the grass and root-feeding animals really manage to feed and live in that area. Since there wasn't a single grass to be seen on the ground. Someone might as well solve this mystery someday. I know it won't be me. The poor little squirrels had just come out of their long winter's sleep previous to this eruption. Now he was homeless with no store, no food, and seldom any water. All sprouting grass and dead three to four feet under that newly fallen volcanic pumice stone, and powdered ashes.

Now these three kayaks which had departed from Kafluk Bay several days previously were expected back any day. No one knew what rate of speed they had made during their journey to Kodiak for much needed assistance

to evacuate presumably hopeless victims of that terror-
ism. Several days had passed since the three kayaks
departed. Then the people started hollering and all voices
get higher than usual. They were saying that there was a
paragútaq coming, which means in our dialect, "steamer."
Pretty soon they said a kayak was coming from that
steamer. So they land and most all the people go to meet
them on their arrival to the beach. We found out these
newcomers was part of the ones that had gone to Kodiak
several days before. Now they brought in good tidings
and said the steamer out there was to evacuate all the
people.

Now people of these two small villages started packing up all their available belongings that was on hand.
Since the biggest part of their property was back home
at their villages [Katmai and Douglas] which was not
obtainable until later during the summer. Now everything was loaded into the small steamer. All the people
boarded the ship and was ready for their journey to—
"Where?" No one had a definite or slightest idea where
they were bound for. All the houses and cabins were now
abandoned. There wasn't a single occupant in any of the
buildings. People were seeking another life, better maybe,
and new experiences, hoping that it wouldn't be one like
a few days back. During the voyage they learned that
they were heading for Kodiak which they have heard
about all their lives. The mountains behind got smaller
and smaller, beaches were now invisible, all the land they
had lived on happily and peacefully was disappearing
gradually. The first port they came to was the town they
called Afognak, where all the passengers discharged. All
were put ashore where some people was guests in some
homes for time being till the next action take place. The
most portion of the people were placed in the schoolhouse and some in the empty houses. We stayed there
for I have no knowledge how many days people spend in
Afognak before the U.S. Coast Guards picked us up to
prospect for a new village location.

Say, Aloysius, this much I will tell you for now. Sometimes I will tell you more....[4]

Reports from the captains of the United States Revenue Cutter
Service (USRCS) reveal a different perspective. The *Manning*, under

the command of Captain K. W. Perry, had just arrived in Kodiak when the ashfall began. Perry and his crew housed and fed the inhabitants of Kodiak on board the ship and journeyed out of port to help residents of outlying villages. At 8:15 p.m. on June 11, the steamer *Redondo*, impressed into service for the Katmai emergency under the command of Lt. Thompson, arrived at Afognak on one of these missions. By then the Kaflia kayakers had made it to the island and told of their plight. Thompson immediately headed the *Redondo* for Kaflia Bay. On Wednesday, June 12, 1912, at 2:30 a.m., the steamer arrived. Thompson reported,

> [I] found natives destitute, but apparently in normal health, and very badly frightened. Volcanic ashes had buried the village to a depth of three feet on the level, closing all streams and shutting off the local water supply.... The village was comprised of natives from Cape Douglas to Katmai, seismic disturbance having caused them to abandon their usual camps and seek mutual protection at Kaflia Bay.[5]

Thompson apparently did not realize that the people had relocated to Kaflia Bay for the season to work at the saltery, and had not, as he assumed, rushed to the bay for refuge following the eruption.

As soon as he arrived, Thompson took 114 people from Kaflia Bay to Afognak, where they were housed in the vacant schoolhouse, in vacant houses, and with residents. They stayed there until the beginning of July.

Eunice Neseth, a well-known Kodiak basketmaker and local historian, was five years old when her parents, an Afognak creole woman married to a Swedish shopkeeper, helped the refugees. Her memories appeared in Lola Harvey's *Derevnia's Daughters* :

> The strangers that were living in the schoolhouse and in the yard around Orloff's place were unlike other people they had known. Papa said they were from way across Shelikof Strait, from a place called Katmai.... Eunice and Enola [Eunice's sister], though curious, were afraid of them....
> These men and women were dark-skinned with dark slit-eyes and black hair, straight and close-cropped. The

Katmai barabaras covered with ash, 1915.
University of Alaska Anchorage Archives, National Geographic Collection, Box 1, 3946

women wore calico dresses and kerchiefs, which lessened
somewhat their scary appearance to the girls. The men,
however, wore dark hats, and coarse dark-colored suits
with heavy knee-high *turbusii*, the skin boots typically
worn by mainland natives. Both girls had seen some children as they ran past the schoolyard, but they were not
going to stop and ask them to play....

When rescue came, [Ivan] Orloff and his wife, Tania,
let some of the people stay in their barn and *banya* [steam
bath]. Others were sheltered at the schoolhouse. The
revenue cutter left an officer in Afognak to oversee the
distribution of rations of food and gear to the refugees....

Herman [Eunice's father] told his family that he had
made arrangements for the Katmai men to carve a number of the crochet hooks [of ivory] and some miniature
skin *bidarkas*, with carved men, to sell in the store. He
thought the work would be a good occupation for the
men, and, of course, he hoped to sell all the items they
could produce.[6]

It was obvious that the Katmai and Douglas Alutiiqs could not
return to their old homes. USRCS vessels made two trips to the two
villages so the residents could retrieve as many belongings as possible, and government officials began considering possible new village
sites. Captain Reynolds, commander of the Bering Sea Fleet and of
the ship *Tahoma*, decided to move the people down the coast beyond Chignik. In a dispatch sent from the *Tahoma* on June 24, 1912,
he wrote,

Recommend the ninety-eight mainland natives now des-
titute and depending on Government aid be located
immediately peninsula westward of Chignik, probably
Stepovak [a bay southwest of Ivanof Bay]. Good summer fishing. Winter trapping and hunting. Should be
moved by July 10th to insure winter supply fish.... soon
self supporting.... Probable cost [of building material] one
thousand dollars.... Agent acquainted with natives possibly Bureau Education should be sent to compel fishing,
building, etc., and handle rations....[7]

Reynold's belief that the people would not fish for their winter supplies without being compelled to do so by a government agent contrasts with Father Harry Kaiakokonok's description of the industrious workers at Kaflia Bay.

The *Tahoma* carried five Katmai and Douglas Alutiiqs with Father Aleksandr Petelin as interpreter on its reconnaissance trip to the area. Captain Perry of the cutter *Manning* followed with the rest of the refugees. Alutiiq elders at first chose Ivanof Bay as the site for the new village. Father Harry recalled in an interview,

> I don't know where we were going, but the people had the Coast Guards give the people quite a long notice for them to make decisions which way they wanted to go. Southwestward or eastward from Kodiak. The people don't know which way to go, which way would be better for them for living; and a lot of people wanted to go further southeast; and some people wanted to go the west. And one lady was so anxious, and she been telling people even when she's got no business, "We go to the west, west,—westward!" Oh! And then her husband, tempting the chief of Katmai, make people go westward and the lady, his wife, advise him to beg him to go westward. Okay, they decide.[8]

In the protected harbor of Ivanof Bay the people set up tents. They began to seine for fish using a net given them by one of the canneries and started to dry fish for the winter, but they soon learned that there were already two Norwegian trappers living at the bay. These men told the people that Ivanof Bay was not a good place for a village, for snowslides occurred, ice formed in the bay in the winter, and land animals were scarce. Father Harry said,

> Oh, the people get excited. "We not going to select this kind of place where we can't go in and out."...The people didn't know any better that they were further down south than where they used to be up here in Katmai and Douglas. Right away the people have a meeting and then they go out and look for location for village. And they selected Perryville, here where we are today. And these two Norwegians, they...fooled the marshal escorting the people.... They all believe it.[9]

George Kosbruk angrily remembered that the Norwegian trappers lied to them, that in fact Ivanoff Bay would have been a prime location for the village. In an interview he said, "That guy, the guy called bullshit. The winter time you got snow right down to the water." [Interviewer's question: "This is what the guy told you?"] "Yeah. And never. Never snow right down there!"[10]

Meanwhile, the residents of Afognak and Kodiak Islands were interested to learn that the mainlanders had found a new village. *The Orphanage Newsletter*, published by the Baptist orphanage on Woody Island, printed an article about the founding of the new village.

> The people of Katmai village..., about one hundred in all, have been taken by the *SS Manning* to Ivanof Bay...where the Government has set them up in housekeeping, furnishing them everything from houses to dories and a seine....
>
> For once in their lives, at least, the people of the new village were thoroughly clean, and with complete new outfits, have a clean start in life.... Taking everything into consideration the people of Katmai are in far better circumstances now than they were before the eruption, and they, at least, have reason to be thankful for the disaster.[11]

As this article shows, the missionaries neither understood nor empathized with the Alutiiqs who had suffered through a terrible ordeal and lost their homes. Instead, they promoted the standard anti-Russian and racist attitudes toward Natives that continued to plague Alutiiqs for the rest of the century.

The 1913 Annual Report of the USRCS tells of moving the village from Ivanof Bay north. In early July the USRCS had left the villagers at Ivanof Bay. On August 1 when the *Manning* returned to check on them, the captain was told that the people wanted to move. Captain Perry agreed and loaded the villagers and their few belongings onto the cutter and took them north to the present site of Perryville. At the new location, the people found a recently abandoned barabara which was dry inside, saw many animal tracks, and were told by a local trapper that the weather was good and fish were plentiful.

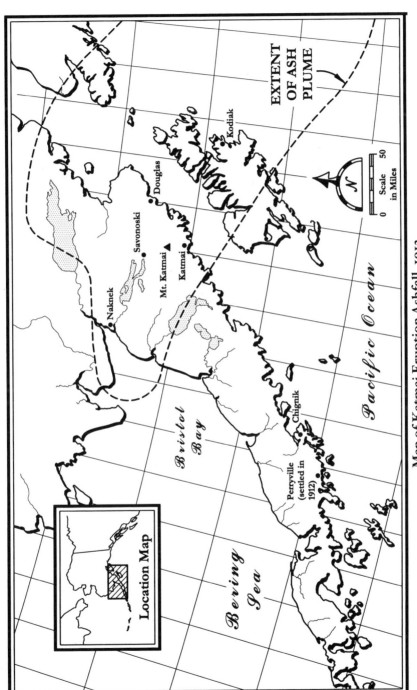

Map of Katmai Eruption Ashfall, 1912

EXTENT
OF ASH
PLUME

Kodiak

Douglas

Savonoski

Mt. Katmai ▲
Katmai

Naknek

Pacific Ocean

N

0   Scale   50
     in Miles

Chignik

Perryville
(settled in
1912)

Bristol
Bay

Bering
Sea

Location Map

USRCS cutters checked on the community now and then during the following summers. In 1913, a year after the relocation, the USRCS Cutter *Unalga* reported that all was well in the village except that there was no church and no bell. The following month the steamer *Yukon* was wrecked on Unimak Island and the captain of the steamer promised its bell to the villagers. The bell was delivered in 1914. Captain Crisp of the *Tahoma* reported,

> I never before saw natives show so much appreciation and before I left the chief gave thanks again for the bell (he can speak a little English), but at the same time he wanted to know when we would bring lumber for a church.[12]

And so the village stayed at the present site of Perryville. However, several villagers soon built winter trapping cabins at Ivanof Bay because land mammals were actually more abundant there than at Perryville. Eventually, in 1965, a permanent village was established at Ivanof Bay.

POST-ERUPTION SETTLEMENTS

Not all former Katmai residents moved to Perryville. Some, like former Katmai chief Nikolai Kalmakoff and his family, resettled in Kanatak, which was to become an important supply base for the northern part of the peninsula and the terminus of an oft-traveled portage to the Bristol Bay community of Egegik. Shortly after the eruption, Kalmakoff returned to Katmai briefly to rescue the icons from the church. His granddaughter Doris Lind recalled his story of the journey; the following account is paraphrased from field notes:

> Nikolai Kalmakoff walked alone all the way from Kanatak to Katmai in February or March, in his *nalugatat*, or knee-high oiled boots. By the time he got to Katmai the heels of his boots had holes in them and he had to tiptoe across the creek to keep from getting his feet wet. He got the icons from the church at Katmai and carried them to the church at Kanatak. Doris remembers one in particular which was a very beautiful icon of the Last Supper on Good Friday.[13]

Katmai chapel after the eruption.
University of Alaska Anchorage Archives, National Geographic Collection, Box 1, 3635

While Alutiiqs from the Pacific coast were relocating to Perryville and other villages south of Katmai, the inhabitants of Savonoski, whose community was completely buried by ash, were also faced with the task of finding a new home. Although all but one family, which remained at Savonoski to fish and hunt ducks,[14] were at Naknek or South Naknek fishing or working for one of the canneries at the time of the eruption, the people learned from American Pete, Savonoski's chief, that their homes had been destroyed. When the eruption occurred, American Pete had been retrieving hunting equipment at what Robert Griggs of the National Geographic Society called "a sort of hunting lodge" for the Savonoski Natives and identified as "Ukak" (actually, the settlement of Ikak). The following statement, attributed to the chief, appeared in a 1921 edition of the *National Geographic*:

> The Katmai mountain blew up with lots of fire, and fire came down trail from Katmai with lots of smoke. Me go fast Savonoski. Everybody get in bidarka [kayak]. Helluva job. We come Naknek one day, dark, no could see. Hot ash fall. Work like hell. Now I go back every year one month, maybe, after fish all dry, and kill bear.[15]

Savonski after the eruption.
University of Alaska Anchorage Archives, National Geographic Collection, Box 4, 3675

Unable to live in their old village, Savonoski people built a new one a few miles upriver from the cannery town of South Naknek, on the southern shore of Naknek River. Dubbed New Savonoski, the village soon boasted a Russian Orthodox church and, within seven years, a large graveyard filled with local victims of the world-wide influenza epidemic. American Pete's widow Pelegia Melgenak and her second husband, One-Armed Nick Melgenak, were the village's mainstays for many years, taking in foster children and seeing to the upkeep of the church. New Savonoski residents continued to use fishing and trapping camps on Naknek Lake near the site of the abandoned village of Savonoski. In the 1950s people began leaving the village for South Naknek so their children could attend school. The settlement was finally completely abandoned in the 1970s.[16]

NOTES

1. By August 1912 National Geographic Society geologists had visited the devastated region. The publicity they gave the eruption captured the national imagination. With great public support, Katmai National Monument was formed.

2. Sanook 1968.

3. Kosbruk 1976.

4. Kaiakokonok 1956.

5. USRCS AR 1912: 125.

6. Harvey 1991: 110–1.

7. USRCS Archives 671, Roll 16.

8. Kaiakokonok 1975.

9. Kaiakokonok 1975.

10. Kosbruk 1975.

11. Quoted in Harvey 1991: 114.

12. USRCS AR 1915.

13. Partnow field notes.

14. Davis recording transcripts 1961:17.

15. Griggs 1921: 225–226.

16. Hodgdon 1981.

6
THE AMERICAN PERIOD, 1912 TO THE END OF WORLD WAR II

Although Alaska had been an American territory for nearly fifty years when Novarupta Volcano erupted, Alaska Peninsula Alutiiqs only became truly Americanized after, and largely as a result of, that event. This chapter explores a period of intense culture change from that time to the end of World War II, which elders consider the beginning of the modern era. The process has accelerated tremendously from the 1950s to the present; in fact, changes in recent decades are so extensive that they deserve separate treatment and are mentioned here only in a postscript.

During the forty-year period immediately before the war, profound changes took place in the region's social structure, population dynamics, economy, education, and belief systems. And the human sphere was not the only one to change: the natural landscape, subject to both cyclic fluctuation and instantaneous upheaval, altered as well. Both kinds of change required that the Alutiiqs continually adjust and adapt.

SOCIAL STRUCTURE

By 1912 the fur trade as formerly practiced was all but dead. The people of the region had been firmly in the grip of the worldwide economy for more than a hundred years under the Russians, and under the Americans had entered into an even greater dependence on cash for food staples and other basic needs. Yet even as they found it impossible to survive without money, they learned that opportunities for earning that money had become more and more scarce. The family rather than the village was becoming the basic economic unit as people traveled far afield searching for jobs. This trend was strengthened by the increasing immigration and in-marriage of Scandinavian fishermen in the region. As noted earlier, with only half the number of extended family members in the picture—since only the mother's family was geographically close—these Scandinavian-Aleut families had fewer and weaker kinship obligations than did their Alutiiq cousins. Their lives revolved around economic pursuits especially suited to the nuclear family. In fact, many first-generation Scandinavian-Aleuts on the peninsula lived away from the villages for months at a time, reestablishing kinship ties periodically but infrequently. Relationships within extended families remained intense, but were escapable in a way not possible in the past. Creole and Alutiiq families also followed this new model of family integration to varying degrees after the eruption.[1]

By World War II, the racism that permeated America had taken its toll on those who were termed "half-breeds," including some Scandinavian-Aleuts. Although many became recognized community leaders, benefiting from their fathers' educational levels and ties with the financially powerful, others did not fare so well. Laura Buchan, a white woman who taught at Pilot Point during the 1940s, wrote,

> The children of mixed marriages, torn by the two cultures, bore marks of the social conflict. They were alert at learning and intrigued by the world Outside [of Alaska], having listened to their father's adventures. But in miserable uncertainty they questioned native traditions and tried to forget their mother's tongue. Loving both their parents, they were hurt by their half-blood status and their need to make a choice at home between contrasting standards.[2]

Buchan observed the seeds of self-hatred, insecurity, and anger at a world that arbitrarily labeled people and deprived them of an innate sense of personal dignity. Sadly, the story repeated itself throughout the peninsula from early in the 1900s through mid-century. I was told many stories of emotional brutality suffered by Alutiiqs at the hands of non-Natives in authority. Racism has left a legacy that continues to damage both individual and community.

Yet for a time the old system of village chieftainship continued in place, particularly in villages that were homogeneously Alutiiq. The village chief or *tuyuq* conferred with his second chief (called the *zakashchik*) and other adult men who formed a village council that made decisions affecting the entire village. Such decisions included where to locate a new townsite for Katmai survivors, what supplies were needed to see the village through the coming winter, and who would perform the work necessary to build a new church or community center. The chief and his council also controlled decisions that would today be considered private matters. For instance, they were responsible for ensuring that all children were well cared for and educated. At one point the Perryville chief and his council decided that a particular widow should be married to an old bachelor. Although the woman had no interest in the marriage, she was forced into it. People were still identified by their village of birth and expected to behave according to the interests of the village rather than their own desires.

One such *tuyuq* continues to be described in oral tradition. At the time of the Katmai eruption, Simeon Takak was the chief of Katmai; with the move to Perryville he became the first chief in that village. Ignatius Kosbruk described the leadership characteristics of both Simeon and his wife Anna, establishing through his narrative a model for past and future community leaders. In the following translation, Alutiiq portions were translated by Ralph Phillips of Perryville.

> I'm gonna talk about—we used to call him "chief." He was from Katmai. Before the eruption of the volcano and here he was chief. Then when the explosion happened he became chief here in Perryville. And they were brought up over by *Manning*. Government boat, I think it was.

So he became chief here in our village. At Perryville. And people respected the chief here. People feared and respected them. He wasn't big like me!

I also knew the chief's wife. People respected people in the past. They listened to each other. Also people helped do what had to be done. The council told them what to do, they did it all together. They finished what they undertook to complete. People used to be happy, I know, when I was a child. Both of us, my wife and I, [knew] people were happy. They helped each other together, before there were gas boats. People used to live well.

That chief was called Simeon. He was married to Anna. They had the same namedays, same month, same day, Simeon and Anna. All the people liked the two of them. And they had lots of respect for them two old couples. They were still together when they came here from Katmai. That's how they used to live for many years, that one being chief. People used to be happy, used to listen to one another, to what had to be done.

That's what those people's council used to do. Simeon was a leader here in Perryville. There were lots of children, lots of children. But during the measles epidemic [in the 1930s] they all died— during that tuberculosis and measles. That's what we knew when we were children. I'm saying on tape how he lived, according to my knowledge.

Simeon used to take care of many children and adults too, all together here when Perryville first became a village. All of them went to eat, they called all the people to eat at holidays. At Christmas, at starring, he was the last in the village to go starring. He took the people along, fed them all. They used to be happy, as far as I am aware. Three stars went out looking for the place where Jesus was born. They went looking for him; they don't do it any more. They went looking for him, but now they don't do it. People used to be happy, knowing them [Simeon and Anna], I remember.

They listened and lived according to their religion. The whole village went to church, filling it up, over there on that little hill [where the school is now].

Then when he died, people changed their way of living a lot. All the people think about him, remember that former chief.

When they were living, the Coast Guard used to come in the spring. [The people] were hungry, they lived here and didn't have anything. There was nothing sweet at all. Tea, sugar, flour were hard to find. They went to Chignik in the fall by kayak; the only store was at Chignik, Alaska Packers. They went to that store with the little money they had, by kayak, going by Dorner Bay. They portaged on their head halfway to the store, then they came home. At Christmastime they would buy groceries. When they got back the chief divided [the groceries] up among the people, and gave them away, whatever they had, whatever they bought. Flour, sugar, tea, milk, they packed on their backs to Dorner Bay. When they got to Dorner Bay they went out, then headed back, arriving at home. People used to be happy and used to help each other.

Then, as far as I remember in 1936 after his death, I don't remember which year he died, I don't know. As far as I remember they died from tuberculosis, both of them.

Then a different chief of the council became leader, still called *tuyuq*. He took over after that and then in the spring the Coast Guard came here. The Coast Guard give people of the village here some things: a hundred pounds flour and sugar, bring 'em right up to his place. Then he was with the council, and they divided up those goods, the flour, sugar, and tea. Coast Guard would bring them in.

Then they divided to the kids, there being lots of them, giving them flour, sugar to the people. That's how people used to live before, how they lived when they didn't have much, before they had a store.[3]

As this narrative illustrates, the shift from communal to individual orientation was gradual and piecemeal on the peninsula. In fact individualism was most common in activities undertaken away from the village. Men, women, or families might travel to Chignik, Egegik, or Port Moller to work for fish processing plants during the summer, or a man and his partner might spend weeks on their trapline. But when they returned to the village they re-entered a close-knit and inclusive social structure based on a combination of precontact and Russian-era practices. This pattern of seasonal contraction and expansion continues today, as families eagerly await the freedom and relative solitude of fish camps each summer, then return to group activities each fall.

POPULATION DYNAMICS

Population Increase

The major demographic fact of the twentieth century on the Alaska Peninsula has been a dramatic increase in the numbers of non-Native immigrants who have come to the area to take advantage of the region's natural resources. In the early years of the century, many were late arrivals of the tail end of the Gold Rush, but this group was soon overshadowed by the thousands who sought wealth in the commercial fishing that was opening up throughout western Alaska.

Many of these immigrants saw the Alutiiqs as savages, childlike, or, at best, backward and ignorant. As mentioned above, they considered the creoles or "half-breeds"—whom the Alutiiqs called "Russians"—to be nearly as bad as they did the Alutiiqs. But how did the Alutiiqs and creoles view the newcomers?

Oral tradition divides the newcomers into three categories: bosses, transients, and potential permanent residents. The bosses included nonresident cannery owners and managers, fur buyers, doctors, some priests (depending on ethnicity and personality—many creole or Russian priests were seen not as bosses but as mediators who eased interaction with the authorities), teachers, and store owners. Most in this category were Caucasian English-speaking Protestants who did not attempt to fit into local Native life, but instead to varying degrees demanded that Natives and creoles adapt to their ways. The stories told about the bosses express an interesting irony: they had economic power, but were culturally stupid. One such story is told by Walter Stepanoff, Sr., of Chignik Bay. In the typical "boss" story, the Alutiiq storyteller comes out on top.

Talking about the old *Star*, every time I think of something. I was just young. It used to stop in and they had a purser, he used to take care of the little place there, where they had candy and stuff for sale. And I had 50 cents, and so I waited when the *Star* came in. A lot of people, locals that stayed here, went aboard.

And I went, and the purser was in there busy so I bought 50 cents' worth of candy, ten bars I think. I got it and in the meantime one guy from here and another guy, they were arguing about something. They got in with the purser, I don't know what it was over. Probably it was over some freight or something.

And the purser had all this change in this cigar box, and they were arguing and I was just young and I stopped and I was listening. I probably stopped with my mouth open, probably watching them. And they were arguing, and the purser he was kind of tall and he looked over and he saw me still standing there. He dug in the box, threw 50 cents up and I took it and I left. I guess he thought I was waiting for my change. I got my 50 cents back and I took off.

I get a kick out of that when I think about it.[4]

Walter's uncle Spiridon Stepanoff was even more direct about the newcomers' lack of common sense. Some wealthy Caucasians had decided to travel by canoe from Nushagak down the Bristol Bay shore of the peninsula to Port Heiden and Unangashik. They were then planning to cross the peninsula by way of Black and Chignik lakes and paddle down the Chignik River to Chignik Lagoon. Once there they intended to buy a gas boat for the trip across Shelikof Strait to Kodiak.

They never made it. I don't see why they traveling in that little canoe up in Bristol Bay. Come from, I don't know, from Nushagak or somewheres. They come all the way down. That little canoe. Three men.

They knowed it, you know. They wired down they was coming here. The canneries down there, they know they was coming. They wire down.

I was gonna buy gas boat, a little gas boat from superintendent, you know, big skiff. But they need it; I try to buy it. And all he says, "Can't sell that," he says, "because millionaires coming down through the lake to here." Says, "This boat, they gonna take that boat, skiff, from here to go back to Seattle along the coast. Once these fellas get here."

I said, "They're crazy to use that boat; too small!" But when he was there, you know, and it started to blow. That week, same week, and they started to blow, even the hurricane, northwest, you know. And that's the time they drownded up here....

And when it calmed 'em, they find 'em up here. The superintendent in Anchorage Bay [the location of the town of Chignik Bay], he told me, they get wire from 'em, you know. They was coming. He was saving that skiff for them fellas. They was prospecting oil.[5]

The second category of immigrants to the Alaska Peninsula, the transients, included, most notably, Asian cannery workers. Spiridon Stepanoff's recollection of the treatment of the Chinese workers is reproduced in the preceding chapter. In the following transcript, a continuation of that account, SS refers to Spiridon Stepanoff, DK to the interviewer, Don Kinsey.

DK: What'd they do, bring all those Chinese up on a boat?

SS: They had a big sailing ship, you know. They come up in a sailing ship, and bring their whole outfit. And then the ships stay up here all summer. When they get through, they load it up, and everybody goes into the same ship, go down again, load and all.

DK: They take them all back then?

SS: Yeah. Till the next year. Now they come up in the steamers. Steamers used to bring 'em up. And then the steamers wait till the fall, take them out with them again....

Mealtime, Chinamens come up, you know, and have a little bowl, with the two sticks [chopsticks]. He goes into the cook.

Cookhouse open, outside, you know. They go, hand his plate in there, they go in the pot, you know, rice put it, fill it up, rice, that's all. Go out, they eat with the two sticks, you know, in their mouth, drink their water, and wash his cups, and goes and he put it back in his room.[6]

When the schooners and steamboats traveled to Chignik each summer with the cannery workers, they also carried live pigs, sheep, goats, and cows to use as food during the summer. August Pedersen remembered selling bear feet and bear gall to Chinese cannery workers in exchange for leftover food at the end of the summer. In this transcript, AP refers to August Pedersen, LS to Alaska Department of Fish and Game interviewer Lisa Scarbrough.

LS: Did you used to bear hunt?

AP: Yeah. My old man used to cure the skins. Fix them all, stretch them all, and he'd give 'em to some friends.

LS: What was your dad's name?

AP: Pete Pedersen, Marius "Pete" Pedersen. He used to give the Chinamen the feet and the gall. They used it for medicines, and in the fall, they would be pretty decent, them years, you packed live animals. Pigs. They'd give you a pig, a live pig. Maybe old canned salmon. They'd give you them "dents" they called it, 10, 15 cases, though, and maybe a couple hundred pounds of rice. They had all them bags from China. That made a big help, you know, for a family of our size, so every year we would get 'em three or four bears, cut the feet and the gall off....

They just wanted the feet for eat. They don't spoil, the damn feet stand all winter like that and they don't spoil. It's that gristle. But that gall, they brought it to China, they said that was used for medicine.[7]

Mike Sam remembered the international food choices the Asian workers and other immigrants made possible:

When we were young, mess hall you had two choices. Chinese mess hall or American mess hall. Kids, in the morning after breakfast, [would] go down with a can, you know, gallon cans. Leftovers, they give you to take home. All summer a woman didn't have to cook if you don't want to cook. Because noontime, they go down. Dinnertime, go down.

We used to switch, you know. But Americans usually dump all different kinds in one can. Chinese and Filipinos just separate, you know, put in same can but they put that paper inside.

And then they'd pull 'em out. They were all good, good food. What we don't eat we give to the dogs, dogteam.

For Chinese [they] had Chinese cook, Filipinos had a Filipino cook, Mexicans had their own cook. Same mess hall, three [cooks].[8]

Another group of transients, Caucasian fishermen, continue to exert a major influence on the economy and society of the Alaska Peninsula. In fact, seasonal immigration rates had reached unforeseen levels by 1970. During the preceding decade, the numbers of out-of-state fishermen had almost tripled, from 300 in 1960 to more than 800 in 1970.[9] Summer populations in the Bristol Bay fishing communities of Naknek, Egegik, and Pilot Point, and the Pacific center at Chignik, are also swollen by the return of Alaskan fishers who spend their winters in Anchorage or other urban centers. The passage of the Limited Entry Act by the Alaska State Legislature in 1973 slowed the increase in out-of-state fishers, who by 1976 leveled out at about 22 percent of Alaska commercial fishing permit holders.[10] In the Bristol Bay fishery, these seasonal residents harvest herring and salmon during the summer, then return to their homes in the Lower 48 or other parts of Alaska in the winter.

The third category of immigrants, those who were potential permanent residents, included other fishermen and trappers, many of whom were Scandinavians, as discussed in the preceding chapter. A number of men in this category married local women and stayed on the peninsula where they raised families.[11]

Villages

During the twentieth century, as in the past, villages were deserted and sprang up as economic opportunities came and went. Kuyuyukak was abandoned sometime in the 1920s. Polly Shangin recalled that what remained of the Kuyuyukak population moved to Kanatak with her when she married her first husband. Ralph Phillips translated the description Polly gave of her early life at Kuyuyukak:

Polly's mother Periscovia was from Port Heiden. She died when Polly was an infant. Polly herself is not sure where she was born, whether in Meshik [Mashiq] or Kuyuyukak. [She was born in about 1910.] She came to her senses in [i.e., her first memories are about] Kuyuyukak, a small village on the coast between Chignik and Kanatak. Only four families lived there the whole time she was there.

From Kuyuyukak they used to portage through Aniakchak Pass and go down to Meshik in kayaks, and spend the summer there doing whatever jobs they could get. Then in the fall they'd go back the same route, through creeks, to the river, then they'd portage and carry kayaks, go through a lake, and through Aniakchak Pass. The last lake they came to was a lake near the ocean. From there they'd go by kayak along the shore to Kuyuyukak.

Sometimes people from Kanatak came to Kuyuyukak in kayaks. Kanatak people invited them to visit and the Kuyuyukak people would travel in their own kayaks. At that time, there was no school in either Kuyuyukak or Kanatak.

The last time they visited Kanatak, a marriage was arranged for Polly. She was about fourteen. When she married a man from Kanatak, the whole village of Kuyuyukak decided to settle in Kanatak too.

After Polly got married, they used to portage to Becharof Lake, then down to Egegik. When Kanatak people stayed on Becharof Lake on the way to Egegik, they stayed in a little bay called "Mehátuq." Further on, at the rapids in the Egegik River, the husbands would drop the women off at the side of the river and let them hike past the rapids, while the men took the boats through. Then they'd pick their wives up at the other side of the rapids. From Egegik they portaged back to Kanatak and spent the winter there.[12]

Chignik Lagoon elders remember hearing that there was a terrible epidemic that killed most of the people in Chiginagak Bay where Kuyuyukak was located. Julius Anderson and Clements Grunert of Chignik Lagoon explained to BIA anthropologists in 1991 that along the eastern shore of Cape Kuyukak there was an old Native village—perhaps Polly Shangin's Kuyuyukak—that had been occupied before their time. Known by Clements and Julius as "Chiginaga," it was located on a small stream opposite a series of offshore reefs and islets. The largest island was called "Bird Island." Pink salmon spawned in the stream, providing a regular food supply. There had been a church which burned down. Only the altar stood when Julius last saw it.

Mike Sam remembers seeing the ruins of what is probably the same village in Chiginagak Bay:

MS: Chiginagak, used to be a village there in fact. On the right-hand side when you go in, you'll see a little kind of a rocky point, you know, not very wide and a big beach there, big beach on one side of it. And the back, that's full of alders there. Everything is down. They say, my grandpa [Innokenty Kalmakoff] used to tell me there used to be a big village there, he used to live there many years ago,...in the village, Chiginaga. I remember that now....

I wasn't even born yet when my grandpa lived there when he was a young fella. In fact my grandpa told me he got married right in this place, Chiginaga Village, you know, years ago.[13]

August (Skinnix) Pedersen remembered the epidemic that was said to have killed almost everyone in the village. In the following transcript, AP refers to August Pedersen and OS to Chignik Lagoon resident Olga Sam, wife of Mike Sam and friend of Pedersen's.

Egegik children, 1917, in front of a sod barabara.
MSCUA, University of Washington, Cobb Collection 4175

AP: There were villages all along. There was one there by Chiginagak, only two guys got out of it. Annie Benson, do you remember her? Annie Benson?

OS: Oh yeah.

AP: Her father, Lowell, Frank Lowell, he had a trading post there [nearby Port Wrangel?]. And then the whole village caught measles or something, you know, they had bad habits them years. You'd go bad (unclear) they all died of pneumonia, only two people. They set fire to the village and two of them walked in. That's only two lived.[14]

Mitrofania was also abandoned, though not because of an epidemic. Originally established as a sea otter hunting camp, the village was inconveniently located to take advantage of commercial fishing. Supply ships bypassed the village. There was no work in Mitrofania Bay. Spiridon Stepanoff's family moved to Chignik in 1919 to work in the canneries. Soon other families followed. The Phillips family moved to nearby Perryville, and other families moved to what is now called "the Old Village" at Chignik Lagoon.

Once a thriving community with its own church and large cemetery, the Old Village at the lagoon was abandoned in the 1920s after the worldwide influenza pandemic killed most of the inhabitants. Innokenty Kalmakoff, grandfather of Mike Sam and father of Artemie Kalmakoff, was the last person to move away from the village.

Kanatak became a boom town in 1922 during a flurry of oil exploration when it

> was changed in a short time from a settlement of from 10 to 15 whites to a boom town with tents, cabins, and frame buildings numbering a hundred or more and with a population of 150 to 200, which has been augmented by still others arriving on every boat.[15]

The town remained an important supply site for other small communities on the Pacific coast of the peninsula until the 1930s. By

Kanatak, 1922.
*Seiffert Collection, 85–122–830, Archives and Manuscripts, Alaska and Polar Regions
Department, University of Alaska Fairbanks*

then most of its inhabitants were Alutiiqs who used the village as a
base for winter trapping, then traveled across a low mountain pass
to Becharof Lake, down Egegik River including a stretch that contained
dangerous rapids, and into Egegik, where they worked summers at one
of its two canneries or the saltery. Although the portage was not
used to transport commercial loads of canned salmon or equipment,
government engineers planned to transform it into the route by which
the autumn loads of salt salmon could be carried to ships docking at
Kanatak on their way to Seward and points south. The portage was
already essential to the bicoastal people of Kanatak who transported
supplies to traplines each winter and moved household goods back
and forth across the peninsula each spring and fall at the beginning
and end of the commercial fishing season. For these reasons the Army
Corps of Engineers sought and obtained permission to blast the rocks
from the Egegik Rapids to make travel safer for Kanatak residents.
The requesting report explained,

> The traffic consists principally of the local inhabitants
> moving in the spring from the Pacific side of the penin-
> sula to the Bristol Bay side for the fishing and canning

season and their return in the fall. The natives move all their possessions with them on each move. In addition to the local inhabitants there are about 200 transients who make use of this route, as it decreases the time to make the trip from Kanatak to Bristol Bay by 6 days over the time required by ship around the peninsula.[16]

Kanatak was the site of a 1937 murder investigation initiated by residents who suspected that a freezing death was actually the result of foul play. Called to investigate the case, Commander Ricketts of the U.S. Coast Guard described the village as follows:

> When we arrived at Kanatak we found it a tiny, bare, windswept village. The roof of the principal building, a general store, was held down by an array of heavy steel cables. They were designed to keep the fierce winds through the mountain passes from blowing the whole building away.
>
> The hundred or so local inhabitants lived in small wooden houses near the store.... A small stream flowed through a gravelly lagoon. Some distance away there was a spot where small boats could be somewhat sheltered from storms.[17]

Family at Kanatak, 1920s.
Anchorage Museum of History and Art B64.1.354

Chignik Fourth of July, 1937.
  Alaska State Library, Childs Collection, PCA 37–4

Perryville Bears baseball team. The Bears regularly played the Coast Guard team whenever it moored at Perryville.
   Photo courtesy Alaska State Library; Melville Collection

Kanatak's population increased during the late 1930s and 1940s during a period of renewed oil exploration, but the village was abandoned in the mid-1950s when drilling activity ceased.[18]

Other villages were also abandoned. On the Bering Sea shore, Ilnik, home of Harry Aleck and his family, and Bear River, birthplace of Dora Andre, disappeared in the 1940s.

The Chignik area became and has remained the economic center for peninsula Alutiiqs on the Pacific coast, while Naknek and, later, King Salmon, served similar functions for Bristol Bay residents. Not only did Chignik boast a summer school, canneries, shipping docks, a post office, and stores, but people could also find entertainment. Christine Martin remembers watching movies inside a cannery building at Chignik Lagoon. When she was young, Father Hubbard, known as the Flying Priest, occasionally flew his plane into Chignik on his way to explore the Aniakchak caldera. Christine recalled,

Oh, Father Hubbard. I remember that one plane would come around and my aunty [Dora Lind Andre] or my dad would say,

"Look, there's a plane." And they would say, "Oh, that's Father Hubbard." We didn't know who Father Hubbard was, we just see that plane flying around.

And pretty soon, I think it must have been Father Hubbard showed a movie, a Bible movie, 'cause they said he was Father Hubbard. It was a good movie. All about Jesus, from Adam and Eve, New Testament....

That one time I remember, they had a movie across the lagoon. There used to be a big cannery there. I remember, they took us there. And we went to this big building, lot of people in there, watching a silent movie. It was a clean, nice movie. Like a joking one.[19]

Movies were popular in Perryville as well. Elia Yagie ran a movie house, specializing in cowboy and Indian movies, which were local favorites.

ECONOMY

Subsistence and the Continuation of Tradition

By the fall of 1912 the large fur companies had closed their posts on the peninsula, the Kaflia Bay saltery was destroyed, Katmai survivors were living in new and unfamiliar areas, and few Alutiiqs were part of the fishing industry in the Chignik area. Most people continued to feed, clothe, and shelter themselves much as their ancestors had done by hunting and trapping animals and gathering plants. In the early 1920s Polly Shangin, later of Perryville, was a young girl growing up in the tiny village of Kuyuyukak, northeast of Chignik Bay. Polly Yagie and Ralph Phillips translated Shangin's account of squirrel trapping.

Polly used to follow her sister and go trapping all day for squirrels when they first came out. All day they'd sit by their traps watching them. And when they got a squirrel they'd kill it and put the trap back in again. That way they'd have skins and meat. They never used to waste anything. They'd skin that night and put meat separate, stretch the skin and dry it out and make coats out of them.[20]

The residents of the new village of Perryville learned about their territory by personal exploration, but also from the more seasoned inhabitants of the area, the creoles from Mitrofania and the *tayawut* from Unga Island. In time there were a number of intermarriages between these people, so that many of today's Perryvillers can claim ancestry from the Aleutian Islands, Kodiak, and Russia, as well as Katmai and Douglas.

Elia Phillips's parents moved to Perryville from Mitrofania in the 1920s. Although they were known as "Russians" by other Perryvillers, Elia's family lived off the sea and land like their neighbors. Elia remembered hunting sea lions off nearby Spitz Island when he was a young man.

> But we used to go out and get 'em, yes, I used to be with them. We used to go out in power dories in springtime or fall. We'd go out to Spitz Island out there. Have to go way out there, you know. You see that island out there, and we're lying next to it. We used to go in that and get a load of sea lions for the whole village. Maybe two or three dories would go out. And come home, everything's all cleaned up, [unload the] dories, dump 'em over, everything, the flippers are taken care of. We come ashore, just come up and give 'em out to everybody.

> Spitz Island [is] that little island way out there. You see them way out there. I think it's called Spitz Island. That's the one with a lot of 'em [sea lions] out there....

> It's a rookery. There's a table rock, like a table, right next, on the west side of it. You could see it when it's clear. That's where all the sea lions used to be on top of that.

> Anyone who was interested [would] go out there. We used to go out in bunches, you know, so if somebody break down, they'd take care of each other. That's how our old people taught us....

> I went down there four, five, six times, maybe, long time ago. That's the only place we learn from, is from our elders.

[It was] mostly .30-30s they had then. Then those big rifles came out, like .30'06 or .270, .243. But mostly Winchesters, they used to call them, .30-30s. Winchester rifles. They're still in use.

We just go right up to [the sea lions on the table rock]. With the dories, you know, they're above us there and they start jumping all over the place, they come out right next to you, growling, they're hollering, or something. They're noisy!

[We'd pick a] smaller animal. They used to get the smaller ones. They won't touch the big ones. That'd be waste. Any animal that I know of, the one they go for most is the smallest one, you know. Not a cub or anything like that, but smaller animal, you know. The large, they're just like—I don't know what you call it—can't chew on 'em. Like rubber.

They used to go out in the springtime mostly. It would have been too tough for 'em to go out there in the winter anyway. With the equipment they had, you know. Dories. Take a long time. Mostly springtime they used to go out there.

Soon as they shoot 'em they pick 'em up. They've fallen into the water. They wait until they're in the water, you know. They wouldn't shoot 'em up on the rocks, there's too many of 'em there.

Just go right up to 'em after they've been shot, they float, some of them float, some of them sink right now. And they put them right into the dories. Pull 'em right in the dories. What they can't put into the dories they tow up to the beach and then cut it up and put it into 'em.[21]

Mike Sam also described the hunting "those Perryville guys" used to undertake off Spitz Island. He remembered, "They [sea lions] used to go round and round. You get those sea lions going, they jump, you know. They just keep jumping, jumping. You get a couple of 'em, then hook 'em, take 'em home."

In the new village of Perryville the people continued to live by traditional beliefs about respect for animals and generosity to others. Ignatius Kosbruk told a story about Ivan Ozuwan, nicknamed Wánkánguaq (literally, "Little Ivan"), who once failed to live up to

Alutiiq ideals. The following English translation of the Alutiiq original was provided by Ignatius Kosbruk. Italicized portions were originally told in English.

When people first got here [Perryville] they used to go trapping. They didn't used to take their wives before. That's how it was organized.

One time there were two boys here: Wanka, and the other boy was his partner Gus. Once they were out trapping at Sayutaq—that's what we call it—Driftwood Bay. The two were trapping there, with Wánkánguaq. *He was the oldest. He musta been the oldest one. He don't let them boys go with him, he took one river and trap all by himself and let these other boys take another route. And he get all the mink.*

He got lots of mink and the boys didn't get any. *He was so greedy. He took the best part of the river for trapping.* So once when they didn't get any [one of the two younger] partners said they should trap among his traps. That time they got some. *They made the best of him. They set their traps between his traps. And that's the only time they get mink. He was greedy. He took the best part of the river for mink.*

Well, they trapped, going along with Wánkánguaq. *But he was here. They used to live here. And he was greedy.*

Now once one boy, maybe, Gus [was the one with him]. Wánkánguaq wasn't there [at the camp]. When he went to check on his traps, then the boy [Gus] cooked seal meat. When the cooking was done they were waiting for him, and finally he [Wánkánguaq] arrived. They were eating seal. Wánkánguaq sat down in his chair right across to eat. Suddenly then Gus said, "You're unhappy? *How come you don't eat?*"

Then Wánkánguaq said, "Why did you eat the part I love, my favorite part? You must have eaten it!"

Then he didn't eat at all, all day. So in the morning Gus just drank tea and just pushed his cup away. He went over the portage behind the island. When he got there, there's a little bay. It's always been there. Seal always like that place. He got there and saw a seal in the bay.

Then he went over to get closer to it. He shot it right in front of him. It drifted right ashore immediately. When it came ashore, he just pulled it up. He removed the sternum part of the seal, he took it out.

He didn't take any other part of the seal, and went home. He took the part of the seal meat Wánkánguaq liked so much back with him. Then when he got home, he went in, and said, "Here." He put it on top of the table. Then he didn't say nothing, another word. "Here's the part you were stingy for!" He was silent after that. *He didn't say, not one word! Oh yeah, that was something.*

That's all.[22]

This narrative illustrates the traditional value of generosity. It also shows that traditional methods of social control were still in use in twentieth century Perryville. Wánkánguaq, a man who had shown no consideration for others, made a fuss over the fact that Gus had eaten his favorite cut from the seal. In response, Gus shamed him by going to much effort to provide that favored morsel to his elder partner.

The Alaska Peninsula is home to a large subspecies of brown or grizzly bear known as the Kodiak Brown Bear. For centuries, perhaps thousands of years, men tested their courage and skill by hunting these bears. Boys learned not only how to track and kill them, but also to show respect before and after the hunt. For instance, in the past all hunters performed a ritual after killing a bear, and some still perform it. The hunter cuts off the bear's head and faces it to the southeast. He places a stick in its mouth and grass in its ears, and stuffs its eyeballs into its nose. This follows traditional beliefs, which held that all animals have a *sua* that hears, sees, and is aware of humans. It is the *sua* that decides whether to allow humans to kill the animal. If humans do something disrespectful to the bear, the *sua* will know about it and seek revenge. The hunter may be mauled in the future, or bears may avoid people altogether, depriving them of bear meat and grease. By plugging up a bear's mouth, nose, and ears and removing its eyes the hunter keeps the bear's *sua* from sensing what is done to its body, thus keeping humans and bears on good terms.

Besides treating the bear's head in a respectful way, there are general rules hunters must follow. These include:

- Be clean before you hunt bears. Many hunters take steam baths before a bear hunt, and all take a steam afterward.
- Don't talk about the bear hunt ahead of time.
- Don't brag about how good you are at hunting.
- Be prepared; know what to do. Bears have many habits that hunters must learn. For instance, they have been known to double back behind hunters. Most bears are also known to be left-handed. People are told to beware of bears with white ears or a white collar, for they are said to have special powers.
- Don't waste the meat. In the past people ate the meat and fat, used the hide for bedding, and made rain parkas out of the intestines. Nowadays people take bears only for the meat and grease. No one makes the beautiful and practical bear gut parkas, which have been replaced by rubber and Gore-Tex.
- Don't allow uneaten parts of the bear (the hide, claws) to be chewed by dogs or left around the village.

Ignatius Kosbruk recorded some of the rules he followed during his hunting days. In this transcript, IK refers to Ignatius Kosbruk, PP to myself.

IK: But the bear hunters, I'll tell you the fact myself. I do myself, I do still believe on that. I never, I never used to believe it, but I have my experience, two or three times in my lifetime. I used to hunt bear and go with old man Wasco [Sanook] and Paul [Shangin]. They never used to shoot the bear without hollering to him.

PP: Without hollering to him?

IK: Yeah, hollering to him first.

PP: What would they say?

IK: They wouldn't—they will just holler.

Alec Angukung and two boys at Chignik, years before his near-fatal mauling.
Alaska State Library, Kenneth Chisholm Collection, PCA 105–3

PP: "Hey!" or something?

IK: "Aaa!" then the bear stood up, and looked at them. They knew the person. But if they don't see you, they'll charge.

If they know it's a person then they wouldn't bother you. And then they shoot him from there. But another thing, I had my experience. Never shoot the bear when she's charging, coming towards you.... You might cripple them and then they'd get the worst of it.[23]

Tales about bears have been told since precontact times; recall Davydov's and Kosbruk's bear who killed the young berry picker, discussed in chapter 2. The most common motif recounted today concerns actual or near injury to the hunters, a result of carelessness, disregard for cultural rules, or ignorance of bear behavior. Bill Lind of Chignik Lake remembered a terrible mauling Alec Angukung of the Old Village on the lagoon once sustained.

I seen people get crippled, though, by a bear, crippled their arm, scars. I seen one guy, too. He didn't die. I was just a kid then. I don't know what year was that. But this guy, [Nick] Nikiforov, old Alec [Angukung] and his boy, Gus [Macauley], another boy, they were hunting [at] Black Lake.

[Alec] used to say—'cause there were boys around, you know— he used to say, "Next time I'll go into the den to get him."

They must have run across a bear [at Black Lake]. Bear went, made a circle back on his track and while they were tracking, old Alec, he was the first guy in the party.

It took his gun right away. Bear shrugged a little bit, on the ground. He's all full of blood. The bear would take him, throw him up in the air, and wait for him like this [arms out like the bear].

And the other guys couldn't do nothing, they were a distance away from him. And they didn't shoot, they were afraid they would shoot Alec. But they just hide inside a deep depression. Yeah, they hide there and they watch him. The bear thought he was dead. He left him for a while, you know, watched him for a while, then left. He left and they couldn't, he didn't move for a while, Alec. So the bear was watching him for a while and he didn't move. He took off again. Bear took off again. Then he went into the alders and he didn't come out, you know.

So Gus and them they grabbed him, you know. That's the only way he got away. The same evening they brought him down the lake, over across there. We were, we used to live across there, you know. And they brought him into our corridor. And it was nighttime, you know, after dark. His son came in through the door and soon as he walked in the door he said he needed some hot water, soon as he walked in. My mother knows right away something's wrong. So they went down and brought him. Them barabaries used to have just a narrow entrance, you know. My uncle wasn't there home, so they brought him in there, in his house.

They wouldn't let us see him, you know. Then Mom took her sheets out and bandaged him up. That guy was, had a busted arm, his ribs were broken, scratched up all over. And they stayed overnight there.

The next day they were gonna catch the tide down at the lagoon. In the morning then, before they leave that time Mom let us go see him. Cause us boys, you know, were small. We saw. It was like he was dead. His face looked pale. His arm was broken, his ribs were broken. His face was all scuffed up, scratched up, you know. Whole body.

He was swollen up so bad he couldn't fit through the door. Wouldn't fit through the door. So they took the window off and brought him out there. Took him to the bay. I don't know how the hell they brought him up. Alec went to Seward, I don't know how in the hell he got out. Mailboat must have been here, I guess. And he was in Seward and he came back.

And his arm was filled with aluminum. Couldn't even straighten it no more. His hands were like this, closed. And he lay. I don't know what was wrong. Leg couldn't straighten out any more, I guess. He just crawled on the floor. That's how he was when he come back. And he died when he was that way, too.

His leg, just roll on the floor to go eat. That's the way, he had no wheelchair.

And that spring we were hunting up there. Black Lake. We had Gus with us. Me and my stepdad [John Andre], Gus must have been with us and Nick O'Domin I think. And they stopped in that place where they had their wood camp. And they find out the same bear, I guess, must have came back, looking for Alec. And he pulled out Alec's clothes only. It tore 'em up. And the clothes were hanging too, in the callidor [entryway]. It took every one of Alec's clothes and tore 'em up.

They said the bear was half gray and half brown. We never saw that bear.[24]

Alec had broken one of the most important rules a bear hunter must follow: he had boasted to an audience of young boys that next time he would "go into the den and get" the bear. Instead, the bear got him. Bill Lind remembered a close call he had himself with a bear when he was hunting in the 1960s or 1970s:

It happened to me once when I was hunting. I think Johnny was with me, teacher [Don Kinsey], Nick O'Domin Sr. Nick O'Domin was down on the flat when we started tracking the bear up the hill. And Johnny was with us and Kinsey. Don Kinsey, the teacher.

But anyway, we were going up the hill and while I'm tracking, coming up, she [the bear] only left one print. That's all she left. And we found out the damn thing had cubs. Damn it! All of a sudden, while we're tracking, you know, the damn thing came down, full bore. I was ahead of the party. I had my gun like this. Shot it eight feet away from me. She rolled down the hill this way. I jumped sideways.

I tumbled over twice. Dropped my cap. And Don said, "Ohhh boy. She almost got you, huh?" He said I was just smiling. I said, "Yeah!" That bear had cubs. I didn't know it.

We left the [cubs]. I killed the mother and we left them.

See, [the bears] were ahead [of us], trying to climb, you know. They were ahead. The mother was the one leaving the tracks, her tracks, like one track. See, when they climb up the hill they use one track. Yeah, I didn't even know it. First time I tracked a female bear with cubs. See she had her cubs ahead of her, you know, first fall of snow, you know?[25]

Walter Stepanoff told about a caribou hunt he and several others were on when they had an unexpected encounter with a bear. As the narrative shows, the men treated the bear with respect, talking to it almost as if it were human.

That was up the head of Hook Bay, I think, the same time we got that big bear. There was a big bear following us. We went up, my two brothers and my nephew and I. And when we got up to the very head, on the flat, we stopped.

And then we started off again. There must have been a big bear on the hillside. We saw, and we passed him. He was sitting down with his legs out. He was big. I told 'em, "Don't shoot him if he don't bother us, we won't bother him." And he was sitting watching us and we had to pass him under the hill and as we were getting closer to him he just shrinked and getting smaller. And when we got underneath of him, we were passing him. He was down real flat, and just like he was sneaking watching us.

And then we passed him and as we were passing him, getting out on the flat, he was coming up slowly and he finally was sitting back up where he was until we got quite a ways from him.

And then he comes down the hill and he starts prowling. And we saw caribou way up ahead and then we wanted to get 'em, so I told 'em, "I don't know what we're going to do, but I ain't gonna have that guy following me," I said, "He's too big."

And we kept going and then when he got, I don't know how far, I'd say about from here to them houses behind of us, and every time we would stop, he would sit down and stop and watch us.

And then when we'd get up and go, well then he'd get up and he kept on. I says, "No, this can't go on, he don't want to scare," I said.

So after we get up to almost where the caribou, I told 'em, "We're gonna have to do something." I said, "I'm gonna have to put him out of commission so we can get the caribou." I had a .375 rifle so

I sat down and he was sitting down. I gave him one shot and that was when he came down. I got him. That's all it took was that one shot. And we took pictures of him afterwards. He was really big.

It was a shame to shoot him but we didn't want to, we didn't want him on our tail, with no way of getting out of it. So we just had to take him. That was a nice big bear though.[26]

When Walter was a boy, he and his brother found a bear in its den. Walter's father boasted that he would be able to get the bear, with unexpected results.

Well, where we shot that bear that spring would have been way up in Dry Creek, about a couple hours' hike from where our home was. And we got him out of a den. He was outside of his den and we got him. My brother and I was up there ptarmigan hunting and we had small guns, we was all the way up and we spotted him.

He was outside [his den], he was in and he was walking so we went home and told our dad about it. "Yeah," he said, "we're going up in the morning and get him."

So we went up but I'll never forget that time. We went up, it was on a steep hillside, and my dad shot at him but he didn't hit him good, and he come down the hill right toward us and the old man caught him just as he raised up to get out of the alders, and he flopped right into the alders and slid right on down the hill. We took the hide and meat that time, we took everything off. It took us a couple of days to get everything down, it was a long pack.[27]

Walter told another story about an encounter with a bear. This one did not result as hoped.

There was a bear here one fall ten years about. He busted into the sheds and everything else. He busted into our shed one night. I woke up. It was nasty, and the door was busted open.

So I shot through the window. I thought he was already in there and I fired a shot. But he wasn't in there, he must have already scooted out and I didn't know it.

And when I shot the bullet, I had this sink, it was a brand new one, in there. And I popped a hole in it.

Well, here's the hole here. I patched it over. I was surprised; I was in the next morning, I went, "Oh, no, punched a hole through my brand new sink. It wasn't even used!"

But I didn't shoot him, he busted into my brother's shed one night and then he shot it when he saw it. But then it ran out and it ran away.

And then they found him next morning up behind here. He was dead, so my boy and I, he was just small, him and I went up with a camera.[28]

Like Walter Stepanoff, Sr., almost every hunter has had personal encounters with bears. Ralph Phillips recorded this narrative, first in Alutiiq and then in English:

Well, I really don't remember the year me and my son David went hunting this bear here. Anyway, it was the, oh, middle part of October. Went back of Three Star Creek. Then we climbed a hill. And we stayed there for about three, four hours, and it was blowing, fifty, sixty miles an hour northwest, cold, you know. And then finally, I told my son, "It's too cold. I think we better give up."

So I started climbing down. I was gonna go home. And halfway down, my son hollered to me, "There's one coming down from the little island." So I climbed back up and we watched the bear go down that river. That bear took his time looking around for fish, silver salmon, you know. From that small island creek he moved to Middle Creek where the silvers go in, and looked around there for a while. And then he crossed that creek and I told my son, "Well, we'll go down here and wait for him by that little creek."

Not very far away from the main creek, we were in the grasses, you know, the grasses were about two feet high. We were waiting. We didn't have to wait long. I was looking toward the main creek and pretty soon I see my son motioning to me, and there was the bear, not even five feet away from me, coming towards, straight towards me. Bear didn't know where we were. And, so I stand up and shot the bear, crippled it. He stood up right by me growling and waving its arm. I told my son to shoot it again, and make sure he hit it in the right place. Both of us shot, the bear took off about ten feet and dropped dead.

And while we were cutting it up it started getting dark. We just cut it open, took the guts out, and just took enough meat for cooking. And our Hondas were about fifteen minutes away from where we were. So we hiked back and went home. And next day, about five, six of us went back there and cut it up, took the fat out first. And brought it all back. When we got back, we distribute the meat out and the fat. Then we had one day left to be in Perryville, me and my family usually spend the winter in Anchorage. So, start cooking fat and put it away, to take along. And we had everything packed, all our dry fish and subsistence food we take along. And everything was ready, you know. We just wait till next morning instead of taking our stuff across to the field we left with the plane when he got here.[29]

Caribou and Reindeer

Although bears enjoy a special status in Alutiiq tradition because of their natural and spiritual powers which are in turn conferred on the hunter, caribou have provided an equally important source of food throughout this century. The Alaska Peninsula herd winters on the tundra between Pilot Point and South Naknek on the peninsula's west coast and spends spring and summer farther south in the Port Heiden area, sometimes crossing a pass near Ivanof Bay into the Pacific coast region. The herd has been augmented by stray domestic reindeer, remnants of a herd imported by the federal government in the early twentieth century.

In about 1910, as part of a government project that was headquartered in Nome, reindeer herds were established at Ugashik and nearby Pilot Point (Aisaq) to supplement winter hunting and trapping. The program was touted as a modern way to improve the economic wellbeing of Alaska Natives by turning them into entrepreneurs. Unfortunately, the reindeer herding experiment failed to live up to its advance billing. First, although the program sought to augment local food sources, there was no food shortage on the Alaska Peninsula at the time. Second, the government wanted to modernize Alaska Natives by bringing them into the cash economy. Again, this was an unnecessary endeavor, for Alaska Peninsula Alutiiqs had been part of a cash economy for more than a hundred years. Still, they had historically been laborers rather than owners, so a program designed to move them into the ranks of entrepreneurs might have been of benefit. But about a third of the reindeer remained in government or Saami ownership, while the rest were divided among Native owners. Although by 1920s the largest herd was owned by Sarah Hansen, an Alutiiq woman who had been born at Pilot Point, the bulk of the Native-owned deer belonged to the Iñupiat families that had been moved into the area as herders.[30]

By the 1930s, the reindeer experiment was showing signs of disarray. Herds left to roam in the summer merged with each other and ownership disputes arose. Wolves and coyotes preyed upon the deer. Trappers killed untended reindeer for food. Owners sold the meat under the table rather than negotiating the maze of government permits. The corral season conflicted with trapping season. Alutiiq and Iñupiat crews often failed to cooperate with each other. And after 1945, caribou began to move into the Ugashik area and quickly absorbed the reindeer herds.[31] The program's most lasting effects were changes in the size and color of the caribou (the deer are markedly larger and lighter than others) and the permanent settlement of several Iñupiat families in the area. Despite its problems, the program did provide a reliable part of the diet of northern peninsula residents for a time. Carvel Zimin of South Naknek explained how it worked:

CZ: The government brought in a bunch of reindeer, and the Lapplanders used them. And of course with the reindeer, you had to buy the meat.

PP: Did they have yearly harvests?

CZ: Yeah. The Lapps stayed with the reindeer all summer, and they'd come in, and the head guy'd come in and ask who wanted reindeer, and whatnot, and they slaughtered for whoever wanted—no refrigeration. So they kept 'em alive. In fact right where my house is here is one of the places to slaughter the reindeer. They brought 'em right into here, right here, this next house over—this whole area right here. And somebody wanted one or wanted two reindeer, they slaughtered 'em and some of the people wanted the skins for mukluks or for wear and you got the skins too.[32]

Fishing and Cannery Work

After the 1912 eruption, Pacific coast Alutiiqs joined the many Caucasian immigrants who had settled in Chignik, Sand Point or Unga. Ugashik, Egegik, Pilot Point, and Port Moller on the Bering Sea side also attracted seasonal workers to their canneries. Other industries drew people to other communities. For instance, oil was found at Kanatak and Cold (Puale) Bay, coal and gold at Unga. August (Skinnix) Pedersen used to transport Perryville people to Unga to work at the canneries each summer. He remembered this about Unga:

> Well, a long time ago they had a gold mine there [Unga], you know, and there it was working.... It's way up in the bay, it's in a kind of lagoon like, and the village is sitting right in the mouth of it. It goes dry at low water. But up in the head there's a gold mine they had long ago. Now it started up a few years ago and they're doing pretty good at it. They started up that old gold mine and, there's quite a bit. It's surprising what they're getting out.
>
> But it wasn't the gold mine so much. The canneries in Squaw Harbor was operating and then there was two in Sand Point, see, and then the traps around there, and then they were fishing.[33]

Until the 1920s few Alutiiqs worked for canneries in the Chignik area, for several reasons. First, cannery owners held that the Scandinavian and other immigrant fishermen were better at fishing than were local Natives. Second, once fish traps were placed inside and just outside Chignik Lagoon, the canneries had no need of fishermen. Instead, they hired tenders for the fish traps and canners to process the catch. The former fishermen were given the jobs of maintaining the traps, while Asian workers at first did most of the indoor work. The priest for the lower peninsula, Father A. Kedrovskii, described daily life in 1911 for Unangan, Alutiiq, and creole workers living in the Belkofsky region near the western end of the Alaska Peninsula:

> The day of the local inhabitant, both in summer and winter, begins quite early: from 4:00 or 5:00 in the morning. Toward 10 or 11 he eats lunch, then at 3:00 in the afternoon, when he drinks tea, he "rests," at 5:00 dines, and at 7:00, undresses for the night.

> Creoles, side by side with the Aleuts [Unangan] and Eskimos [Alutiiqs], also lead this very life with interest. It's true, in several settlements, where culture and civility started to take, [theirs] is the most affable and most intelligent and respectable existence, but usually the picture of the life of the creoles is such as painted above....

> This is the present occupation of the Natives: hunting for land and sea animals, fishing, hunting for wild game—all this for household use (they sell only from 5 to 20 red fox hides per year to traders, for the sum of $5.00 for all), and partly daily work (seldom) in the trading companies, where they are kept safe, but the last few years [some] also work in fish canneries.

> Permanent [cannery employees]—working the whole summer season, get wages with room and board of $35.00 per month and a percentage of 1/3 of a cent per each box of fish [packed], of which each factory delivers 65,000 and more. The last category of workers work for four or five months for $350 to $450. In infrequent instances, such a sum falls to Natives, especially to the creoles, but mostly it falls in the pockets of the whites—scum from Europe, imported from California by the fishery companies, or themselves settled earlier in other parts of Alaska....

> Amongst all the Aleuts and Eskimos interest in this work is increasing.... The local inhabitants of Chignik and surrounding villages, (Eskimos) in numbers from 100 to 150 annually, from time to time, sometimes for a month or months at a time [work in the canneries]....

At mining works (gold at Unga and quarry mining at Chignik) one almost doesn't see Natives. However, for tens of white people there is now enough work to be paid from $2.50 to $3.00....[34]

It was to find this type of cannery work that Wasco Sanook of Katmai was sent on a journey in the early 1900s, described in an earlier chapter.

During the 1920s and '30s canneries began to hire local Alutiiqs and creoles in larger numbers for work in canneries and as fish trap tenders. Olga Kalmakoff was grateful that people could earn money, but remembered the hardships children suffered when both parents had to work. She recalled some childhood experiences in the 1920s and '30s:

I had a lot of friends in Perryville, like Effie Shangin and Polly Yagie, they were my friends. Like we would go do our chores and go help each other so we could go play dolls and play house. And we used to have Ignatius [Kosbruk] for our guitar player. Like we would go play dancing, you know....

Polly Yagie. I think we didn't bring our dolls here [when there was a cannery at Ivanof Bay]. So we would play with bricks as our dolls. And we'd talk to them. And we'd make mudpies, and we used to have fun.

I was raised in Perryville by Jenny Shukak and Efrim Shukak. They were very nice people and they brought me up like their own.... And I thought Jenny was my real mother, and I loved her. She passed away last summer in Anchorage when I was there.... I think most of my relatives died from tuberculosis or that epidemic they had.

Jenny [who later married Harry Kaiakokonok] bought [my toys] for me. I remember I had a big doll. It was porcelain. And I used to feed it. And it got stale! I remember that.

I remember when she [Jenny] was working in a floating cannery. She took me along and this one girl. And I used to cry a lot, I was scared in that boat.

Two little girls, they would leave us in our room. And we would dress up, powder up, use their powders and whatnot. And when they lose us they would look for us in the ship. You know, we'd roam around. And you know she was trying to make money so she could get us clothes. That's the way she worked.

Then they started going to Squaw Harbor [Unga Island] to work. That's where I was born. They would go on the boat. And come back.[35]

In many families, both parents worked for the cannery. Men usually worked as caretakers, stevedores, or fish trap tenders while women canned the fish. Christine Martin remembered her first annery job:

I started working in the cannery maybe '36 or '37. I was fifteen. I was only fifteen. And when I first start to working too my dad went to the cannery and I went with him. And I was standing watching those other ladies working on the fish. And pretty soon this guy come, took me by my hand, and took me to the canning machine. And he showed me how to put those lids on the machine. And he walked away.

So I stayed there and I did what I was told to do. I was always like that, doing what I was told to do.

Then maybe five they quit and I went home. And I play out, even I was fifteen years old, we play out, like playing balls. And pretty soon towards evening when I went in my dad said that I have to go to bed early 'cause I have to get up early. And I said, "Oh, why do I have to?" I didn't know I had a job!

So in the morning I got up and I got ready and I walked the beach to the cannery. They put me same place there.

So that was how I started working. I didn't ask for it. I worked all my teens, fifteen, sixteen, seventeen. And then I worked all my twenties and thirties.[36]

While people earned money working for the canneries, they also had to put up fish for their own winter use. Walter Stepanoff, Sr., described the beach seining he and others did in Chignik Lagoon.

> [People set nets not from boats but] off the beach. You leave one end on the beach, you used to run out and hold the hook. There used to be salmon jumping and they'd pull it down and into the beach and they'd catch the other end and start pulling.

> I was sixteen when I got out of school and the first day I worked in the cannery. The first year it was a dollar a day. No, it was more than that, I worked two years, two years and a half. I guess I was a deck hand on the small tender there and before I got in the army I worked in the trap gang for two years.[37]

Kukak Bay cannery, 1953.
National Park Service

Mike Sam also remembered beach hauling for salmon. He recalled a major technological advance when August Pedersen's father, Marius (Pete) Pedersen, devised a way to set a net from a boat.

> They finally learned how to round haul, you know. This old man, Pedersen, [Skinnix] Pedersen's dad, he...made the round hauls. We used to go out to work it and [got] a lot of fish! But we had nothing to make the seine go out at the end, you know. And one of my uncles told 'em, "tie the tack bucket and throw it," you know.
>
> Yeah, tried it. And seine go out, you know. Seine go out there but then, hell of a time picking that five-gallon bucket full of water! Too hard!
>
> So they went to see old Pete up here, where they have the house. And he had a "frog." He made some frogs out of wood. Kind of angle 'em like this, and with the handles on 'em. Nail it at the two ends, drill a hole in a 2 x 4, put line in and tie a knot, tie it onto the seine.
>
> They float. But [they] pull the seine out, you see. They still use it around here, you know, some of them guys. But now they just got a skiff going, a skiff puts it out.[38]

Meanwhile, on the other side of the peninsula, the residents of New Savonoski and South Naknek fished, worked for canneries, and caught and preserved fish during the summer. In addition, each fall they traveled upriver to Lake Naknek, where they harvested spawned-out red salmon (called "redfish") as had their ancestors before the Katmai eruption. Fred T. Angasan, Sr. of South Naknek (TA) described part of the yearly cycle as follows:

> TA: The first thing I remember was in the spring, like in March or April, we traveled up to...catch whitefish and dolly varden with nets. We used to come back with boatloads in the day from here.
>
> PP: That would be a day trip?

TA: One day trip. And go back in the evening. And then that's beginning in the spring. Now in the fall, the first thing I remember was traveling all the way up here.

PP: Okay, and this is at Brooks Camp [in Katmai National Park]?

TA: This would be about September or so, when it first starts getting cool. The frost is just starting, and they'd use nets and fish along all the way up to the falls, Brooks Falls, at Brooks River. And they'd catch maybe—I think I remember catching about 5000 reds.

PP: In what period of time?

TA: September, in about three, four days. That's why people went up there, because all the fish were concentrated in this river, and they'd make just one drift and catch 500 or so and then split them up and hang 'em up.... Or somebody stand on the beach and walk the other end of the net down. You'd take the net and row down in the skiff and load up 500 fish at a time, and maybe we stayed up there until, well I think I remember was when this part was white—Dumpling Mountain. They'd look at this mountain to see if it's getting colder or not.... Because by that time all your fish are done and ready to eat. That would be maybe the first trip in September.

And then they'd come back after the fishing was done to hunt bear. They'd use the bear for dog food and stuff, because people used dogs in those days for their transportation and stuff. They didn't really eat the bear because bear tastes like something horrible, fishy taste to it and only dogs ate that. And they'd go and catch maybe five or six bear and then go home with the bear. That'd be sometime in October when it's cold.[39]

Because the redfish harvested at Brooks Camp was lean, it dried quickly and easily. People prepared it both for human consumption and as dog food. Carvel Zimin of South Naknek described the difference as follows:

Well, you just look at 'em. The older ones had mold on 'em and spots and whatnot. And they were thinner. They'd spawned out longer, and then the ones that had just spawned would be a little bit heavier in the meat. The meat would look, it would be a little bit better. And those were the ones you kept for yourself, what we called the eating fish. But then toward the middle of the winter, and so you ran out of the eating fish, then you went to the dog fish and looked for the best ones you could find, because it was food. And it was a type of food that we liked. The summers spent fishing for food and money allowed families to buy staples so they could take part in what soon became the primary wintertime occupation, trapping.[40]

Furs

In the 1920s and 1930s fashions around the world turned to fur hats, coats, blankets, and stoles. A new era in the fur trade began. The twentieth century industry required techniques unlike those used during the previous two hundred years. Whereas in the past large hunting parties harvested the furs, by this time individual families ran traplines in the mountains and along river drainages, or managed family fox farms on unpopulated islands. Instead of seeking sea otter pelts, men, boys, and occasionally women and girls trapped fox, lynx, beaver, land otter, muskrat, mink, and the rare bear. Both transient and permanent peninsula residents—Scandinavian-Aleuts, Alutiiqs, "Russians" and Caucasians alike—trapped and sold furs.

The only modes of winter transportation available on the Alaska Peninsula to early twentieth-century trappers were foot and dog team. Families bred large dog teams and fed them from the surplus of salmon caught during the summer commercial fishing season. Mike Sam recalled, "The [canneries] used to leave a bunch of canned salmon for people [at the end of the season].... They would even use 'em for dog food, you know.... There was so much to eat."

Carvel Zimin of South Naknek recounted his experiences trapping in the 1940s and 50s:

And we'd come up from town with our dog team and we left the dogs here and we would walk the creek. It was a one-day walk. And we'd get there just about dark. And then we'd—the beaver we got, we would just pull the skins off the meat because we didn't want to carry the whole carcass. And then we'd walk back down again and check our traps, and then we got back down to the cabin, depending on the amount of furs we'd spend a day, two days, and we'd flesh our skins and stretch 'em. We had 'em stretched on the outside of the walls of the cabin. We had plywood stretchers, whatever it took to make a round beaver pelt, you know.[41]

Zimin also remembered the fur buyers who traveled to remote villages each spring:

In our area, and into Dillingham, they had traveling fur buyers that came through. They came out of Anchorage and they'd fly through the villages, certain times of the year, and they bought the fur. How they used to do it years ago, like when I was telling you trapping up at Paul's Creek and Smelt Creek and that, we'd get our furs, and then I can remember as a kid two fur buyers. Generally they traveled in pairs. And these two guys would come to my dad's house, and they'd look at the skins, each one'd look at the skins, and they'd take a piece of paper and they'd write a figure, how much they'd give for the pelts. And then they'd both hand the figure—the piece of paper to my dad and my dad'd look and naturally he would take the highest bidder. And I kind of think they had it all figured out, you know, "One time, well I'll do this, one time I'll do that." But that's how they worked it. And they both traveled in the same airplane. [laughs] And it looked like competition.

But they'd come out into the villages, cause it would cost my dad money to go to Anchorage, or even to go to Dillingham. And these traveling buyers, on an average, I believe, paid a little bit more than the buyers in Dillingham. They'd come sweeping through, you know, and they'd head right back to Anchorage with their planes loaded.[42]

The most common yearly cycle for peninsula Alutiiqs on both the Pacific and Bristol Bay sides was to trap in the winter and work for the cannery as fisherman or processor in the summer. This meant that there were few children in the villages during the trapping season, but many during the summer. Thus, many of the village schools operated during the summer.

During the wintertime people made only occasional trips away from their trapping cabins to go "to town"—Chignik or Chignik Lagoon in the south, Egegik or Naknek in the north—to the store and post office. Carvel Zimin described his periodic trips across the Naknek River to the store in the town of Naknek:

> When I was a young guy we'd hitch the dogs up, before daybreak in the wintertime, I don't know, maybe—well, say Christmas, we were going to go Christmas shopping. The Alaska Packers cannery had a store here. And it was a store with no heat. So you can imagine if you went down to buy canned vegetables or something, they would be frozen. And so we'd hitch the dogs up before daybreak, and we'd take off up to New Savonoski—the Savonoski village, and then we'd cross there, and there was a trail, but it was a lot further inland than the highway. And then we'd go on down to, well Naknek Trading now, it was the Red Salmon Canning Company owned it, so we called it "Red Salmon." And we'd go in and we'd shop for an hour or so and then we'd go out and we had to carry sleeping bags in the sled, course your regular tarp that you always kept in the sled. And you bundled everything up in there, the freezables and whatnot, and you'd take off back home, and you always got back here after dark. In other words, one whole day went to go shopping. And then if it was lucky, the river would be frozen up by PAF cannery, and if we were lucky enough to be able to cross there, then it would cut the time down considerable. It was, back in those days, this was the way we lived.[43]

The peninsula was dotted with traplines. Elders remember that there was one in almost every valley on the Pacific coast, and each creek and river drainage along the Naknek River. Each trapline was operated by a single family or pair of trapping partners. Families on the Pacific coast lived in permanent camps from September until April.

Spiridon Stepanoff's brother William and his wife Mary Naumoff Stepanoff had a trapping camp at Ocean Beach, northeast of Chignik. The family lived in a sod barabara during the winter, spending their spare time reading, sewing, and preparing food and clothing. Their second son, Walter Stepanoff, Sr., drew a diagram of his family's barabara and explained how it was built:

> Here's what we called the corridor or callidor where you go in. There was a…main room, our kitchen and living room you would call, and there was two bedrooms, separated. And there was another room where the boys stood. My mom and dad in another room and my sister in another.
>
> They dug it out, made it level, and after he built the siding up, we embanked it with ground and then the roof was just made regular with rafters and 1 x 12s or 1 x 6s. And we covered it with building paper.
>
> I would say that one was built in the 30s or the very early 40s.[44]

Stepanoff Family Barabaras, Chignik Area
Drawings After a Sketch by Walter Stepanoff, Sr.

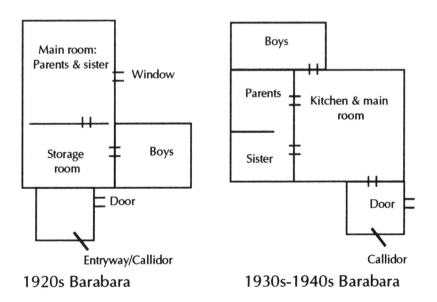

1920s Barabara

1930s-1940s Barabara

Children George, Walter, Sr., Julia, and William (Bill) Stepanoff had their own traplines. Julia Stepanoff Boskofsky, now of Kodiak, remembered one experience when she and her brothers went after a land otter. The following is an excerpt from the author's field notes:

> One time when Julia and her older brother Walter were walking along their trapline, they saw an otter trail. They both said, "I'm going to get that one, it's mine!"
>
> So Walter set a trap at the bottom of this little hill, right in the water, and Julia set one on the other side of the hill at the bottom. Then they went home. When they returned the next day the otter had been on the trail but neither of them had caught him.
>
> For three days this went on. Then their father said he would get the otter. They showed him where the trail was. He told them he'd teach them a lesson *after* he got the otter. He put his trap right at the top of the hill.
>
> The next day he went back and he had the otter. He asked his children where they had put their traps. They told him they had put them in the middle of the trail. Their father had put his on the side. He asked them to explain how the otter walks. Its feet are on the side, and it slides on its belly! That's why he was able to catch the otter and they weren't.[45]

When Mike Sam was a small child his parents died. His grandparents, Innokenty and Barbara Kalmakoff, adopted and raised him. Mike remembered trapping with his grandfather up Chignik River to Black Lake and staying at their cabin, located at Sword Point above the river.

> Most of those Natives, a long time ago, when the fox was right, that's all they do, trap. Make a living. Everything was cheap. Can of coffee, you'd get a pound of coffee, 50 cents a can. One hundred dollars in them days go a lo-o-ong way.
>
> Like I told you, I went fishing, a dime a piece, them big red salmon.

We buy the traps. Number 1, number 2 trap, number 3 trap. Number 3 trap is a big fella, for a wolf and wolverines and land otter.

But you get a number 2 trap, you use it for fox. And number 1 trap, you use that for mink.[46]

In addition to obtaining furs by trapping, some Alaska Peninsula residents owned or operated fox farms that produced a steady supply of fox pelts. The practice had begun during Russian days: fox farms required an isolated and self-contained spot—generally a small island that was escape-proof. A few foxes were transported to the island to breed, and feed boxes doubling as live traps were left close to the shore. The Alaska Commercial Company had continued the practice, establishing fox farms on the Semidi Islands in the 1880s.[47] Each fox farm was operated by a single individual or family, who sometimes lived on the island, sometimes on the mainland nearby. These people took food to the animals, monitored the population increase, harvested the foxes each year, prepared the furs for sale, and sent them to a factory or sold them to a traveling buyer.

The village of Perryville operated a community-owned fox farm on Chiachi Island, across the short channel from the village. Managers were required to make twice-weekly trips to the island with food for the foxes. Mary Phillips and her first husband, Tikhon Kosbruk, tended the fox farm for a time. She and second husband Elia Phillips explained how people accustomed the foxes to going into the traps:

MP: That island out there (Chiachi) used to be blue foxes. Farm. My first husband and I, we used to go with the skiff and feed the foxes. My husband used to feed 'em with dried fish. He used to make bunch of 'em. And we used to go by skiff. Go around that spit we call here. That's where the house is. And we used to go way around.

[We went out] twice a week when the weather was nice; we used to do it with my kids when they were small.

They had boxes, you know. We put [the dried fish] in the box and them boxes had doors.

EP: They had doors in front. They kept the door open. But if they were gonna get fox, the door would slam on the fox.[48]

There were a number of other fox farms in the Chignik and Perryville areas. For instance, Jacob and Paul Islands were at one time farms for blue foxes. Up until World War II Lars Hansen leased Chanikliuk Island near Castle Cape. Axel Carlson and his wife had a cabin and fox farm on the southwest side of Kumlik Island, locally called "Axel's Island." On nearby Unavikshak Island, known as "Charlie's Island," Charlie Olson harvested foxes. The Benson family leased Ugaiushak Island for fox farming, but the mother, Annie Lowell Benson, died when her two sons were still young. They were sent to live in the Jesse Lee Home in Unalaska where, as a schoolboy, Benny Benson designed what became the Alaska flag in a territory-wide contest. The Pedersen family farmed foxes on Nakchamik Island from 1925 to 1935. The family lived in a two-story house on the shore of a lagoon on the eastern side of the island and captured foxes in several traps near the house.[49]

During the trapping and fox farming era that lasted until World War II, many families lived isolated lives. They looked forward to visits from distant neighbors and relatives, an anticipation recounted by those who remembered traveling for two days for a week-long visit. A family might make the journey because they had run out of flour and had heard that relatives had a surplus left from the past summer's purchases. Or they might travel for Russian Christmas, called *Sláwiq*, to go starring.

Christine Martin recalled her father packing her into a dogsled and journeying across the peninsula from Chignik Lake to Ilnik on the Bering Sea. Once there, they visited Christine's uncle, Aleck Artemie, and her cousin, Harry Aleck. The village also received a visit from the fur buyer, who gave Christine her first airplane ride. In the following transcript, CM refers to Christine Martin, PP to myself.

CM: When I was about, maybe eight or nine, my dad went to Ilnik and he took me along. And he would put a big canvas on the sled and some blankets and pillows and let me sit in there. And here we were on our way to Ilnik. It must have been what, 1930?

And we were there for a while. He said he was taking me to see my uncle but I didn't know who he was. I was scared 'cause I didn't know anybody there. And I thought we were going to get to a big village, and there was only three or four houses when we got there.

PP: Was it just you and your dad?

CM: Me and my dad and there was another sled with, I forgot who they were now. Anyway, there was two dog teams.

PP: Could you see out?

CM: Sometimes I would open up, you know. And when the weather was stormy and snow storm, you know, he would wrap that canvas over my head. And here I would keep trying to look out, you know. Keep opening my face.

And pretty soon we got to Ilnik. I remember it was dark in the evening.

PP: Did it take just one day to get there?

CM: No. Maybe two. We had to stay overnight in some houses at Second [Black] Lake. 'Cause there was some people up there, way up there, wintertime. They go up there for trapping....

Seemed like in springtime, it must have been springtime when we came back.

PP: Did you come back by boat?

CM: No. By dog team.

Oh, that's when I had my first plane ride up in Ilnik where there were only three or four houses. It wasn't a city! And that is where I had my first plane ride.

It was—a little plane came, a wheel plane. They called it "Fur Buyer." Some guy come there to buy their fur, like foxes and minks, and some other fur....

And when I was flying up, flying in the plane, I looked down, and I saw little houses down there and I told my dad, "Look, Dad, there's play houses down there!" And my dad, he laughed and he said, "No, that's the houses we're staying in!" That was my plane ride.[50]

EDUCATION

The first schools were opened on the Alaska Peninsula in the 1920s. Operated by the Bureau of Education, a federal agency, and later the Bureau of Indian Affairs, their sessions were coordinated with the seasonal patterns of the people. For instance, the Chignik Bay school was open only during the summer. Julia Stepanoff Boskofsky, who grew up in Chignik Bay, remembered going on Fourth of July picnics with the teacher and the rest of the school children. August Pedersen remembered the Chignik teacher Lena Anderson. In the following transcript, AP refers to August Pedersen, PP to myself.

AP: You didn't have no winter school, see, you only had summer school. People would be traveling around, see, and then around the first of April, school would run until about the end of August.

PP: And where would the teachers go?

AP: They'd go home. They'd leave.... A lot of 'em were from Outside. Mrs. Anderson, Lena, she was schoolteacher here for years and all the time I was going to school, and she lived around Seattle, I think, somewheres around there. They'd come up for the summer, pretty rough going them years.[51]

In contrast, Perryville School was open during the fall, winter, and spring, but some families spent winters at trapping camps away from the village. Some parents left their children with relatives staying in Perryville, while others took the children with them to camp.

Kanatak School including class of adults and chief, 1925.
National Archives

Government schools sowed the seeds of an immense and irrevers-
ible change in Alutiiq life. When Alutiiq-speaking children first began
attending schools in Perryville in 1922, they were taught by white
teachers, most of whom had been hired from the contiguous United
States to work in what was considered a remote location. The primary goal of education at the time was to teach the children to speak
and read English. Teachers' personal styles varied, but many were
remembered for punishing their students for speaking the Native
language or misbehaving—though the children often could not understand what they had done wrong. Olga Kalmakoff of Ivanof Bay,
and her son Joe Kalmakoff, remembered some of the maltreatment
students faced for speaking Alutiiq in school:

OK: We were put in the corner or go inside a closet.

JK: I remember Herman going into the closet. They forgot about
him one time, I know. It was probably a little two by two foot
space there, it was a broom closet where it was, there, sitting
next to a heater. I guess they put him in the early afternoon and
forgot about him. It was after suppertime they finally started

looking for him and there he was in there still waiting to be freed. Wasn't locked or anything, he was just scared, I guess.[52]

OK: I went to a corner lot of times. Or put in a little broom place. They let us be in there and close that door, and hard to breathe in there, in a closet, in a little tiny closet. And that woman teacher, if [students] have curly hair or makeup, she would make them wash up and really beat them.[53]

As a result of this treatment the students resolved not to speak Alutiiq at home when they grew up, hoping to save their children from similar experiences. Through this process the language was well on its way to extinction by the 1950s. When the generation of post-war baby boomers went to school few of them could speak Alutiiq.

Schools had another important effect on life on the peninsula: they determined where people would live. For instance, there was no school in the village of New Savonoski, established by refugees

School children at Perryville, 1939–41.
Alaska State Library PCA 222–370, Leslie Melvin Collection

from the old village that had been destroyed by the ashes of the Katmai eruption. The nearest school was seven miles downstream in the cannery town of South Naknek. As New Savonoski children reached school age, their families moved, one by one, to South Naknek. In 1979 the last resident of New Savonoski closed up his house and moved out permanently.[54]

The education system imposed restrictions on Alutiiqs, but it was also manipulated by them. In the 1960s Dora Lind Andre and her extended family built homes at the site of a modern winter trapping camp and an ancient settlement at the mouth of Chignik Lake. An environment rich in salmon and close to an important bear area, the location seemed ideal. Residents successfully petitioned the state for a school on the grounds that the village contained more than the minimum number of children necessary.

ORGANIZED RELIGION

Until World War II, despite massive changes in almost all aspects of their lives, the Alutiiqs of the Alaska Peninsula were confident in one constant: unanimous adherence to the Russian Orthodox faith. But after the war, even this seemingly unassailable area of life began to change. In 1949 the first evangelistic Slavic Gospel Church missionaries came to Chignik, and shortly afterward two women from the same sect settled in Perryville. The missionaries are remembered as friendly, generous, and well-liked. But when they converted a number of people away from Orthodoxy, the community of Perryville split into two factions. From 1912 many Perryvillers had maintained trapping cabins and fishcamps at Ivanof Bay, and several times over the years the village council had considered relocating the village there. Finally, a disagreement over the way the village was run and the issue of religious freedom led a group of six families, all members of the Slavic Gospel Mission, to move permanently to Ivanof Bay in 1965.

Other peninsula villages have experienced similar missionary activities leading to an ever more diverse religious picture. In addition, teachers, who generally live in the villages for only a few years and then return to their homes elsewhere in the state or nation, belong to a variety of religious denominations. The result is that although Russian Orthodoxy is still dominant in many Alaska Peninsula villages, it is only one of many active churches. This new religious pluralism has brought peninsula villages more in line with practices in the rest of the United States, but has also acted as an assault on village unity and a force for an individual, as opposed to community-wide, locus of identity and allegiance.

DISASTERS, NATURAL AND HUMAN

Natural and human disasters figure prominently in the oral tradition of the Alaska Peninsula. Catastrophic volcanic eruptions, earthquakes and tsunamis, as well as epidemics and oil spills, have required the people to adjust often to loss of life and economic opportunity.

Ironically, the village of Perryville, refuge for survivors of the Katmai eruption, is located at the base of another active volcano, Mt. Veniaminov. Emil Artemie remembered an eruption of that volcano that occurred when he was a boy. Raised on stories of the Katmai eruption, he was understandably nervous about the experience:

> Yeah, anyhow, my uncle Paul Shangin (he used to take me out all the time) and I were out cod fishing. Cod fishing disappeared, you know. They were abundant before and they just start disappearing. I was eight maybe; no, ten, probably. We were way out. We were so far out we could see the volcano over the top of the island. Way out in the open. And real nice weather, you know, sun shining, clear sky. They were back of the clouds here and there but it was flat calm. This must have been around spring, I think. Or late in the fall. I don't remember.

> Anyhow, this big puff of smoke—I didn't notice that. My uncle hollered to me, he was looking, it was smoking, in Native, "*Puyulek nuthetuq!*" he said. And it was really smoking. "Mountain blew up, volcano blew up." That's what he said.

> Boy, I was scared, you know. When we started heading ashore, I didn't want to go ashore 'cuz we'd be closer to it! We went ashore

anyway. It still bothered me, there was a volcano up there that blew up, big puff of smoke created on top of it. It was a bright sunny day.

Anyhow, that evening it was a big flame up there. They were like one of those fireworks you see. And according to the Coast Guard, the flame went up to 10,000 feet that time.

The ashes start falling in Perryville and we never got no daylight for about a couple of days. It remained dark. The ashes continually falling. [When] I was a kid, there was no gas. We had to pump water, you know, made it from here just about to Randy's house [about 100 feet], pack water, five gallon cans. Pretty soon my hair started really getting stiff, you know. I was wondering why. There was fine sand. It got into your head, and you had to wash your head. Man, you could smell it. Kind of a, like a powder, gunpowder smoke in the air. Stayed coming down. It didn't seem to create that much in the ground though.

And then we were all ready to come to Chignik that spring. We would go to Chignik, get away from the smoke, you know. And I didn't realize that darn thing was right behind us [in Chignik]. Still right behind us![55]

In this seismically active region, earthquakes are also common. Ignatius and Frieda Kosbruk told about a major one that occurred in 1939 before they were married. They were at separate trapping camps at the time.

IK: You want to hear about that 1939 earthquake? Some of the people were here. We were westward at our trapping grounds. Also my [future] wife was there at that beach with the swells. I was westward with Harry Kaiakokonok and his wife. Before we got married.

There was a terrible earthquake. I never see anything like that. It was so terrible. Harry sent us to the village to Paul Shangin's—I think we ran out of salt or something. I tried. We went over, we hike over. And when we get to the big river—boy, it was funny. We were okay when we went over, but when we get to this river, boy, golly, I told Spiridon, "We'll never cross this creek." We didn't know it was going to have earthquake. And it was all dirty and muddy. We didn't try so we turned back.

Then when we were going back, I was wondering why I walked with big, high steps. My partner said, "How come I walk funny?" Suddenly we stopped. Sure enough, it was earthquake. My goodness. And we tried to get out on top of the ridge so we see the sea. Boy, the sea was just like mountains, water coming up bubbles. Oh, it was terrible.

FK: Me too. It was when I was married the first time. We spent the winter at Back Bay.

IK: That same year—

FK: Same year, when I first get married to other man. Suddenly the earthquake struck. We got the dogs outside. They were tied up outside the barabara. This unmarried girl said, "Where's my *nacaq* [head covering]?" Even she don't get married, she asked for *nacaq*....

Suddenly we saw them waves just coming up, dry, just like a big swells. Just like the barabary's gonna cave in! We went outside. And here the church bells were ringing without nobody touching them. It was 1939.

IK: Yeah, there was an earthquake. People didn't do anything to the bells. Church bells were ringing. We were westward at the trapping grounds. Rocks were rolling there at my place at Anchor Bay.... Big rocks were rolling all over farther east at Ivan Bay and Ivanof Bay. There was an earthquake, the whole works. I've never felt one like that since, never seen one like that before or after; neither of us. Then we got married. Before we got married, the earthquake of 1939 occurred. It was scary.

And we didn't know nothing about tidal waves. We didn't know anything about tidal waves. And we had no warnings or no radios or nothing. But we survived but there was no water come in. But in Ivanof Bay they did, huh? Not too much though. They had a little tide, tidal wave in Ivanof Bay but not too bad. And it was all the way, all the way to Wányaq and to Ithiq. The boys were trapping, that's why, that's how strong it was, all the way along.

And they even felt it down in Sand Point, too, I guess. That was a scary earthquake.

That's all.[56]

Health care—both traditional and that associated with post-contact epidemics—forms another part of the oral tradition among Alutiiq elders. Both male and female practitioners were skilled at massage and bleeding for the treatment of conditions as varied as heart ailments, boils, and arthritis. Midwives skillfully assisted women in childbirth. But perhaps the most important healing tool was the steam bath, locally called a *banyu*, where therapy was generally performed. Archaeological and historical evidence indicates that the people of Kodiak Island and the Alaska Peninsula used saunas lined with rocks before the coming of the Russians, as early as AD 1100.[57] The steam bath itself is therapeutic both as an aid to physical health and cleanliness, and as a necessary step in spiritual health. In fact, in traditional Alutiiq thinking the states of physical and spiritual health

Mike Sam's *banyu*, Chignik Lagoon, 1990.
Patricia Partnow

are closely related: physical ailments were often signs of a mental or spiritual imbalance, while moral or ritual mistakes often resulted in physical afflictions. Even today, both before and after hunts and important religious rituals, participants take a steam in the *banyu*.

Besides healers, in previous centuries the Alutiiq people were treated by *kaḻagalget*, or shamans. As the story of Puglálria in Chapter Three indicates, by the twentieth century these people had converted to Christianity, but some still practiced traditional skills. By the 1940s most people had come to fear the shamans, considering them less interested in helping and curing others than furthering selfish or evil desires for power, revenge, or wealth.

During Russian days, in larger settlements traditional medicine had been supplemented by the services of a physician's assistant, called a *feld'sher*. In posts like Katmai, which had no resident *feld'sher*, the Russian or creole *baidarshchiks* were trained in rudimentary medicine. Thus in 1837 Ivan Kostylev was able to manufacture a smallpox serum that saved the population of the village. During the American period the Alaska Peninsula villages were visited periodically by doctors, but even in the twentieth century only the cannery town of Chignik Bay could boast a resident physician. Alutiiqs were accustomed to seeking medical treatment in any of a number of ways from a variety of practitioners.

Unfortunately, no one was prepared to deal with "the Great Sickness" of 1900, an influenza and measles epidemic that spread throughout western Alaska.[58] It took a heavy toll in the Bristol Bay area, as Doris Lind remembered hearing from her grandmother. She was told "so many people died that the people stopped crying for them. Babies were sucking from their dead mothers' breasts. They dressed the dead in squirrel skin parkas and buried them in a mass grave." The village of Aisaq (today's Pilot Point) was one of the most severely decimated. In fact, only three Alutiiqs survived: the *tuyuq's* daughter Sarah Hansen, who later came to own the largest reindeer herd in the Ugashik/Pilot Point area, and her two uncles.

The village of New Savonoski, like many others on the peninsula, was also hard hit by the worldwide influenza pandemic of 1918–19. Teddy Melgenak, originally from New Savonoski but now of King Salmon, remembered the story his grandmother, Pelegia Melgenak, told him about the epidemic. The following is paraphrased from field notes:

> There is a large communal grave at New Savonoski with a huge cross on it. This is where the victims of the 1918 flu epidemic are buried. Pelegia remembers that she and her husband, One-Arm Nick, were having tea at home one day when a neighbor came in and joined them. She left and soon afterward some medical people with masks covering their noses and mouths came in and reported that the neighbor, and many others, had died. "But we just had tea with them 5 or 10 minutes ago," they protested, "and now they're dead, just like that."
>
> Pelegia and Nick gathered dog excrement and put it in a big wooden drum, then covered it with a wooden lid. They burned it in front of their house. In this way they protected themselves from the flu infection.[59]

In 1932, a deadly measles epidemic struck the peninsula, this time concentrated at the twenty-year-old village of Perryville. Many of those who died were mothers with young children. Jenny and Harry Kaiakokonok, who by this time was village chief, took over the care of a number of the newly orphaned children. The mother of Elia Phillips and Effie Shangin was one who died in the epidemic. The two remembered that she died within an hour of her eight-month-old baby daughter and was buried with her. Frieda Kosbruk's and Clydia Kosbruk's mother also died. Frieda herself had the measles. She remembers seeing the spots on her forearms as she washed clothes outside in the spring. Her future husband Ignatius Kosbruk remembered that only three men were untouched by the epidemic, the teacher Mr. Burke, the Orthodox priest Father Kochegin, and one other. The three went around the village packing water and lighting fires for the ill. They were relieved to find people starting to recover just as the supply of firewood was running out.

Tuberculosis has afflicted Alutiiqs since Russian times, and perhaps before. Many current residents of peninsula villages spent years in hospitals in Sitka, Seward, Unalaska, or Anchorage undergoing treatment for the disease. In fact, tuberculosis was at its worst in the years immediately following World War II. It was only during the second half of the twentieth century that effective medicines were developed to cure and control the disease.

The most insidious and persistent disease to strike Alaska Peninsula Alutiiqs is alcoholism. Although Davydov claimed that Koniags made and drank fermented liquids before the coming of the Russians, it is more likely that alcohol was unknown in precontact days.[60] During the eighteenth century, alcohol abuse was a problem among the Russian population of the colony more than among Natives. By the nineteenth century, however, Unangan and Alutiiq Natives had been taught the art of brewing *kvass*, a fermented drink made from fruits, berries, or roots. Each village or permanent settlement likely had at least one *kvass* brewery, some more than one. Thus even during the years when the sale of alcohol to Natives was forbidden or restricted (between 1818 and the 1820s and between 1842 and 1867), peninsula Alutiiqs had no difficulty obtaining liquor.[61]

The American era of free enterprise brought with it a steady traffic in alcohol. Ships stopped at ports up and down Alaska's coast, taking special advantage of the new cannery operations. Smugglers and licensed traders alike sold drink to peninsula residents. A particular problem was binge drinking, which was by no means universal, but common enough to produce comment and complaint. For instance, during the 1880s in the village of Douglas ACC post manager Vladimir Stateev denounced the general drunkenness he observed, and ten years later the itinerant Orthodox priest lamented its widespread effects and expressed relief that the closing of the ACC peninsula posts in 1901 and 1902 would make sugar for brewing beer or *kvass* unavailable.

In the 1970s village health care changed from the old system of reliance on local healers and occasional visits from physicians. For the first time health aides from among the local population were trained and hired to serve each village. Today the aides can call on physician's assistants stationed in regional centers such as Chignik Bay, or doctors in Anchorage, King Salmon, or Dillingham. In addition, traveling dentists, mental health counselors, and physicians visit the villages on rotating schedules.

POSTSCRIPT: WORLD WAR II AND LIFE AFTER THE WAR

If the twentieth century as a whole represents a march toward Americanization, the postwar period is a 100-yard dash to the finish line. Today's elders consider World War II the watershed between the old rural lifestyle and modern American culture. During the war itself the Alaska Peninsula was almost instantly transformed from an isolated corner of the world to a teeming crossroads. Afterward, transportation, communication, and American cultural influences expanded in unforeseen directions and dimensions, tying peninsula communities to the rest of the state and the world.

The war brought hundreds of sailors and GIs to the port at Chignik Bay, and thousands of soldiers to the new air bases at Port Heiden and King Salmon. Young men from the peninsula served in the armed forces throughout the territory and world, while more women than ever before worked in canneries on the peninsula and Kodiak. USO dances became popular pastimes and a chance for local women to meet young men from the Lower 48. During and immediately after the war a number of romances and marriages occurred as a result of these meetings, the aftermath being the departure of many young women from the peninsula to destinations to the south.

Emil Artemie observed the GIs at Chignik Bay as they struggled to adjust to a foreign environment. His narrative describes a changing world—a metamorphosis of Chignik Bay from familiar and predictable landscape to an unrecognizable but exciting scene:

> But during the war, you know, there were deserters. They turned in one or two of them, going out in the rafts. Either they jump overboard with a life raft or something. Picked up one or two of them, one time, one skipper here, down the bay. Turned 'em in. The Army boat had 'em fishing or something. They were outsiders.
>
> You'd be surprised the kids that were in the service during the war. Just kids, some of them. Eighteen years old. And some of 'em had never seen an ocean in their lives. We could tell. They used to stop down the bay, and they ask me one time, a couple of them came ashore and I was at the beach working on a skiff or

something. "Can we walk to Seattle from here?" "I suppose you could but it's going to be a very long walk," I said. I figure they thought there might be a highway out on the other side of the mountains, maybe. Anyway there was four or five of them took off. Seen them packing their gear, into an old skiff they got holed up under the dock in the afternoon. But they took off, pretty soon I seen them, there at the ridge of the mountain down the bay. You look up there, there's a ridge, you know. That was them cruisin' around out there. They come back in the evening, to their boat, and their skipper just say, "Welcome back, boys."[62]

When the war ended, men and women went back to their homes on the Alaska Peninsula, hoping to return to life as usual. But the village life they had left was gone; dizzying technological advances changed both the scenery and customary activities. For instance, while peninsula economics continued to be dominated by commercial fishing, the process itself altered immensely after the war, due both to new technology and the 1959 banning of fish traps. Processing

A boat owner prepares nets for the next salmon opening, Chignik Lagoon, June 1990.
Patricia Partnow

plants began to freeze as well as can fish, and without fish traps the plants depended once again on fishermen in boats to bring in the salmon. Many Alutiiqs and Scandinavian Aleuts started their fishing careers operating company-owned boats immediately after the war, and gradually earned enough money to buy their own vessels.

Meanwhile, as word spread about the rich fisheries around Kodiak Island, Bristol Bay, and the Alaska Peninsula, outside fishermen came to the peninsula during fishing season. Each fall they left to spend the winter in other parts of Alaska, the Lower 48, or Hawaii. As in the early days of the canneries, fishing towns were completely transformed each summer from quiet villages to bustling commercial centers, only to return to a semblance of pre-war days when the fish were processed and the hordes of workers left. The surrounding villages experienced the opposite effect: in the summer they were all but abandoned as fishermen left and families moved to fish camps, then expanded again in the winter when residents returned for school, hunting, trapping, and social events.

Fox farming and fur trapping nearly disappeared during the war. Trapping enjoyed a temporary resurgence during the 1950s, but now at the beginning of the twenty-first century few Alaska Peninsula residents trap, and no one can live on the money earned from trapping alone. The fur industry's postwar dependence on fur farms in locations close to the centers of commerce in Europe, Canada, and the United States has undercut the trapping industry in Alaska.

With the demise of the fur business, families had no need to stay in isolated camps, as they had done during the first part of the century. They returned to villages, a move that resulted in a new stable population base. This allowed for the opening of schools and establishment of village governments throughout the region.

Another major change after the war was a marked improvement in transportation and communication with the rest of mainland Alaska. First radio, then telephones, later television, and finally, in the 1990s, satellite TV, became available in peninsula villages. As a result residents—particularly teenagers—experienced Elvis fever, Beatlemania, punk rock, and MTV. This sudden and intense Americanization alarms elders, who see no way of countering their grandchildren's infatuation with the dominant media image of consumerism and individualism.

The technology associated with subsistence hunting and gathering also advanced markedly and rapidly after the war, in large part because faster and more reliable modes of transportation became available for sale to individuals just as the commercial fishing industry was peaking and providing residents with ready cash. All-terrain vehicles, snowmobiles and airplanes have made hunting both more accessible and expensive. These machines, and the equipment needed to harvest the animals, require considerable outlays of money for purchase and upkeep.

Salmon drying on Polly Yagie's porch, Perryville, September 1990.
Patricia Partnow

Despite these profound changes, two aspects of subsistence have remained relatively constant from prewar years: the economic importance of hunting, fishing and gathering for peninsula residents, and the integration of subsistence activities and the values that accompany them into the social system. The Alaska Department of

Fish and Game began gathering statistics about subsistence use in peninsula villages in 1975, and has continued to conduct periodic surveys to determine types and amounts of foods harvested for private consumption. The figures are startling: in 1989, for instance, each resident of the five villages in the Chignik region consumed an average of between 208.9 (Chignik Bay) and 489.9 (Ivanof Bay) pounds of subsistence foods.[63] Similarly, in 1992–93, each resident of South Naknek consumed 296 pounds harvested by subsistence techniques.[64] In contrast, Anchorage residents ate an average of 10 pounds of subsistence foods per capita in 1989.[65]

As people gather subsistence foods today, they continue to use them to promote and preserve values and customs associated with Alutiiqness. Subsistence hunting forms an integral part of the self-definition of peninsula people. Daily lives are taken up preparing for the hunt, undertaking it, processing the meat afterward, and discussing the experience. To a lesser extent those Alutiiq men and women who have moved to Anchorage, Fairbanks, or other urban centers try to remain involved with the subsistence lifestyle by returning to the peninsula for the summer commercial fishing season. When fishing is closed for periods throughout the summer, they spend their time at family fish camps putting up subsistence fish and gathering berries. Similarly, many urban Alutiiq families return to the village for fishing and berry picking during the summer. The emphasis on the food quest is reinforced in the folklore of the region. Not only do most traditional stories unfold in the context of hunting or fishing, but the vast majority of personal memorates that are shared around kitchen tables also revolve around hunting and gathering experiences.

Another dimension of the Alutiiq subsistence ideal involves partaking of the foods that were obtained through personal effort. Feasts held throughout the year feature what the community thinks of as Native foods. These occasions include Orthodox name days or saints' days, *Sláwiq* feasts, and potlucks. Family members who have moved away from the village are similarly involved in subsistence activities. They relish the packages of wild foods from relatives living in the villages and send back fresh fruits and vegetables and frozen turkeys in exchange. Potluck dinners, which may be occasioned by anything from a board meeting or year-end party of a Native organization to an arts festival or the arrival in town of a fresh halibut catch, are an essential part of most urban Native gatherings. The food is discussed, described, and explained in detail. Women exchange recipes and compliment each other, but the greatest recognition is an empty serving dish at the end of the feast.

Federal and state governments continue to play a dominant role in the lives of Alaska Peninsula Alutiiqs. Lands traditionally used as home sites or in subsistence harvests, such as those now contained within Katmai National Park and Preserve and Aniakchak National Monument, have been placed in federal ownership and protectorship. As of this writing, the regulation of subsistence harvests throughout the state is in the hands of the federal government, in the wake of the Alaska State Legislature's failure to pass regulations in keeping with federal law.

But the government action with the widest repercussions for Alaska Peninsula Alutiiqs occurred in 1971 with the passage of the Alaska Native Claims Settlement Act (ANCSA). The act's intent was to compensate Natives for lands taken by governments or private individuals, and to clarify title to all land in the state so that a pipeline could be built to transport oil from the North Slope to the port of Valdez. The act's effects were far different from any imagined at the time, for they involved the alteration of the very nature of the relationship between people and land. During precontact days Alutiiqs were territorial in that they guarded the exclusive right to use the territory around their villages, but they had no concept of land ownership as understood in the Western world. The attitude toward the land was one of stewardship and usership rather than ownership, entailing not only rights but also responsibilities. For instance, if a person did not use a portion of land over a period of years, he lost his right to it. Similarly, if the land and its resources— particularly the game animals—were abused or ignored, the person's hunting luck would be lost and he would be unable to provide for his family. Thus people tried to use and respect their land in ways that their elders told them were proper.

In Russian days ideas about land use and ownership changed less than might be supposed. Although the Russian crown claimed the right to rule the entire territory, it did not pretend to own any land except that on which the RAC had built settlements. Natives were removed from land they had previously controlled only at the sites of trading posts and administrative centers. Most Alaska Natives continued to live in ancestral settlements as before. Those in the Aleutians, Kodiak Island, and the Alaska Peninsula had far less freedom to harvest the resources surrounding their villages than formerly, but the primary factor curtailing their land use was control of labor and time, not territory.

It was only during the American era, with the influx of large numbers of immigrants, that pressures for mining rights, transportation corridors, and home sites raised the issue of land ownership. At first the question was answered by denying Natives the right to own land while issuing permits and land patents to Caucasians who filled out the proper forms. On the Alaska Peninsula, this occurred primarily in the cannery towns, but during the first part of the century there was still enough unsettled land that those Alutiiqs who felt they were being crowded needed only to moveover a bay or two to continue their subsistence pursuits or trapping.

Eventually, however, it became apparent that the question of who owned which bits of land needed to be settled legally. With the passage of ANCSA, some land was ceded to newly formed Native corporations, which were to administer both the land itself and payments for lands given up. The twelve new regional corporations were intended to correlate as closely as possible with traditional cultural boundaries in hopes that they would eventually be seen as pseudo-tribal organizations. Unfortunately, the state's Alutiiqs were divided among three corporations. Those who live on the Pacific coast of the Alaska Peninsula are closely related in history, language, culture, and kinship to Kodiak Islanders, but they became part of the Bristol Bay Native Corporation along with Naknek River and Bristol Bay Alutiiqs, many Yup'ik speakers, and a few Dena'ina members. Kodiak Island forms its own, separate corporation, Koniag, Inc., and the

Alutiiqs of the Kenai Peninsula and Prince William Sound were placed in the Chugach Alaska Corporation.

As important in the lives of Alutiiqs as the effect of becoming instant shareholders is the underlying philosophy of the act. Land is now a commodity, a good to be bought and sold, fenced and planted. Owners can control who may travel and hunt on their own land, but they must also ask permission of others if they wish to cross a neighbor's land. While traditional subsistence needs required a family to travel great distances to hunt, fish, and gather, ANCSA divided lands into townships and lots. Joe Kalmakoff of Ivanof Bay spoke of the change in attitude toward the land:

> The people never ever thought of it as owning the land, but rather sharing it. There was no boundaries. It was like, everybody respected each other. It was no saying, "Well, this is my place," you know. And "you can't go beyond this." There was never nothing like that. Never any real conflict as far that went, because everybody shared pretty much everything.

> After Land Claims came a division, a real division. That's where it was. It was a bad thing in my way of thinking. It separated the people amongst themselves and from anyone. Real estate, ownership of real estate and boundaries was probably the worst thing that could ever happen to a unique people. Land. The relationship.

> Everything, all the resource was so much respected, that it was better managed than by the state or federal government.

> My grandpa was really strict on that part. He said, "You're the managers. You're responsible. You take care of the land that you live by. You never better be abusive toward the land or its people that you need to help you take care of the land."

> Always one needs the other one to exist. Everything has its balance. Nature has its balance. Course, that's being people of nature, the subsistence way of life, that's really deep down.

> Like there's a better way of managing rather than human beings being the dominant living. Saying that there is a reason for it to

be there, because it exists there since the beginning of time. And everything exists for a reason. Nature has its own balance.[66]

Kalmakoff and his neighbors have adapted to the act and its effects and are currently striving to make the corporations both profitable and responsive to the social and cultural needs of their shareholders. Their level of success will become a vital part of the next part of the history of Alaska Peninsula Alutiiqs.

AFTERWORD: HISTORY MADE AND REMADE

Today, Alaska Peninsula Alutiiqs are expressing a renewed interest in their ethnic identity and cultural heritage. Some have formed the Council of Katmai Descendents, an organization dedicated to preserving traditional knowledge and objects, and others have established a Kanatak Tribal Council with similar goals. Many have helped plan and launch a pan-Alutiiq exhibition, *Looking Both Ways*, with the Smithsonian Institution's Arctic Studies Center. A number of peninsula Alutiiqs are involved in archaeological work, subsistence studies, genealogical research, museum work, and oral history projects. Through these endeavors, they continue to make history, not just by living it, but by telling and writing it for future generations.

I anticipate that their work and words will redesign the way Alaska's history is presented. These authors will invent new ways of integrating the old *unigkuat* and *quliyanguat* into a new story, determining a unique balance among the disparate voices of the past. I believe their stories, like the ones presented here, will use as their starting points the people's relationship with the land and sea, for it is this relationship that provides a sense that the past still lives in the present. Mary Jane Nielsen of South Naknek expressed this sense when she described the emotional attachment that she, a descendent of Savonoski, Douglas and Katmai residents, felt when visiting the abandoned village of Douglas. She explained that the experience evoked what she could only describe as a "cellular memory." As she stood in the shallow grass-filled square pit that had once been the church, she realized she was on the site of the altar—a spot forbidden to women in the Russian Orthodox church. She moved back and thought she could hear singing in Alutiiq, music she had not heard since her grandmother Pelegia Melgenak had died. The feeling that overcame her was so intense that she had to cover her face with her jacket. By the time she returned home to South Naknek she was exhausted.

It is this feeling of physical, spiritual, and eternal attachment to the land that will be expressed in new histories written by Alutiiq authors. Now that the Alutiiq language is gasping for life, religious unity has been torn, and more and more people are leaving the villages by their own choice, it is this knowledge of untold years of residence that orients and defines the people.

In fact, I believe these histories of the future only *seem* new and different; they will actually be a continuation of the creative process by which Alutiiq people have redefined themselves, their pasts, and their futures since time immemorial.

NOTES

1.   Cf. Mishler and Mason 1996 for a discussion of this phenomenon in Old Harbor on Kodiak Island.

2.   Buchan and Allen 1952: 98–99.

3.   Ignatius Kosbruk 1992.

4.   Walter Stepanoff 1990a.

5.   Stepanoff 1969.

6.   Stepanoff 1969.

7.   Pedersen 1990.

8.   Sam 1990.

9.   Petterson 1981: 4.

10. Petterson 1981: 7.

11. Cf. Mishler and Mason 1996 for a discussion of the effects of Scandinavian intermarriage on the social system of an Alutiiq/Creole settlement on Kodiak Island.

12. Shangin 1992.

13. Sam 1991.

14. Pedersen 1990.

15. Report of the Governor of Alaska 1923: 30.

16. US House of Representatives 1933: 14.

17. Ricketts 1980.

18. Orth 1967: 492.

19. Martin 1992.

20. Shangin 1992.

21. Elia and Mary Phillips 1992.

22. Ignatius Kosbruk 1992c.

23. Ignatius Kosbruk 1992d.

24. Bill Lind 1991.

25. Bill Lind 1992.

26. Walter Stepanoff 1990.

27. Walter Stepanoff 1990.

28. Walter Stepanoff 1990.

29. Phillips 1992.

30. Kramer 2000.

31. Morseth 1998: 134ff.

32. Zimin 1998.

33. Pedersen 1990.

34. AOM 1911: 273–4; 323–4.

35. Olga Kalmakoff 1992.

36. Martin 1992.

37. Walter Stepanoff 1990a.

38. Sam 1990.

39. Angasan 1998.

40. Zimin 1998.

41. Zimin 1998.

42. Zimin 1998.

43. Zimin 1998.

44. Walter Stepanoff 1990.

45. Partnow field notes.

46. Sam 1990.

47. Porter 1890: 53.

48. Mary and Elia Phillips 1992.

49. Nielsen 1976.

50. Martin 1992.

51. Pedersen 1990.

52. Joe Kalmakoff 1992.

53. Olga Kalmakoff 1992.

54. Hodgdon 1981: 7.

55. Artemie 1992.

56. Ignatius and Frieda Kosbruk 1992.

57. Davydov 1977: 154–5.

58. Fortuine 1992: 215ff.

59. Partnow field notes.

60. Davydov 1977: 176.

61. Fortuine 1992: 280ff.

62. Artemie 1992.

63. Alaska Department of Fish and Game 1990.

64. Alaska Department of Fish and Game 1995.

65. Alaska Department of Fish and Game 1989: 14.

66. Joe Kalmakoff 1992.

REFERENCES CITED

Abalama, Nick. 1990. Interview by Marie Meade for Bureau of Indian Affairs, May 23.

Afonsky, Bishop Gregory. 1977. *A History of the Orthodox Church in Alaska 1794–1914*. Kodiak: St. Herman's Seminary Press.

Alaska Commercial Company (ACC). 1868–91. Correspondence of the Kodiak Post. Microfilm. University of Alaska Anchorage Archives.

Alaska Commercial Company/Douglas. 1885–95. Log books for the Douglas Post. Archives, Alaska and Polar Regions, Rasmuson Library, University of Alaska Fairbanks.

Alaska Commercial Company/Katmai. 1883–1903. Log books for the Katmai Post. Archives, Alaska and Polar Regions, Rasmuson Library, University of Alaska Fairbanks.

Alaska Department of Fish and Game. 1989. Alaskans' Per Capita Harvests of Wild Foods. *Alaska Fish & Game* 21(6).

———1990. Household Survey. Anchorage: Division of Subsistence.

———1995. Subsistence in South Naknek. Anchorage: Division of Subsistence.

Alaskan Russian Church Archives (ARCA). Microfilm. University of Alaska Anchorage Archives (originals in Library of Congress, Manuscript Division).

Aleck, Virginia. 1993. Interview by Patricia Partnow. Chignik Lake, Alaska, January 13.

Alekseev, A. I. 1990. *The Destiny of Russian America 1741–1867*. Translated by Marina Ramsay. Kingston, Ontario: The Limestone Press.

Angasan, Fred T. 1998. Interview by Patricia Partnow for National Park Service. South Naknek, Alaska, January 26.

AOM (See Pravoslavnyi Amerikanskii Vestnik').

Arndt, Katherine L., 1999. Katmai Station, 1883–1889: The Journals of Nikolai R. Fomin. Paper presented at Alaska Anthropological Association 26th Annual Meeting, Fairbanks, Alaska.

Arndt, Katherine L. and Richard A. Pierce. 1990 [1802, 1817–1835]. Records of the Russian-American Company: Calendar of Communications Received by Chief Managers, 1802, 1817–1835 (ms.). Fairbanks: University of Alaska.

————1990b [1826–1830]. Records of the Russian-American Company: Calendar of Communications Sent by Chief Managers, 1826–1830 (ms.). Fairbanks: University of Alaska.

Artemie, Emil. 1992. Interview by Patricia Partnow. Chignik Lake, Alaska, January 24.

Beach, Rex. 1940. *Personal Exposures*. New York: Harper and Brothers.

Bergsland, Knut. 1994. *Aleut Dictionary/Unangam Tunudgusii*. Fairbanks: Alaska Native Language Center, University of Alaska Fairbanks.

Black, Lydia T. 1977. The Konyag (The Inhabitants of the Island of Kodiak) by Iosaf [Bolotov] (1794–1799) and by Gideon (1804–1807). *Arctic Anthropology* 14(2):79–108.

————1990. The Creole Class in Russian America. *Pacifica* 2(2):142–155.

————1991. *Glory Remembered: Wooden Headgear of Alaska Sea Hunters, with a Reprint of Aleut Hunting Headgear and its Ornamentation, by S.V. Ivanov, 1930*. Juneau: Alaska State Museums.

Boas, Franz. 1919. *Tsimshian Mythology. Bureau of American Ethnology Annual Report* 34. Washington: Government Printing Office.

Buchan, Laura and Jerry Allen. 1952. *Hearth in the Snow*. New York: Wilfred Funk, Inc.

Clark, Donald W. 1987. On a Misty Day You Can See Back to 1805: Ethnohistory and Historical Archaeology on the Southeastern Side of Kodiak Island, Alaska. *Anthropological Papers of the University of Alaska* 21:105–132.

Clark, Gerald H. 1977. Archaeology on the Alaska Peninsula. *University of Oregon Anthropological Papers* #13. Eugene: University of Oregon.

Crowell, Aron L. 1996. Precontact Koniag Ceremonialism on Kodiak Island and the Alaska Peninsula: Evidence from the Fisher Collection. *Arctic Anthropology* 29(1):18–37.

Crowell, Aron L., and Mann, Daniel H. 1996. Sea Level Dynamics, Glaciers, and Archaeology along the Central Gulf of the Alaska Coast. *Arctic Anthropology* 33(2): 16–32.

Davis, Nancy Yaw. 1986. *A Sociocultural Description of Small Communities in the Kodiak-Shumagin Region. Minerals Management Service Technical Report* No. 121. Anchorage: U.S. Department of the Interior, Minerals Management Service, Alaska Outer Continental Shelf Region.

Davis, Wilbur. 1961. Recording, Mount Katmai, Alaska Eruption. Tape and transcript at University of Oregon archives.

Davydov, Gavriil I. 1977 [1810–1812] *Two Voyages to Russian America, 1802–1807.* Translated by Colin Bearne. Kingston, Ontario: Limestone Press.

Desson, Dominique. 1995. Masked Rituals of the Kodiak Archipelago. Ph.D. diss., University of Alaska Fairbanks.

Drucker, Philip. 1966. Some Variations on the Potlatch. In *Indians of the North Pacific Coast.* Edited by Tom McFeat. Seattle: University of Washington Press, 102–107.

Dumond, Don E. 1971. A Summary of Archaeology in the Katmai Region of Southwestern Alaska. *University of Oregon Anthropological Papers* #2. Eugene: University of Oregon.

———1981. Archaeology on the Alaska Peninsula: The Naknek Region, 1960–1975. *University of Oregon Anthropological Papers* No. 21. Eugene: University of Oregon.

———1987. Prehistoric Human Occupation in Southwestern Alaska: A Study of Resource Distribution and Site Location. Eugene: *University of Oregon Anthropological Papers* No. 36. Eugene: University of Oregon.

———1988. The Alaska Peninsula as Superhighway: A Comment. In *The Late Prehistoric Development of Alaska's Native People.* Edited by Robert D. Shaw, Roger K. Harritt, and Don E. Dumond. Alaska Anthropological Association Monograph Series No. 4. Anchorage: Alaska Anthropological Association, 379–388.

———1995. Archaeological Reconnaissance in the Chignik-Port Heiden Region of the Alaska Peninsula. *Anthropological Papers of the University of Alaska* 24(1 & 2):89–108.

Dumond, Don E. and VanStone, James W. 1995. Paugvik: A Nineteenth-Century Native Village on Bristol Bay, Alaska. *Fieldiana Anthropology*; new series, no. 24. Publication 1467.

Efimov, A. V., ed. 1964. *Atlas Geograficheskikh Otkrytii Sibiri i Severozapadnoi Amerike XVII–XVIII* [Atlas of the geographical discoveries in Siberia and northwestern American, 17th–18th centuries]. Moscow: Nauka.

Ellanna, Linda J. and Andrew Balluta. 1992. Nuvendaltin Quht'ana: *The People of Nondalton*. Washington: Smithsonian Institution.

Elliott, Capt. Charles P. 1900. Salmon Fishing Grounds and Canneries. In *Compilation of Narratives of Explorations in Alaska*. Washington: Government Printing Office.

Erlandson, Jon, Aron Crowell, Christopher Wooley, and James Haggarty. 1992. Spatial and Temporal Patterns in Alutiiq Paleodemography. *Arctic Anthropology* 29(2):42–62.

Fall, James. 1987. The Upper Inlet Tanaina. *Anthropological Papers of the University of Alaska* 21(1–2):1–80.

Fedorova, Svetlana G. 1973. *The Russian Population in Alaska and California, Late Eighteenth Century to 1867*. Translated and edited by Richard A. Pierce and Alton Donnelly. Kingston, Ontario: The Limestone Press.

Fienup-Riordan, Ann. 1990. *Eskimo Essays*. New Brunswick: Rutgers University Press.

Fortuine, Robert. 1989. *Chills and Fever: Health and Disease in the Early History of Alaska*. Fairbanks: University of Alaska Press.

Gideon, Hieromonk. 1989. *The Round the World Voyage of Hieromonk Gideon 1803–1809*. Translated and with an introduction and notes by Lydia T. Black; edited by Richard A. Pierce. Kingston, Ontario: The Limestone Press.

Golder, Frank A. 1903. Tales from Kodiak Island. *Journal of American Folklore* 16: pt. 1, 16–31; pt. 2, 85–103.

Golovin, P. N. 1979 [1862]. *The End of Russian America: Captain P. N. Golovin's Last Report 1862*. Translated by Basil Dmytryshyn and E. A. P. Crownhart-Vaughan. Portland: Oregon Historical Society.

Griggs, Robert F. 1921. Our Greatest National Monument: The National Geographic Society Completes its Explorations in the Valley of Ten Thousand Smokes. *National Geographic*, September, 219–292.

Harvey, Lola. 1991. *Derevnia's Daughters: Saga of an Alaskan Village*. Manhattan: Sunflower University Press.

Hefner, Robert W., ed. 1993. *Conversion to Christianity: Historical and Anthropological Perspectives on a Great Transformation*. Berkeley: University of California Press.

Henn, Winfield. 1978. Archaeology on the Alaska Peninsula: The Ugashik Drainage, 1973–1975. *University of Oregon Anthropological Papers* No. 14. Eugene: University of Oregon.

Hodgdon, Teresa. 1981. Old, New and Now Savonoski. In *Uutuqtwa*. Naknek: Bristol Bay High School.

Holmberg, Heinrich Johan. 1985 [1855–1863]. *Holmberg's Ethnographic Sketches*. Translated by Fritz Jaensch and edited by Marvin W. Falk. Fairbanks: University of Alaska Press.

Izmailov, Gerassim. 1787. Log of the vessel *Tri Sviatitelia Vasilii Velikii, Grigorii Bogoslov, i Ioann Zlatoust*. TsGAVMF (Navy archives), St. Petersburg, fond 870, opis'1, delo 1784.

Kaiakokonok, Harry O. 1956. Story. Photocopy of ms. originally published in *Island Breezes*. Sitka: Public Health Service.

———1975. Interview by Michael J. Tollefson. King Salmon, Alaska, April 29. Unpublished transcript provided by Katmai National Monument.

———1975a. Interview by Michael J. Tollefson and Harvey Shields. Perryville, Alaska, October 22. Unpublished transcript provided by Katmai National Monument.

Kalmakoff, Joe. 1992. Interview by Patricia Partnow. Ivanof Bay, Alaska, April 3.

Kalmakoff, Olga. 1992. Interview by Patricia Partnow. Ivanof Bay, Alaska, April 2.

Kan, Sergei. 1988. The Russian Orthodox Church in Alaska. In *Handbook of North American Indians*. Edited by William C. Sturtevant. Vol. 4, *History of Indian-White Relations*. Edited by Wilcomb E. Washburn. Washington: Smithsonian Institution, 506–21.

Kashevarov, Vasilii. [ca. 1833]. *File on Kodiak District of the Russian-American Company*. Transcribed by Svetlana Fedorova and draft translation by Lydia T. Black. Unpublished manuscript.

Kawashima, Yasuhide. 1988. Colonial Governmental Agencies. In *Handbook of North American Indians*. Edited by William C. Sturtevant.

Vol. 4, *History of Indian-White Relations*. Edited by Wilcomb E. Washburn. Washington: Smithsonian Institution, 245–254.

Khlebnikov, K. T. 1979. *Russkaya Amerika v Neopublikovannykh Zapiskakh*. Edited by R. G. Lyapunova and S. Fedorova. Leningrad: Nauka.

———1994. *Notes on Russian America: Parts II–V: Kad'iak, Unalashka, Atkha, the Pribylovs*. Translated by Marina Ramsay and compiled, with an introduction and commentaries, by R. G. Liapunova and S. G. Fedorova. Kingston, Ontario: The Limestone Press.

Kitchener, L. D. 1954. *Flag Over the North: The Story of the Northern Commercial Company*. Seattle: Superior Publishing Co.

Kosbruk, George. 1975. Interview by Michael J. Tollefson and Harvey Shields. Perryville, Alaska, October 21. Unpublished transcript provided by Katmai National Monument.

———1975a. Interview by Michael J. Tollefson and Harvey Shields. Perryville, Alaska, October 22. Unpublished transcript provided by Katmai National Monument.

———1976. We Were Very Lucky. *Elwani* 1(1):16–19. Kodiak: Kodiak Aleutian Regional High School.

Kosbruk, Ignatius. 1992. Interview by Patricia Partnow. Perryville, Alaska, March 24.

———1992a. Interview by Patricia Partnow. Perryville, Alaska, March 26.

———1992b. Interview by Patricia Partnow. Perryville, Alaska, March 30.

———1992c. Interview by Patricia Partnow. Perryville, Alaska, April 7.

———1992d. Interview by Patricia Partnow. Perryville, Alaska, November 10 and 11.

———1992e. Interview by Patricia Partnow. Perryville, Alaska, November 13.

Kosbruk, Ignatius and Frieda. 1992. Interview by Patricia Partnow. Perryville, Alaska, March 31.

Kramer, Bobby Jo. 2000. Personal communication with author, Anchorage, Alaska, July 5.

Krauss, Michael E. 1980. *Alaska Native Languages: Past, Present, and Future*. Fairbanks: Alaska Native Language Center, University of Alaska, Fairbanks.

Langsdorff, George H. 1968 [1814]. *Voyages and Travels in Various Parts of the World*, Vol. 2. Amsterdam: DeCapo Press.

Lantis, Margaret. 1938. The Mythology of Kodiak Island, Alaska. *Journal of American Folklore* 51(200):123–172.

Leer, Jeff. 1985. Prosody in Alutiiq (The Koniag and Chugach dialects of Alaskan Yupik). In *Yupik Eskimo Prosodic Systems: Descriptive and Comparative Studies*. Edited by Michael Krauss. Alaska Native Language Center Research Papers Number 7. Fairbanks: Alaska Native Language Center, University of Alaska, Fairbanks, 77–134.

Lind, Bill. 1991. Interview by Lisa Scarbrough and James Fall for Alaska Department of Fish and Game. Chignik Lake, Alaska, December 5.

———1992. Interview by Patricia Partnow. Chignik Lake, Alaska, October 22.

Lind, Doris. 1992. Interview by Patricia Partnow. Chignik Lake, Alaska, October 20.

———1993. Interview by Patricia Partnow. Chignik Lake, Alaska, January 13.

Lisiansky, Urey. 1968 [1814]. *Voyage Round the World in the Years 1803–1804, 1805, and 1806*. Ridgwood: The Gregg Press.

Litke, Frederic. 1835. *Puteshestvie Vokrug Sveta Sovershennoe po Poveleniia Imperator Nikolaia I, na Voennom Shliupe Seniavine v 1826, 1827, 1828, i 1829 godokh: Otdelenie Morekhodnoe s Atlasom* [Voyage completely around the world by command of Tsar Nicholas I, on the battlesloop *Seniavin* in 1826, 1827, 1828 and 1829: navigation section with atlas]. Sanktpeterburg: Kh. Gints.

Maclean, Norman. 1992. *Young Men and Fire*. Chicago: University of Chicago Press.

Martin, Christine. 1992. Interview by Patricia Partnow. Chignik Lake, Alaska, October 19.

Merck, Carl H. 1980. *Siberia and Northwestern America 1788–1792*. Translated by Fritz Jaensch and edited, with an introduction, by Richard A. Pierce. Kingston, Ontario: The Limestone Press.

Mishler, Craig and Mason, Rachel. 1996. Alutiiq Vikings: Kinship and Fishing in Old Harbor, Alaska. *Human Organization* 55(3): 263–269.

Morseth, Michele. 1998. *Puyulek Pu'irtuq! The People of the Volcanoes: Aniakchak National Monument and Preserve Ethnographic Overview & Assessment*. Anchorage: National Park Service.

Moser, Jefferson F. 1899. The Salmon and Salmon Fisheries of Alaska. *Bulletin of the U.S. Fish Commission* 18:1–178.

Mousalimas, Soterios A. 1992. The Transition from Shamanism to Russian Orthodoxy in Alaska. Ph.D. diss., Oxford University.

Nielson, Helen. 1976. It was a Simple Life I Led. *Elwani* 1(1):108–116. Kodiak: Kodiak Aleutian Regional High School.

Oleksa, Archpriest Michael J. 1990. The Creoles and the Contributions to the Development of Alaska. In *Russian America: The Forgotten Frontier*. Edited by Barbara Sweetland Smith and Redmond J. Barnett. Tacoma: Washington State Historical Society.

Orth, Donald J. 1967. *Dictionary of Alaska Place Names*. Washington: United States Government Printing Office.

Oswalt, Wendell. 1967. *Alaska Commercial Company Records: 1868–1911*. College: University of Alaska.

Partnow, Patricia H. 1990. Russian American Schools. Unpublished manuscript.

———1992–93. Field notes.

———1993. Alutiiq Ethnicity. Ph.D. diss., University of Alaska Fairbanks.

Pedersen, August. 1990. Interview by Patricia Partnow and Lisa Scarbrough. Chignik Lagoon, Alaska, June 5.

Petroff, Ivan. 1900. Population, Resources, Etc. of Alaska [From United States Census Report of 1880]. In *Compilation of Narratives of Explorations in Alaska. U.S. Congress, Senate, Committee on Military Affairs*. Washington: U.S. Government Printing Office, 55–284.

Petroff, Ivan (under the name Boris Lanin). n.d. *Presentiments: An Alaskan Reminiscence*. In Bancroft Library, University of California. Photocopy viewed in the collection of Richard Pierce.

Petterson, John S. 1981. *Limited Entry and the Bristol Bay Native: Problems and Prospects*. Paper presented at the Alaska Anthropological Association Annual Meeting.

Phillips, Elia and Mary. 1992. Interview by Lisa Scarbrough for Alaska Department of Fish and Game. Perryville, Alaska, November 13. Also present were Susan Savage (National Park Service) and Patricia Partnow.

Phillips, Ralph. 1992. Interview by Patricia Partnow. Perryville, Alaska, March 24.

Pierce, Richard A. 1984. *The Russian-American Company: Correspondence of the Governors: Communications Sent: 1818*. Kingston, Ontario: The Limestone Press.

———1990. *Russian America: A Biographical Dictionary*. Kingston, Ontario: The Limestone Press.

———1990a. The Russian-American Company Currency. In *Russian America: The Forgotten Frontier*. Edited by Barbara Sweetland Smith and Redmond J. Barnett. Tacoma: Washington State Historical Society, 145–153.

———nd. Russian-American Company Correspondence, 1836–1867. Unpublished notes.

Pinart, Alphonse L. 1872. Itinéraire aux Iles Aléoutiennes (d'Ounalashka à Kadiak) (map).

———1873. Eskimaux et Koloches: Idées Religieuses et Traditions des Kaniagmioutes. *Revue d'Anthropologie, Paris* 2:673–680.

———1873a. A Voyage on the North-West Coast of America from Unalaska to Kodiak (Aleutian Islands and the Alaska Peninsula). *Bulletin, Societe de Geographie* 6:6. Unpublished translation by Gerald Clark.

Polonskii, A. n.d. *Perechen Puteshestvii Russkikh Promyshlennykh v Vostochnom Okeane s 1743 po 1800 g.* [Inventory of voyage of Russian Promyshlennik in the Eastern Ocean from 1743 to 1800]. Unpublished ms. Archive of the Russian Geographic Society, Academy of Sciences, Russia, St. Petersburg, R 60, op. 1. No. 2, Verso 79 – Folio 82. Unpublished translation by Lydia T. Black.

Portelli, Allessandro. 1991. *The Death of Luigi Trastulli and Other Stories: Form and Meaning in Oral History*. Albany: State University of New York Press.

Porter, Robert Percival. 1893. *Report on Population and Resources of Alaska at the Eleventh Census*. Washington: U.S. Government Printing Office.

Pravoslavnyi Amerikanskii Vestnik' [*American Orthodox Messenger*] (AOM). 1896. From the Travel Journal (for 1895) of the Priest of the Kodiak Church of the Resurrection, Tikhon Shalamov. Draft translation by P. H. Partnow. Vol. 1:57–58, 118–119.

———1898. Short Church Historical Description of the Kodiak Parish (from the archives of the Kodiak Church). Draft translation by P. H. Partnow. Vol. 2:265–6, 508–510.

————1899. Report on Kodiak Parish. Draft translation by P. H. Partnow. Vol. 3:91, 160.

————1902. Report of the Voyage of Vasilii Martysh, Taken in 1901. Draft translation by P. H. Partnow. Vol. 6:431–3.

————1904. Excerpts from Travel report of Vasilii Martysh on a Trip Taken in 1902. Draft translation by P. H. Partnow. Vol. 8:13–15, 32–34.

————1911. Oldtimers of Alaska by Father A. Kedrovskiy. Draft translation by P. H. Partnow. Vol. 15:273–4, 323–4.

————1916. Priest Aleksandr Petelin: Obituary. Draft translation by P. H. Partnow. Vol. 19:572–3.

————1926. Vol. 27:119.

————1972. Bishop Nestor. Draft translation by P. H. Partnow. Vol. 68:111–3.

Prucha, Francis Paul. 1988. Presents and Delegations. In *Handbook of North American Indians*. Edited by William C. Sturtevant. Vol. 4, *History of Indian-White Relations*. Edited by Wilcomb E. Washburn. Washington: Smithsonian Institution, 238–244.

Report of the Governor of Alaska. Governor to the Secretary of the Interior. Washington, D.C.: Government Printing Office. 1923.

Ricketts, Commander. 1937. Kanatak Murder Trial, December 31, 1937. Story told in 1980. Archives, Alaska and Polar Regions, Rasmuson Library, University of Alaska Fairbanks; Commander Noble G. Ricketts Collection, Folder 3.

Roscoe, Fred. 1992. *From Humboldt to Kodiak*. Kingston, Ontario: The Limestone Press.

Russian-American Company (RAC). 1821. *The Second Charter of the Russian-American Company*. Unpublished translation by Richard A. Pierce.

————1842–63. Ochet' Russisko-Amerikanskoy Kompaniy Glavnovo Pravleniya [Reports of the chief management of the Russian-American Company]. Photocopies supplied by Richard A. Pierce.

————1844. *The Third Charter of the Russian-American Company*. Unpublished translation by Richard A. Pierce.

Sam, Mike. 1990. Interview by Lisa Scarbrough and Patricia Partnow. Chignik Lagoon, Alaska, June 5.

————1991. Interview by Matthew O'Leary and Joe Bartolini for Bureau of Indian Affairs, April 2.

————1992. Interview by Patricia Partnow. Chignik Lagoon, Alaska, June 2.

Sanook, Barbara Shangin. 1968. Recorded interview by Don and Julia Kinsey. Chignik Lake School, January 13. Translated by Doris Lind and Virginia Aleck.

Seton-Karr, Heywood. 1887. *Shores and Alps of Alaska*. Chicago: A. C. McClurg.

Shangin, Polly. 1992. Interview by Patricia Partnow. Perryville, Alaska, March 25. Translated by Ralph Phillips and Polly Yagie.

Shanz, Alfred B. 1893. Chapter VI: The Fourth or Nushagak District. In *Report on Population and Resources of Alaska at the Eleventh Census*. Edited by Robert Perceval Porter. Washington: U.S. Government Printing Office, 91–98.

Shelikhov, Grigorii I. 1981 [1793, 1812]. *A Voyage to America 1783–1786*. Translated by Marina Ramsay and edited, with an introduction, by Richard A. Pierce. Kingston, Ontario: The Limestone Press.

Spurr, Josiah Edward. 1898. Field notes (unpublished).

————1900. *A Reconnaissance in Southwestern Alaska in 1898*. Washington: Government Printing Office.

Stafeev, Vladimir. nd. Diary. Draft translation by Marina Ramsay and edited by Richard A. Pierce. In press. Fairbanks: The Limestone Press.

Steller, Georg Wilhelm. 1988 [1743]. *Journal of a Voyage with Bering 1741–1742*. Edited with an introduction by O. W. Frost. Stanford: Stanford University Press.

Stepanoff, Spiridon. 1969. Interview recorded by Don and Julia Kinsey. Chignik Lake, Alaska. Transcript by P. H. Partnow.

Stepanoff, Walter Sr. 1990. Interview by Patricia Partnow and Lisa Scarbrough. Chignik Bay, Alaska, June 2.

————1990a. Interview by Patricia Partnow and Lisa Scarbrough. Chignik Bay, Alaska, June 4.

Tanner, Z. L. 1888. *Bulletin of the United States Fish Commission*, Vol. 8. Washington: U.S. Government Printing Office.

Teben'kov, M. D. 1981 [1852]. *Atlas of the Northwest Coasts of America*. Translated and edited by Richard A. Pierce. Kingston, Ontario: The Limestone Press.

Tikhmenev, P. A. 1978 [1861]. *A History of the Russian-American Company*. Translated and edited by Richard A. Pierce and Alton S. Donnelly. Seattle: University of Washington Press.

———1979 [1863]. *A History of the Russian-American Company Vol. 2: Documents*. Edited by Richard A. Pierce and Alton S. Donnelly. Kingston, Ontario: The Limestone Press.

United States. 1900. Census of Alaska, Roll 1832.

———1910. Census of Alaska, Roll 1750.

United States House of Representatives. 1933. Egegik River, Alaska: Letter from The Secretary of War. Document 51; 73rd Congress, 1st Session.

United States Revenue Cutter Service (USRCS). Archives 671, Roll 16. Records and Communications. 1912. Annual Report of the Revenue Cutter Service. Washington: U.S. Government Printing Office.

———1915. Annual Report of the Revenue Cutter Service. Washington: U.S. Government Printing Office.

VanStone, James W. 1967. *Eskimos of the Nushagak River: An Ethnographic History*. Seattle: University of Washington Press.

VanStone, James W., ed. 1988. *Russian Exploration in Southwest Alaska: The Travel Journals of Petr Korsakovskiy (1818) and Ivan Ya. Vasilev (1829)*. Fairbanks: University of Alaska Press.

Veniaminov, Ivan. 1984 [1840]. *Notes on the Islands of the Unalashka District*. Translated by Lydia T. Black and R. H. Geoghegan; edited, with an introduction, by Richard A. Pierce. Kingston, Ontario: The Limestone Press.

Vick, Ann, ed. 1983. *The Cama-i Book*. Garden City: Anchor Press.

Wells, E. 1891. Our Alaska Expedition: Conclusion of Mr. Wells' Narration. *Frank Leslie's Illustrated Newspaper*, New York: Sept. 19:106.

Wrangell, Ferdinand P. 1980 [1839]. *Russian America: Statistical and Ethnographic Information*. Translated from the German edition of 1839 by Mary Sadouski and edited by Richard A. Pierce. Kingston, Ontario: The Limestone Press.

Yesner, David R. 1985. Cultural Boundaries and Ecological Frontiers in Coastal Regions: An Example from the Alaska Peninsula. In *The Archaeology of Frontiers and Boundaries*. Edited by Stanton W. Green and Stephen M. Perlman. Orlando: The Academic Press, 51–91.

Zimin, Carvel. 1998. Interview by Patricia Partnow for National Park Service. South Naknek, Alaska, January 27.

Zimmerly, David W. 1986. *Qajaq: Kayaks of Siberia and Alaska*. Juneau, Alaska: Division of State Museums.

INDEX

ABOUT THE AUTHOR

Patricia H. Partnow is an anthropologist with thirty years of experience living and working in Alaska. She moved there directly from graduate school in 1971 and spent three years in Juneau working at the Alaska State Museum designing learning kits that went to rural schools. When she moved to Anchorage in 1974, she became involved in bilingual education and curriculum development, eventually spending thirteen years with the Anchorage School District's Indian Education Program designing and publishing curriculum and student readers about Alaska Native cultures. She then returned to university studies (University of Alaska Fairbanks) to earn her doctorate in anthropology, concentrating on oral tradition and questions of ethnic identity in the Alaska Peninsula. She is the author of a number of articles and chapters in journals and books. In 1999, Dr. Partnow became vice president of education at the Alaska Native Heritage Center. She currently serves as senior vice president of programs and education at the center. She has two grown children, various pets, and a few house plants.

ACKNOWLEDGEMENTS

I wish to thank the many people whose time and efforts made this book happen. First, I thank the wonderful people of the Alaska Pensinsula whose stories are the heart of this volume. They fed and housed my body, mind, and soul. This is their book, to the extent that they are willing to claim it. Some are gone, but all remain in my memories and in some small part through this book. They include Ignatius Kosbruk, Frieda Kosbruk, Doris Lind, William Lind, Christine Martin, Virginia Aleck, Emil Artemie, Susan Shangin, Olga Kalmakoff, Joe Kalmakoff, Polly Shangin, Polly Yagie, Ralph Phillips, Mary Phillips, Elia Phillips, Walter Stepanoff, Sr., August Pedersen, Aleck Constantine, Mike Sam, Mary Jane Nielsen, Vera Kie Angasan, Fred Theodore Angasan, Sr., Teddy Melgenak, Carvel Zimin, Sr., and Bobby Jo Kramer. Second, I wish to acknowledge the faculty of the University of Alaska Fairbanks for their time, expertise, and advice. These people are my mentors, peers, and friends. They include Dr. Lydia Black, Dr. Jeffrey Leer, Dr. Phyllis Morrow, Dr. Richard Pierce, and Dr. William Schneider. Third, I would like to acknowledge those who supported me during my research, including Peter Partnow, Dr. Jeffrey Partnow, friends Dinah Naske and Dr. Claus-M. Naske, and colleague Lisa Hutchinson-Scarbrough of the Alaska Department of Fish and Game, Subsistence Division. Thanks also to Dr. Aron Crowell for permission to use photographs from the Arctic Studies Center's (Smithsonian Institution) *Looking Both Ways* exhibition. Cartographer Vanessa Summers drew beautiful maps for this book, for which I thank her. Many other people helped throughout the years of research and writing. They are archivists, librarians, researchers, state and federal employees, and fellow anthropologists whose direction, leads, and suggestions I greatly appreciate. Finally, I want to express my gratitude to editors Deirdre Helfferich and Carla Helfferich of the University of Alaska Press for shepherding this book to its publication.